# Machine Gun

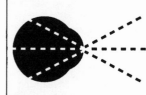 This Large Print Book carries the
Seal of Approval of N.A.V.H.

# Machine Gun

The Story of the Men
and the Weapon that Changed
the Face of War

## Anthony Smith

Thorndike Press • Waterville, Maine

Published in 2004 by arrangement with
St. Martin's Press, LLC.

Thorndike Press® Large Print American History.

The tree indicium is a trademark of Thorndike Press.

The text of this Large Print edition is unabridged.
Other aspects of the book may vary from the original edition.

Set in 16 pt. Plantin by Elena Picard.

Printed in the United States on permanent paper.

**ISBN 0-7862-6346-6 (lg. print : hc : alk. paper)**

# Machine Gun

As the Founder/CEO of NAVH, the only national health agency solely devoted to those who, although not totally blind, have an eye disease which could lead to serious visual impairment, I am pleased to recognize Thorndike Press★ as one of the leading publishers in the large print field.

Founded in 1954 in San Francisco to prepare large print textbooks for partially seeing children, NAVH became the pioneer and standard setting agency in the preparation of large type.

Today, those publishers who meet our standards carry the prestigious "Seal of Approval" indicating high quality large print. We are delighted that Thorndike Press is one of the publishers whose titles meet these standards. We are also pleased to recognize the significant contribution Thorndike Press is making in this important and growing field.

Lorraine H. Marchi, L.H.D.
Founder/CEO
NAVH

★ Thorndike Press encompasses the following imprints: Thorndike, Wheeler, Walker and Large Print Press.

# Contents

# Acknowledgements

Where would we be without libraries? More to the point, and in this particular instance, where would I have been without the libraries — and the ever-helpful librarians — of the Imperial War Museum, the National Army Museum, the Connecticut State Library, and the recesses of the London Library? To all of them my enthusiastic thanks. So too with the Public Records Office, that astonishing cornucopia of rich pickings so promptly available. Friends were also besieged whenever they knew of something, or of someone who could provide a small but critical detail. And there were friends who provided hospitality, such as Roberta and Dick Huber, most splendidly housed (on Charter Oak Place in Connecticut's Hartford) within easy reach of so much Colt and Gatling memorabilia. Authors may seem to work on their own, and occasionally may do so, but far more probable is their exploitation of everyone and everything available, such as libraries, librarians, friends, and friends of friends. These all know my debt to them, and so do I, most avidly.

# Foreword

# Death of an Inventor

The date was 24 November 1916. A heavily bearded and elderly naturalised Briton lay dying in Kent, breathing raucously through a bronchial device of his own creation. This American-born inventor should, perhaps, have been listening more acutely to the death rattles of thousands upon thousands of men on the European mainland. He would have heard them giving their last utterances in a variety of languages, such as Russian, German, Italian, and certainly English. And he might have pondered the fact, with his own last breath, that he — more than any other individual — had given a terrible twist to the old human preponderance for going to war. He and his inventiveness had utterly transformed the killing business.

By the time of that one man's death, the Battle of the Somme, started with such high hopes twenty-one weeks earlier, had been officially and miserably concluded, with a toll for the Allies of 700,000 dead, wounded and missing. British conscripts had not been involved in the slaughter, since the victims had been almost entirely those who had rushed to volunteer when hostilities began. Over on Germany's eastern front, the war's savagery had been as great, and Czar Nicholas II would not stay on his throne much longer: he had taken personal control of the army in 1915 and would therefore receive blame for subsequent disasters. Gallipoli's ten-month horror had been terminated, leaving 25,000 Allied dead, 76,000 wounded, and 13,000 missing. There were still two more years of war to wreak their havoc, to kill as had never happened previously, to mow men down in horrific style. Some 9,000,000 were to die before its conclusion, with artillery and rifles taking their toll, and the new deployment of machine guns being hideously effective.

Rapid-firing weapons were certainly not new. The man in Kent had done his earliest work on them back in the early 1880s, but their power and destructive capability had still not been fully installed within many a military mind, not least those in charge of the Somme offensive. As a scythe cuts through corn, or a mower mows the grass, Lord Kitchener's volunteers were to succumb as never before. Neither in their method of attack, nor in its basic principles, did they stand a chance. In a new kind of war they had attacked in an old kind of way. They were not asking to be slaughtered, but it might have seemed that way. As a German gunner wrote after that first day of July in the middle of the war:

When the English started advancing we were very concerned; they looked as though they must soon occupy our trenches. We were amazed to see them walking, we had never seen that before. . . . The officers were at the front. I noticed one of them was strolling calmly, carrying a walking stick. When we started firing we just had to load and reload. They went down in their hundreds. We didn't have to aim, we just fired into them.

The man in Kent, dying in his bed so peacefully save for that difficulty in breathing, had been at the forefront of this new form of killing machine. No one before him had made a fully automatic machine gun, needing only a finger on its trigger to despatch its box-full of bullets with terrifying haste. There had been earlier attempts, with earlier weapons and designs, but nothing so remorselessly automatic in its virulence. In the early 1880s, when this middle-aged inventor was recently arrived in Europe from New York City and deciding to produce a weapon which all its armies might desire, he had designed a single-barrelled, water-cooled, recoil-operated gun capable of firing 600 rounds a minute. With one man using a single finger, plus other men assuaging the gun's appetite with belts of ammunition, the device was a masterpiece of killing capability. Visitors had flocked to the inventor's workshop in London's Hatton Garden, notably the Prince of Wales and his entourage, men such as the Duke of Cambridge, the long-time head of the British Army, and Garnet Wolseley, the most famous and revered of British generals. They each revelled in the weapon's ability (and noise and smoke), but were uncertain of its relevance in any major war. It might be useful, perhaps, in quelling the hordes so frequently encountered in colonial skirmishes around the globe. It might do quite well in those distant spots, but not in any proper war.

Hiram Stevens Maxim, the inventor in question, was not greatly troubled by the lack of British sales. The prime advantage of Europe, as against the American homeland he had vacated, was its considerable number of potential purchasers. No one in the 1880s then foresaw a further European war (with the Crimean war, and even the Franco-Prussian conflict, well embedded in the past), but the European nations did possess substantial armies, usually via conscription, and these armies were in steady and competitive need of better weapons. Therefore, after designing and manufacturing his lethal gun, Maxim had set off with this creation to visit likely clients.

He did not relax and wait, as so many of his inventive kind will do, for the world to beat pathways to his door. He beat the paths himself, knocking on a range of doors at every opportunity. Switzerland provided his first big success, its authorities astonished (and delighted) by the killing power of his new weapon. Italy, Spain, Portugal, Austria-Hungary and Russia swiftly followed suit, with their several kings, emperors, marshals and admirals adding their distinguished names and titles to the Maxim order book.

One big omission, which happened to

possess Europe's largest and most powerful army, was Germany. Prince Wilhelm of Prussia, the future Kaiser, had spent time in England, notably during the celebrations for Queen Victoria's Golden Jubilee, educating himself about the rapid-firing guns on offer, and he liked very much what he saw. His cousin, the Prince of Wales, soon also to become head of state (as Edward VII), then helped to clinch an Anglo-German deal by travelling to Berlin with both Hiram Maxim and a Maxim gun. Wilhelm was ecstatic, and received permission to develop the Maxim weapons within his realm, providing he sent royalties according to the numbers made. Little did Britain's Prince, or the inventor so delighted by the sales, know (or suspect, or even imagine) that British soldiers might fall victims to the direct descendants of those Maxim guns — dying in their many tens of thousands — before a few more years had passed. (The authorities also did not know, or apparently consider, that Germany might perfidiously make many more of the weapons than it cared to acknowledge via those royalties.)

At the time of this commercial exchange, and during the closing years of the nineteenth century, no one appreciated who might be fighting whom should a new war begin. There were so many pacts and alliances, international rivalries and loyalties, that the entangled concordances were difficult to unravel, let alone visualise in operation should something happen to disturb their equilibrium. Forecasters within Britain might assume that France, as traditional opponent, would be the most likely enemy in those days before the *entente cordiale* had been stitched together. As for Germany's aspirations, these were not then widely anticipated. Neither was Russia's impending turbulence or the possibility of a Balkan killing by an anarchist upsetting the entire apple cart. Absolutely no one was imagining the kind of conflict about to engulf the continent.

Therefore Maxim's enthusiasm for selling guns wherever possible, and to every enthusiastic army, was not (quite) as cynical, and disloyal, or even as treacherous and traitorous as it might seem. After some twenty-five years in other trades, when he had sold whatever product he could to any would-be purchaser, he had become a gunmaker. Therefore he then became a gunseller. As a friend in Vienna had casually advised: 'If you wish to make a pile of money, invent something that will enable

17

these Europeans to cut each other's throats.' He had done so, and then he did so. Even the forthright friend could never have imagined quite how much money, or how much death, would be entailed.

It is difficult to know if the inventor was ever concerned by the gruesome ability of his invention. Maxim's autobiography, *My Life*, gives no hint whatsoever of any troubled thinking. It does reveal the man, as all personal narratives will do, both between the lines as well as on them, but self-doubt is not in evidence. Indeed, the book could stand as the most conceited of its kind there has ever been. Praise abounds, all heading in the same personal direction. Criticism is also rife, but directed elsewhere. There are also curious omissions. He married twice, but his first wife is nowhere mentioned. His second, and much younger partner, is permitted to exist within the volume, but only very occasionally and *en passant,* as it were, when 'Lady Maxim and I' were going somewhere. There were also three children — somehow, but no details in his book about their existence, or how and when they came to pass. (In fact, the one son and two daughters arose from his first marriage, the second being without issue.) As a book of revelation, the autobiography scores only modestly, save in its steadfast braggadocio and its lack of conscience about making money, and fame and honour, from wholesale killing machines.

Hiram Maxim's final hours, and his life's eventual conclusion at his home in Kent, were scarcely noticed among the maelstrom of events swirling worldwide at that time. Franz Josef, ruler for sixty-eight years of the Austro-Hungarian empire, had died one week earlier. Woodrow Wilson had just been re-elected for a second term as a Democratic President of the United States. Gregori Rasputin, Russia's invidious and domineering monk, was about to be assassinated, and David Lloyd George would become Britain's new prime minister within a week. In the trenches, as a third Christmas loomed, no one believed the forthcoming festival would witness the war's conclusion as had been optimistically imagined two years earlier. In short, there was ample reason why one old man's death in bed south-east of London created little comment when the death of innumerable young men among mud and filth was such a commonplace.

In any case, there was not yet a universal understanding that Maxim's invention in

Hatton Garden thirty-two years earlier had heralded a new form of war. Even the army — or particularly the army — had still not fully absorbed what had come to pass. There was continuing talk of bravado and dash, of élan and esprit being the crucial elements of winning wars. There was still too little comprehension of the effect which several machine guns could produce, each remorselessly firing one dozen rounds a second into advancing crowds of unprotected infantry. Men at the Somme walking across no man's land were showing their steadiness under fire just as men at Waterloo had also stood still, or walked in rows, before they too died; but ragged fire from muzzle-loading muskets bore no relation to well-aimed salvoes from modern machinery.

Without doubt a revolution had occurred. Hiram Maxim's actions, initiated to make a pile of money from militant Europeans, have immortalised his name in the slaughter business; yet he was not the first, any more than he has been the last, to be thinking along such lines. Rapid-firing weapons, by no means fully automatic, had been developed — and used — long before Maxim had entered the fray. Many names and devices had been involved during those earlier years. For example, to name but one who played a major part with his own creation, there had been Dr Richard Gatling.

# Chapter 1

# A Doctor's Contribution

Richard Gatling did it, so he said, to save life. In 1861, when starting upon this endeavour, the inventor of the first effective rapid-firing (but not automatic) machine gun would, in his opinion, be a philanthropist, with a considerable feeling for his fellow man inspiring him to create the weapon. The logic behind this nineteenth-century sentiment stated that, if a hundred men were sent to shoot at one hundred of the enemy, there would inevitably be much death. Some of the fatalities would be caused in action by the men themselves, by their shooting and hacking at each other, but most of them would result from disease. The Crimean war, ending five years earlier, had made this point only too emphatically, and the war between North and South in the United States was about to make it all over again.

If, therefore, a single weapon could spew bullets as accurately and as lethally as a hundred riflemen could do, there would be much saving of life. Fewer men would be employed to kill just as many of the enemy, and the losses from disease would, in consequence, be much reduced. An invention of this kind would therefore be humanitarian, leading to fewer casualties on one's own side and still killing very many of the enemy. A similarly optimistic view had also been expressed in other quarters, such as newspapers. When a man invents a process, stated one American editorial in 1852, 'by which a whole army could be killed . . . the lion and the lamb will lie down together . . . Wars among civilized nations would cease forever . . . The inventor of such a machine would prove a greater benefactor of his race, than he who should endow a thousand hospitals.' The creator of the first rapid-firing gun would therefore be of service to humanity, and one man in particular was determined to provide that humane beneficence.

Richard Jordan Gatling, this wishful philanthropist, was aged forty-three when he witnessed troops returning from early engagements of the U.S. Civil War. From his home in Indianapolis he had seen the soldiers depart, and had then watched some of them return as wounded or dying men, having also left many of their number behind them. 'Most of the latter lost their lives, not in battle, but by sickness and exposure incident to the service,' as he later wrote. In Gatling's buoyant mind a machine with the requisite 'rapidity of fire' would, to a great extent

supersede the necessity of large armies, and consequently, the exposure to battle and disease [would] be greatly diminished . . . I thought over the subject and finally this idea took practical form in the invention of the Gatling Gun.

Many a creator of novelties is more excited by their creation than their possible usefulness, but Richard Gatling was essentially pragmatic. He had studied medicine (although he never practised) mainly because, aged twenty-seven, he had nearly died from smallpox which had then become more severe when complicated by pneumonia. At the time he had been on board a ship voyaging from Cincinnati to Pittsburgh, and his illness had been unhappily aggravated when this vessel became ice-bound for two weeks. After the thaw, his subsequent mood was not improved by a seventeen-year-old sister dying, this death following those of two other sisters, who had succumbed at the ages of twenty-nine days and twenty-five years. If medical men were apparently, and so blatantly, inadequate, might it not be wise to study their trade oneself? He therefore attended medical colleges in Indiana and Ohio before graduating from Ohio Medical College, Cincinnati, in 1849. That, in essence, was Richard Gatling's practical attitude to life. If death in the family was a problem, he should learn how better to prevent it. If battlefield disease was paramount, he should find a way of circumventing it. To concentrate his mind yet further on the matter of prevention, the smallpox he suffered had caused him to grow a beard thereafter in order to hide, as far as possible, the resulting pock marks on his face.

Gatling had been brought up near Murfreesboro in Hertford County, North Carolina. His father, Jordan Gatling, was a farmer and also an inventor. He had finished his life in 1848 owning a fine home, 1,200 acres and twenty slaves, eleven of whom were women and children, and had been one of the largest and most prosperous land-owners in the county. On this property stood the gin house, which contained novel machinery for separating cotton from its seeds. Gatling senior had taken out patents in 1835, the first of their kind, for his cotton planters and cotton thinners. Assuredly he passed to his son a wish, as well as a skill, for making life easier — and probably more profitable.

This talent for improvement by the very individuals who would first gain from such advances was peculiarly American. 'There has to be a better way of doing this' might have been the catch-phrase enunciated up and down the land; 'so let's find that way, and do it ourselves.' If sowing and covering cotton seed was a problem, well, let us fix it. If thinning cotton plants was also difficult, then let us try to find a more efficient way of achieving it. And then patent the invention. And possibly make some extra money for having dreamed up a solution which everyone in the same line of business would surely want. (It is even argued that the famous Gatling gun was, in essence, no more than a seed planter and a rotary cultivator, the two major inventions of Gatling Senior. Instead of dropping seeds at regular intervals there would be bullets, with everything performing in a similarly rotary manner.)

That inventive father and his wife, Mary Barnes, produced three daughters and four sons. The girls did not do well, with all three dying before their father. Three of the boys left home on reaching adulthood, leaving only James with their mother. He is said to have been short on social graces but, as compensation, was undeniably long on courage. Three decades before the Wright Brothers successfully took to the air, James was leaping from a barn's upper door, having strapped wings of corn-leaves to his arms. Almost simultaneously, in a flurry of leaves and dust, he was soon landing on the ground with badly twisted ankles. Rather less damagingly, James Gatling also made model aircraft from wood and paper, and he remained convinced all his life that human beings would eventually achieve what he was failing to do. His greatest aerial construction, known locally as 'The Old Turkey Buzzard', did leave the ground one day in 1873, with James at the controls, and it travelled for a hundred feet before meeting a 'hefty-sized' elm, leaving the pilot injured and his plane a wreck. Of course he was mocked, being labelled 'the fool who thought he could fly', and he was later maddened yet further by his brother's fame and fortune with the Gatling gun.

Within the Gatling family there was plainly an inclination towards invention, and James was not as daft as others believed when hearing only of his aerial adventuring. He acquired several patents for agricultural products, and improved the farm he had inherited. He made it more prosperous in several directions, but he was still called 'odd-ball', 'fiery' and 'generally eccentric', these traits becoming yet more apparent as he grew older. He even had a fight one day, when aged fifty-seven, on the steps — no less — of the County Courthouse. Official retribution was understandably swift, with each antagonist promptly ordered to forfeit $20 for contempt of court, even if they had got no further than the steps of that locality.

In the end, although barn door leaps and stationary trees might have been the death of him, it was James's lack of social graces which proved more critical. He refused one day, presumably tactlessly — as was his way, to give a carriage ride to a local man named William Vann. This refusal must have been severe because Vann immediately threatened murderous revenge, and was not long in putting his outspoken words into violent action. On the following day, while he fed his hogs, James was not only shot but also clubbed to death. Vann's crime had been observed, and his trial took place at nearby Winton, with most businesses in the area closed for the entire proceedings, so popular was the event. A death sentence was pronounced, but then commuted to life imprisonment by the state's governor.

Within a few years Vann was paroled, perhaps because his victim's shortage of social graces was still so vividly remembered, with everyone recollecting how very irritating the former James Henry Gatling had been. That definite lack, and the irritation it surely caused, may also explain why James's three brothers left the family homestead as soon as possible, departing for nearby Northampton County (Thomas), for Kansas and then Canada (William), and for St Louis, Missouri (Richard). When the difficult James was murdered in 1881 there was still an untried, and unflown, flying machine within the family barn. That building then burned down in 1905, thus incinerating a former rival to the Wrights' 'Flyer' which had been so successful two years earlier in another part of that same state of North Carolina. This family history is certainly intriguing but also helpful in explaining the enterprising climate of the times and the creative spirit which partnered it: 'I may only be a farmer, but I'm a whole lot more than that. Just you wait and see.'

Richard Jordan Gatling's first attempt at invention would never have assisted his father's farm (save, it was hoped, financially) but would certainly fulfil a need. The U.S. Government was advertising during the early 1830s that it would offer substantial financial reward for any device which would propel warships from beneath water level rather than vulnerably above it, as with paddle-wheels and sails. Richard Gatling devised a screw propeller, then an entirely novel concept. He tried it out on the farm's pond, discovered that it worked, and refrained from travelling to Washington for a patent until better weather arrived the following spring. More than 200 miles were involved and, with travel then a difficult business, wintry journeys were hardest of them all. After arriving at the capital's patent office, and upon presenting his model, he quickly learned that a certain John Ericsson had delivered a nearly identical model only a few months earlier. In effect, the seventeen-year-old boy had lost his first fortune by waiting for nicer weather.

The speed with which many nineteenth-century individuals started to fashion their lives, instead of struggling to achieve diplomas, certificates and degrees, does have its appeal. Four years after the Washington disappointment, while at work as his own store-keeper, Richard Gatling designed and patented a rice planter which was then adapted to handle wheat. This time the young inventor did not hesitate. If he wanted fame or fortune, this was up to him, and he immediately set out to sell his creation. In those days sowing by the broadcast method, the archetypal system, was still paramount. He therefore suggested to each potential client, as a formal sales procedure, that one half of their land should be sown traditionally, and the other half with the Gatling device — which actually buried the seed from enthusiastic birds and winter frosts. The inventor would receive, if the client agreed, all the excess corn achieved via this new creation, its value serving as down-payment on equipment then hungrily desired by the impatient farmer. A fortune lost on the screw propeller by an unfortunate delay was soon being amassed by a seed drill, particularly after it had been exhibited at London's Crystal Palace in 1851 (and the inventor's European rights had been sold to Britain). The lad plainly had an inventive streak, there being little obvious relationship between a ship's propulsion system and the burial of seed.

Then came the disfiguring smallpox attack, and that determination to learn about medicine. In between these studies, Gatling devised a machine for beating hemp so that this plant's fibre could be separated more effectively. And he created a system, alas not patentable, which distributed compressed air by pipeline, thus providing a convenient method for delivering energy to points distant from a main power source. In the late 1850s Gatling also invented a steam plough, a huge thing for churning up soil, although this did not do well, principally because it was introduced at a time when money was tight and expensive machinery not immediately welcome. But this particular creator was soon to acquire a fame which has preserved his name far more than his numerous and beneficial achievements on behalf of agriculture. He was about to watch those weary, sick and hobbling soldiers return from battle, and learn how many of their companions had been smitten by disease rather than the enemy. It was occasion for philanthropy.

The outbreak of war in 1861 was initially exciting, such an event on home ground being so novel. Washingtonians boarded their buggies and gigs to see the fun. They took picnic baskets with them, and headed for Virginia. In the first battle, the Battle of Bull Run, one-sixth of the Union's troops became casualties, and the returning carriages were assuredly partnered by quite a different mood among the sightseers. Optimism and pessimism must have gone hand in hand. It was terrible to see such death and injury, but there was surely argument that Yankee ingenuity would soon create some 'absolute weapon', as the *Philadelphia Enquirer* phrased it, which would 'thrash the rebels'. With America in the 1860s such a gun-using nation, and the right to bear arms so constitutionally ingrained, every northerner — or so it seemed — had an idea how to slaughter the opposition.

The Chief of Army Ordnance, steadily bombarded by new inventions, reacted in petulant fashion by blocking every fledgling scheme, affirming that this 'evil' of bright ideas could only be stopped by 'positively refusing to answer any requisitions for or propositions to sell new and untried arms'. One can see his point. Even by June 1861 the army was sorely afflicted by far too many calibres and types of weapon. According to one 1863 report, the Union military then officially recognised 'seventy-nine different models of rifles and muskets, twenty-three of carbines and musketoons, and nineteen of pistols and revolvers', with almost every firearm requiring different kinds of bullet. Praise the Lord, in short, but make certain to pass the right kind of ammunition. As far as the hard-pressed Ordnance Department was concerned, America's propensity for invention, improvement, modification and individual betterment was no way to run a war.

Contrarily, the nation's President, so famously log cabin-born within Kentucky, welcomed the homespun initiatives. He personally sponsored various inventions which, according to the military professionals, were quite unsuitable. Simultaneously, and in similar vein, *Scientific American* solicited for inventors to come forward with ideas, sound or otherwise:

There is an enormous demand for improved fire-arms, cannon, shells, projectiles, explosive grenades, and military accouterments of all kinds.

There was also great demand for recruits to advance the war. In theory there were hundreds of thousands of militiamen on the rolls to supplement the Federal troops, but their expertise was as varied as the weaponry they brought with them to their training periods. Paul Wahl and Don Toppel, in their book on Gatling's gun, state that these activities were 'generally limited to a one-day annual muster devoted to getting drunk together'. And, presumably, firing off their assembly of weapons somewhat casually at targets, at bottles, at anything which tempted.

Into this confusion of untrained forces, haphazard weaponry, unwarranted optimism, reasonable discontent and stonewalling officialdom stepped Richard Jordan Gatling, with benefaction in mind and considerable mechanical experience behind him, but zero knowledge of matters military. Although he was born a southerner (which would later cause him trouble), his first move to Missouri was followed by a shift to Ohio and then Indiana. The bellicose weapon he devised, allegedly spurred by that idea to save lives, was little more than an amalgamation of two existing weapons. Thomas Edison was later to argue that every so-called invention was, in reality, a modification of some earlier creation, and Gatling certainly examined existing weapons before surfacing with his novelty. It is presumed he took particular note both of the single-barrelled Ager 'Coffee Mill' gun and of the Ripley multi-barrelled design. These were each hand-cranked and, much like artillery pieces, were suspended heavily between two large wheels.

By 1862 Gatling had produced his first gun — without (or indeed ever) acknowledging any indebtedness to earlier products. His prototype's firing mechanism, with a hopper gravity feed (which had given the Ager 'Coffee Mill' its name) was extremely similar to the earlier gun save that, as with the Ripley design (which never actually fired a shot), it had six revolving barrels. The earliest Gatling weapon, whether or not its basic concepts were borrowed, was produced with astonishing speed. The Civil War's first shots (at Fort Sumter) were fired on 12 April 1861. The first major battle, that of Bull Run — whose effects had so shocked the sensitive Dr Gatling, took place on 21 July, exactly

100 days later. Administration of patents is traditionally a lengthy business, but the first official document for a Gatling gun was granted on 4 November in the following year. It therefore surfaced less than sixteen months after survivors from Bull Run had served so chillingly as spur for this 'humanitarian' creation.

More importantly in those frantic days, and long before Patent No. 36,836 had been issued, demonstrations of the gun were being given 'before thousands' of Indianapolis citizens. Indiana's Governor was so impressed that he appointed a military committee to assess the weapon's merits, and it reported favourably:

> We are aware that nothing but actual service in the field, subject to all the casualties of war, can fully establish the utility of any arm, but in this gun, as far as we have been able to judge, everything has been anticipated to render it effective under all circumstances.

The report added, most gratifyingly for Gatling, that his gun's firing system is 'ingenious and simple'. The barrels are fired independently so that 'damage to one does not affect the others'. There are no complicated parts 'and the common soldier can keep it in order as readily as he does his musket'. Firing 'with desirable accuracy' can be made '150 times per minute'. This may be continued 'for hours . . . without overheating'. 'Two men are sufficient to work the gun' and 'two horses can carry it over the ground with the rapidity of cavalry'. It also has 'a very low price'. Therefore some of the weapons should be 'immediately constructed for a fair experiment in the field'.

Armed with this endorsement, Indiana's Governor wrote to the Assistant Secretary of War in Washington suggesting that the new gun merited an official exhibition.

> I cheerfully recommend [Dr Gatling] to you as a gentleman of character and attainments, and worthy in all respects of your kind consideration. Any favour you may be pleased to show him will be duly appreciated.

No reply, let alone encouragement, came back from the nation's capital. Presumably, if the letter reached anywhere besides the Assistant Secretary's desk, it may have encountered that Chief of Army Ordnance, so assaulted by irritating novelty that he was still blocking every fresh approach. (One is reminded here of the — no doubt apocryphal — assessor of inventions with a reputation for 99 per cent accuracy in selecting worthwhile creations. He confessed that his method was simple — he turned down everything.)

Misfortune of a graver sort was soon to come Gatling's way. Having mustered sufficient funds to initiate manufacture, he contracted for six weapons to be made by Miles Greenwood & Co., of Cincinnati. When these were nearing completion, the entire factory, together with all his drawings, patterns and pilot models, was burned to the ground. The unflagging Gatling set about raising more money and asked McWhinney, Rindge & Co., also of Cincinnati, to make a dozen guns. Such setbacks at least provided a convenient opportunity for improvement, and during this time the basic invention was altered, bettered and hastened in its rate of fire. Copper instead of paper was used for the .58 cartridges. This speeded up the action, and the fifty bullets contained in its coffee-mill hopper could then be loosed off in sixteen seconds. This rate of fire, faster than originally claimed, could not be maintained (as if 187 rounds per minute were possible). In practice, fifty rounds per minute might be achieved, with the hopper needing to be recharged after every speedy burst. There were also major defects. Despite the barrels having a tapered and rifled bore, the bullets tended to arrive at their destination not only without any signs of rifling on them, but actually sideways to their line of fire. Dr Richard Gatling still had quite a way to go with his philanthropy.

Newspaper coverage of the weapon's capabilities continued to be favourable. The *Indianapolis Evening Gazette* not only echoed this inventor's original motive, the saving of life, but also stressed the saving of money.

> One of these guns . . . costs $1,500. A regiment of men ready for the field costs about $50,000, and it takes $150,000 to keep a regiment in service twelve months. [One gun] may be considered very nearly equal to a full regiment of infantry.

In an effort to outwit Washington's ordnance blockage, a Gatling agent demonstrated the gun in Baltimore to General F. Butler, known as 'Beast' Butler. He ordered twelve of the Gatling weapons, at a bargain price of $1,000 each, plus 12,000 rounds of appropriate ammunition. He then personally directed their use, but without much skill, when some fighting broke out near Petersburg, Virginia. Butler was not only incompetent (as were so many of that war's generals) but was anti-Lincoln when fighting for the Union and, after various defeats, either resigned his post or was pushed. His nickname of Beast came, allegedly, from New Orleans where, after its capture, he ordered that any women 'insulting' Yankee troops should be treated as prostitutes, but further details of what form this punishment took are lacking.

As for Washington, its embattled Chief of Ordnance, J. W. Ripley, remained steadfastly unimpressed. But Richard Gatling was not merely creative, humanitarian and patriotic — on the Union side; he was also a businessman. In 1863, with the Civil War in full swing, he wrote to the French Royal Artillery suggesting that its nation purchased his weapon. The Europeans immediately replied with enthusiasm, requesting additional details as well as a sample gun. No less promptly, Gatling sent the relevant information, together with suitably flattering endorsements from military men, but with the proviso that 100 of the guns had to be purchased rather than a singleton. This arrogant suggestion never turned into a deal, partly because such a transaction soon became impossible. The United States, somewhat belatedly for a country at war with itself, and needing weapons urgently, then chose to forbid the export of all arms and ammunition.

Also somewhat belatedly, for a man desperate to have his weapon generally accepted, and knowing of the President's outspoken enthusiasm for armament novelties, Gatling wrote to 'His Excellency, A. Lincoln', in February 1864.

<u>It is just the thing needed to aid in crushing the present rebellion</u>. . . . The gun is very simple . . . and can be used effectively <u>by men of ordinary intelligence</u> [Gatling's underlinings] . . . May I ask your kindly aid and assistance in getting this gun in use? . . . Such an invention, at a time like the present, seems to be providential.

No reply came back. Abraham Lincoln was perhaps too occupied, and no longer so busily in favour of novel weaponry. Criticism of his administration, the impending election (of 1864) and the war's horrific progress gave him little opportunity for worrying about yet another weapon, however providential — or for bullying Washington's General Ripley to change his obdurate attitude. A further reason for the President's failure to reply may have been the fact that the gun's inventor had come under suspicion of being in favour of the South.

Gatling's North Carolina birthplace naturally made him suspect, however much he had resided lengthily elsewhere. More disturbingly, it was alleged that he belonged to the Order of American Knights, an organisation sympathetic to the southern cause. It was officially outlawed in 1863, and its leaders were then imprisoned. The O.A.K. soon re-emerged as the Order of the Sons of Liberty, with a membership believed to have reached 250,000. Not all its members favoured the South, and many of them were more disturbed by the increasing power of the Federal Government and of Republicanism in general.

Gatling's determination to manufacture his guns, and the fact that their assembly line was situated at Cincinnati, also increased misgivings about him. The factory was on the northern side of the Ohio river, and rebel guerrilla bands were occasionally operating in the mountainous territory south of the opposing bank. Why had Gatling chosen this difficult border area? Why not further from a front line? One theory suggested that this position made it simpler for the gun man to assist both sides, and therefore to sell his guns impartially, or even arrange for his premises to be successfully raided by the enemy. (What makes this innuendo bizarre, although it was widely prevalent at the time, is the presence on the Ohio's southern side of Kentucky, a community which remained loyal to the Union.)

At all events, Gatling chose to shift his centre of operations, abandoning McWhinney, Rindge & Co., and moving to a firearms manufacturer at Frankford, Pennsylvania. Perhaps the slur about Cincinnati and his loyalties had proved irksome. Perhaps, as seems more likely, the excellent reputation of the Cooper Fire Arms Manufacturing Co. proved most influential — that and the fact the company was based nearer Washington D.C. Or perhaps he merely wished to distance himself from Indiana, since the commanding general of that district had been the first to point an accusing finger at him. Every civil war must be extremely susceptible to suspect loyalties, but nothing concerning Gatling and his possible pro-Confederacy sympathies was ever proven. In any case, he was extremely busy, being conspicuously and fiercely occupied with improvements to his invention. It is easier to suspect that his allegiance lay mainly — if not entirely — with his gun.

So what effect did Richard Jordan Gatling's invention have upon the war which had prompted its creation? Had it been humanitarian, in reducing the need for so many to confront the enemy? And had it aided, as President Lincoln had been advised, in the crushing of the rebellion? In short, was it in the slightest influential in contributing to the war's awesome total of 600,000 dead? And had it lessened, as originally hoped, the number of deaths from infection and disease rather than the war itself? The answer, in brief, is none and no. It altered that war's statistics not one jot, and certainly did nothing to lessen the Union's toll. In fact, so many thousands of those fighting for the North died in battle rather than from disease during the war's first two years that conscription was introduced in March 1863 to keep up numbers. As for its slaughtering of southerners, the gun scarcely saw service in any major fight. 'Beast' Butler's purchased weapons were used when that general became 'Bottled-Up Butler' after the Confederate's General Beauregard had turned the tables briefly in May 1864, but the Gatling guns were no more than moderately relevant during that engagement near Petersburg, Virginia.

Only in January 1865, three months before the war's conclusion, did Gatling achieve a proper and official trial of his gun in Washington. By then it was a much better weapon than he had originally devised — and which he had tried so determinedly to sell. Most importantly, he had overcome its principal weakness, the problem of gas leakage from around its breech following each explosion. There was also a new Chief of Ordnance for the Union, Ripley having at last departed. This newcomer was enthusiastic, but preferred that the weapon should be one-inch calibre rather than .58. If Gatling was willing and able to make such guns, the Army would not only require eight examples, but would conduct proper tests at its Frankford Arsenal, just down the road from the Cooper factory. The inventor was immediately compliant. Many thousands of rounds were soon detonated, most successfully, during these trials. The officer in charge of them was commendably succinct in his final report: 'The gun worked smoothly in all its parts.'

There was, however, one forthright confrontation with Gatlings during the U.S. Civil War. This dramatic act took place, strangely, in New York City. Three of the guns were used to defend the *New York Times*, no less, and they achieved victory without firing a single round. From 13 to 16 July 1863, the island of Manhattan, in particular, experienced terrible rioting, this near anarchy arising in response to the new conscription laws. The cause of the crowd's anger, somewhat justifiably, was the exemption clauses which enabled wealthier citizens, those with a spare $300, to evade the draft. Not only did 50,000 New Yorkers then take to the streets, but 1,000 of them were to die during the furore. Henry Jarvis Raymond, editor of *The Times*, had vigorously condemned the outraged mob within his paper, and he therefore expected retaliation either against his offices, or himself, or both. Three Gatling guns were mounted in appropriate positions, these principally manned by him and Leonard Walter Jerome, a considerable

*Times* stockholder who was, as it happened, the father of Winston Churchill's famous and redoubtable mother, Jennie Churchill. After learning that the newspaper building, although flagrant as a symbol of wealth and power, was well defended, the rioters went elsewhere. (At least they had assessed correctly that a new kind of armament had been devised.) Gatling's guns, and their determined gunners, had therefore won the day.

The War Between the States was not just a hideous conflict. In all manner of ways it was a brand new kind, and it has been called the first truly modern war. Railways played a vital part, hurrying men and equipment from one region to another. The electric telegraph permitted generals to keep in touch with their scattered forces, and then issue orders to them. New kinds of rifle, breech-loading and more accurate, meant that men could lie prone, hide themselves, and annihilate troops, or even cavalry, when enemy consignments were advancing over open ground. Fortune now befriended the defender, and the longer range of rifles caused artillery to retreat, making its form of venom less accurate and usually less devastating. The fight was also a war against peoples, and not just their armies. And it was certainly one of attrition, with Ulysses Grant making the point most straightforwardly:

> I am determined to hammer continually against the armed forces of the enemy . . . until there should be nothing left for him but submission.

Some 4,000,000 men were mobilised on the two sides, and more soldiers died in that war's four years than the United States lost in World War One, World War Two, Korea, and Vietnam combined.

It was difficult for military minds to absorb the various lessons so blatantly demonstrated between 1861 and 1865. With so much change — scorched earth, speedy transport, overall control, massive numbers, rifled accuracy — it becomes understandable that the arrival of the rapid-firing gun tended to be overlooked. It had shown its power, but mainly in trials. By the war's end it had been effectively developed, but had not been properly deployed to show its capabilities. Rather like the earliest, mouse-like mammals which first appeared when great reptiles were so dominant on Earth, the few Gatlings were not seen as harbingers of tremendous

change. Just as millennia would pass before those mammals gained superiority, so
it would take time for the world to realise
quite what a Carolina-born, agriculturally
raised, medically educated and inventive
forty-three-year-old had had in mind
when, philanthropically, he had devised the
first practical, rapid-firing weapon known
to man.

# Chapter 2

# Alchemist, Minister, and Seaman

The Gatling gun may have been the prime rapid-firing weapon of its day, but its creator was not the first to think of despatching more bullets at an enemy than single-shot devices could ever do. Similarly, nothing could be achieved with rapid-fire until cartridges had been well developed, and no cartridges could be fired until gunpowder and detonators had been created. Richard Gatling's 'novelty' undoubtedly rested upon earlier thinking and earlier achievement. It is therefore necessary to retreat in time, first to the eighteenth century and then even earlier. Gatling's gun did not come out of the blue any more than any other gun has ever done. It had innumerable forebears, such as Puckle's Patent, even if this invention may never have fired a round. (According to the *London Journal* of 31 March 1722 it did do

52

so, discharging 'in the Artillery Fields sixty-three times in seven minutes by one man in the rain'. Detonating nine times per minute was good going, and better still in the wet — if the report is true.)

James Puckle was ahead of his time, not by a few years or even decades, but by a century and a half, as if he were recommending tanks to Napoleon or cannons to William the Conqueror. On 25 July 1718 'Mr Puckle, Gent.' acquired Patent No. 418 for a 'Portable gun or machine, by me lately invented called a Defence'. By way of lyrical explanation to his 'Sovereign Lord King George' (who, in knowing only German, may have missed the jollity) this creation was for 'Defending King George your Country and Lawes, to Defending Yourselves and Protestant Cause'. In similar vein Puckle also considered it an excellent weapon 'For Bridges, Breaches, Lines and Passes, Ships, Boats, Houses and other Places'.

Had the gun worked as well as Puckle hoped, it might have defended all manner of installations but, along with its creator, the weapon was far ahead of its day. Essentially it employed a rotating system, with several chambers being revolved manually, and with each one fired when it came into line with the single barrel. How, one wonders, would all of these detonations have been successfully achieved? At the beginning of the eighteenth century, and before the days of percussion caps, there were problems even in igniting a single charge. Striking a flint or using a smouldering length of cord was never easy or trustworthy, and the prospect of setting fire to several cartridges in succession as they became aligned must have been daunting. This difficulty did not prevent the inventive Puckle from manufacturing several of his weapons. A few survivors from that modest production line still exist in England, and there is even one in Russia's St Petersburg, but none — it is widely believed — was ever truly tested. And certainly none ever proved, as their inventor had proclaimed, the impossibility of 'carrying any ship by boarding'.

In Puckle's patent drawings the weapon does look extremely capable. It stands on a robust tripod. It can be swivelled in any direction. It is not unduly heavy, and the revolving system appears workmanlike, whether or not it worked. The feature of the gun to attract most attention, perhaps then but certainly now, is its designed ability for firing two types of bullet. The round sort was for service 'against Christians' and the square kind 'against Turks'. Firing bullets of any shape would have been difficult with this gun, but launching little cubes of metal would have been hardest of them all. Puckle's impressive signature which concludes his patent ends in a flourish of small circles, these presumably referring (as an early logo) to the multiple manner in which the gun might defend 'his Majesties Kingdom of Great Britain call'd England his Dominion of Wales Town of Berwick upon Tweed and his Majesties Kingdom of Ireland'. As the majesty concerned was then four years into his reign but still spending much time in Hanover, and as patents (described in English) were presumably of lesser interest to him than his considerable intrigues with Parliament, it is highly unlikely that George I ever encountered James Puckle, Gent., or the extraordinary 'Defence' this British subject had designed on his and Great Britain's behalf.

The military procedure of standing, or perhaps marching, while the opposition took aim and fired must have caused many an individual to wonder whether there might not be an alternative system which could despatch more bullets at an enemy than were being so stoically received. The lengthy business of firing, reloading, ramming, and cocking and firing, while comrades on either side fell down, must have concentrated all minds still upright most determinedly. There had to be a better way, and various individuals were to assert they had found an answer. According to William Drummond of Scotland, for example, there was a better way, one which he had dreamed up even before Puckle. This person patented (but only in his home nation) a multi-barrelled arrangement 'allowing one man to take the place of a hundred musketeers'. A single fuse moved past the many touch-holes and caused, in theory, a cannonade. In practice this notion never came to fruition, theory being so often ahead of the game. More excitingly, and published in 1663 within the *Transactions* of Britain's newly formed Royal Society, a paper described how to use the force of recoil, as well as the gases within the barrel, to reload a weapon, again and again. The device could be shot 'as fast as it could be, and yet be stopped at pleasure'. In effect it was a machine gun, save that it never left the drawing board.

Throughout the seventeenth and eighteenth centuries that old problem of ignition continued to be paramount even with single weapons, let alone multiple arrangements. Until a patent was drawn up in 1807 for a percussion system, on behalf, curiously, of a Scottish Presbyterian minister, there was no such method for igniting gunpowder. Formerly this could only be achieved either with the glowing 'match', this being a live coal, a taper, or twisted jute suitably impregnated with powder, or it was effected mechanically. With the latter system either a spring-loaded wheel was rotated against flint or a single spring did the same job when compressed and then released. Both methods created the necessary sparks — usually. The rotating wheel was expensive if well made, and all forms of glowing match were conspicuous at night and troublesome in wet conditions. The one-spring system, called a snaphance, was probably imported from Holland. The Dutch *snappen* and *haan* (snap and cock) implies that chicken thievery (and the wish to defend oneself if caught) may have been the spur for such a simple, cheap, unobtrusive, and effective ignition arrangement. Children who fire 'caps' so enthusiastically may little realise what an advance had been achieved when the Reverend John Alexander Forsyth did much the same, and put forward his 'Application of the detonating principle to exploding gunpowder firearms', patenting it on 11 April 1807.

It was indeed an application. The relevant discovery had been made twenty-one years earlier when, merely by banging with a hammer, it was learned how to make an explosion from suitable material. Most suitable of all was mercury fulminate, first detonated in 1799 and then awarded its thunderous name. (Chemically it was ammonium hydroxide mixed with a metallic oxide.) The Rev. Forsyth designed 'pill locks' into which the modest 'pills' of fulminate were placed, first by hand but later merely by pulling back the hammer of the gun. Allegedly Napoleon Bonaparte offered this Scotsman a huge sum for the invention; but why, one wonders, with Britain and France then at war, did the emperor not straightforwardly filch it? Most honourably, however, the minister chose to donate his invention to the British governments and there is even a commemorative plaque to this effect, the only one of its kind, at the Tower of London.

There ought also to be a plaque somewhere in the United States for the American seaman who, after learning about fulminate and its abilities, improved Forsyth's idea by encasing each pill more securely within pewter. Captain Joshua E. Shaw attempted to patent this undoubted advance, but his prolonged absences at sea from his homeland infringed that country's patent legislation concerning residency. This bureaucratic stumbling block at least gave the captain the opportunity to better his invention. He changed the pewter container to one of copper, but not until 1816 did he get his patent from the government — plus $20,000 as an extra sweetener. Within a year the U.S. had arranged for 100 of its Hall rifles, the first breechloading weapon, to make use of Shaw's percussion caps. In consequence, people were suddenly able to fire at each other with greater facility.

The first person in England to define gunpowder had been the alchemist friar, Roger Bacon, in 1252, several centuries before the Presbyterian minister made the old mixture so much more useful with his percussion discovery. And just a few more years had to pass before a nautical man was then able to better the Scottish arrangement. It was therefore a strange alliance which led to modern weaponry. George M. Chinn, gun historian, has aptly summed up this curious and prolonged origin:

It may be said that the combined intellect of three men from the most contrasting professions imaginable, an apothecary, a minister, and a sea captain, prepared the way for the wholesale experiments in the development of weapons.

But those nineteenth-century trials could not have taken place without the basic fact that certain substances, when suitably ignited, react violently. These substances then produce great quantities of gas in a very short time. However much the creation of good detonators sparked off such combustible materials, and then led to an outpouring of novel weaponry during the nineteenth century, nothing would have happened without an explosion at the root. 'Bang, bang!' says almost every child, sometime in its life. And bang, bang provided the fundamental fact of weapon development.

Strictly speaking, nothing can be called gunpowder unless it is used within a gun. To what extent the substance was not only discovered by the Chinese many, many centuries beforehand, and also found helpful, is a matter for happy debate, but China certainly did not use it for firing projectiles. Indeed, its explosive possibilities were even banned, save for fireworks and the like. Within the Gentoo Code of Laws, embedded deep in Chinese history, it is stated that the Magistrate will not make war with any deceitful machine or poisonous weapons. China, with its huge territory and without pressing rivals, could make that sort of edict, and then make certain it was obeyed. Jared Diamond, arch-distributor of absorbing facts, has pondered why a country which had invented 'canal lock gates, cast iron, compasses, deep drilling, gunpowder, kites, paper, porcelain, printing, stern-post rudders and wheelbarrows' should then slip behind 'late-starter Europe'. He finds relevance in its attitude to ocean-going ships. Seven centuries ago, it possessed the most impressive fleets in the world (one even taking Marco Polo, for example, from Peking to the Persian Gulf), but an anti-navy faction then developed. A new emperor, yielding to this group, soon dismantled the shipyards, dismembered the fleets, and effectively called a halt to the former enterprise. In consequence the great fleets swiftly disappeared. Something similar happened with the development, and then the curtailment, of gunpowder.

European explosions began their evolution with the thirteenth-century writings of Roger Bacon (Oxford and Paris) and of Barthold Schwartz (Freiburg and Cologne). Both men are said to have prepared chemical mixtures which caught fire rapidly. Bacon is particularly informative in his *Concerning the Marvellous Power of Art and Nature*. The precise formula he mentions, of saltpetre, charcoal, and sulphur, is eminently combustible, and therefore excellent for magic, pyrotechnics, and showing the power of nature. He never suggests using this force to launch projectiles, preferring to advocate the possibilities of frightening an enemy or merely blowing him up. Both Bacon and Schwartz were diminished by authority, with Bacon even imprisoned by his Order for fourteen years, too many of his works being considered heretical in their outlining of 'certain novelties'. He had asserted, for example, that the holiest Christian celebration at Easter was occurring on the wrong days, the calendar having slipped since Roman times. To suggest that the Church was wrong in any detail, whether small or major, was tantamount to heresy, the gravest crime of all. Not for another three centuries was this error, then even greater, to be admitted and corrected by the Church. As for Schwartz, his current reputation has fallen wretchedly. Modern scholarship believes that he never even lived but was instead created (according to Partington's *History of Greek Fire and Gunpowder*) to demonstrate the Teutonic origin of firearms.

Gunpowder, properly defined as an 'intimate mixture of saltpetre, sulphur and charcoal', served as the only known explosive between its origins, however obscure, and the middle of the nineteenth century. Saltpetre, or potassium nitrate, could be obtained naturally from soil, or by the conversion of sodium nitrate, or by the decomposition of organic substances which happen to be rich in nitrogen, hydrogen, and oxygen. If potassium salts are in this mixture, and conditions are good for transformation, some ammonia and carbon dioxide will be created. Bacteria will then act upon the ammonia to make nitric acid. When this acid comes into contact with ammonia, it produces ammonium nitrate, which will then react with the potassium to form potassium nitrate, so crucial an ingredient for gunpowder. Charcoal was more easily created (and better understood), with thin branches of willow being particularly satisfactory. As for sulphur, this element occurs naturally, but its impurities have to be removed before it too is suitable for gunpowder's creation.

Essentially the powder explodes because saltpetre's considerable quantity of oxygen (potassium nitrate being $KNO_3$) serves as fuel for the burning of charcoal, and therefore transforms this solid substance into the gases of carbon monoxide and carbon dioxide ($CO$ and $CO_2$). There is no absolute necessity for sulphur in the explosive reaction, save that it burns at a lower temperature than the carbon of charcoal. It therefore assists with the combustion of that carbon, and generally aids the process. (It is easy to imagine early alchemists tinkering with, and often deeply regretting, the experimental mixtures which they created, and then combusted, eventually explosively.) The actual percentages of the three ingredients are important in creating a potentially violent mixture, but there are advantages and disadvantages in every successful concoction. Maximum gas production is required for maximum effect, but this needs to be coupled with a minimum of ash production. Speed of reaction is also relevant. The greater the proportion of saltpetre, the slower will be the combustion, whereas increasing amounts of charcoal and sulphur will accelerate it. Charcoal produces more heat, along with the two gases, but sulphur makes the ash. The very best compromise, which leads to the most complete oxidation, is 84 per cent saltpetre, 8 per cent sulphur, and 8 per cent charcoal. (Bacon's recommended percentages were 'six parts of saltpetre, five of sulphur, and five of charcoal', or 37, 31, and 31 per cent respectively. These ratios explain why his formula was best for demonstration, and for magic, and a long way short of modern powder's explosive properties.)

As vital as their percentages, and greatly influential in the eventual reaction, is the manufactured intimacy of these three ingredients. To what level of fineness should they be ground, and then hardened, and finally granulated? Only a pestle was used in the earliest days, but rotating drums were gradually incorporated, and then grinding mills, and finally tremendous presses. Trial and error provided solutions as to how much milling, compressing and general intimacy achieved the best results. (Yet again, it is easy to imagine the whole procedure going horribly wrong, with countless individuals — and even their more distant accomplices — belatedly learning what should not be done.)

Once the so-called black powder had been suitably prepared, it was ready to become gunpowder. Mixtures can explode without being confined, but constraining their reactions makes them greatly more effective. From 1346, and for the next 500 years, that old formula of 84 per cent saltpetre, 8 per cent sulphur, and 8 per cent charcoal (with slight modifications) reigned supreme. It blasted all manner of projectiles, and its detonations were heard on almost every battlefield. It made castles suddenly less secure, their formidably impressive keeps and battlements no longer so impregnable. Eventually, as the nineteenth century progressed, chemists learned how to create far more powerful explosions, these proving safer (for their users) and more destructive in a thousand different ways; but nothing, until the creation of atomic bombs, was quite so revolutionary as that fourteenth-century addition to the ground-based armoury of war. It must have been terrifying to realise that the old rules had been so violently transformed. Instead of sharp steel and pointed arrows ruling the fight, with a few extras like catapults and assault towers, men could suddenly be blown apart or severed by a cannon ball.

The year 1346 witnessed the Battle of Crécy. The English longbow won the day of 26 August when Edward III's army routed Philip VI's of France, even though outnumbered four to one. English archery had proved supreme against the lightly armoured opposition. England's longbow would continue to win battles for a while, but at Crécy, among the noise of conflict, there was also the occasional sound of detonated gunpowder. Historians sometimes disregard the fact, with so much else proceeding during the turbulence of those times, but the English king had also brought some cannons with his bowmen, their operation on the field of battle being the first generally accredited use of artillery in a major engagement. The guns did not fire projectiles of any kind, but undoubtedly made a bang. Such weapons were known as stampede cannon, their purpose being to terrify the horses and also frighten men. The explosive roar was all the greater for being initiated within iron tubes encased in wood. The huge quantities of smoke also liberated by each detonation helped to create additional anxiety.

It is intriguing that multiple-weapon systems were developed about the time when explosions were first being used in war. During the latter part of the fourteenth century several iron tubes were linked together, each packed with explosive. They were then filled with pebbles, and eventually fired simultaneously. Known as ribaulds, as organ guns, or *chars de cannon,* these various devices were also loaded with iron balls and then with single rounded stones to be hurtled at the enemy. Now that fire-power had arrived, visibly as well as audibly, everyone wanted more and more of it in any form that worked. Even breech-loading guns were devised, an advance which would not re-emerge until the nineteenth century.

The 1400s witnessed the development of even greater weapons. Huge cannon, allegedly firing half-ton stones, were used during the vanquishing of Constantinople in 1453. Louis XII of France employed a weapon with fifty barrels. Leonardo da Vinci invented a fan-shaped device, its projectiles intended to spray an area, and its ignition touch-holes arranged conveniently close to one another. Despite the willingness of gunpowder to explode, and the military enthusiasm for making use of it, the problem of setting fire to it still remained a sticking point. Combustion had to be initiated without doing greater harm to those despatching the missiles than to those receiving them. Hence everything waited in attendance until the reverend and the sea captain put their wits (so distantly) together to create percussion caps.

The United States, as a nation, bore little relation to others. Its new arrivals were fanatics for improvement, for gadgetry, and novelty. Wherever there was need, there was invention. Europe was nothing like so single-minded in this respect. For one thing, it had servants and labourers and employees to do the menial tasks. Why bother about better reapers, binders, haymakers, potato peelers, apple corers, and every kind of labour-saving device when labour was relatively so available? When the telephone was invented (by a Scotsman in America), a City of London man famously stated: 'Why bother with such a thing when we have plenty of messengers?' The United States was perennially short of every form of worker — from the outset. There was so much to do in that new land, so much change to initiate, so many possibilities. No wonder it imported slaves from Africa and made powerful use of them. In any case, so many of America's immigrants from Europe were determined to fend for themselves, to hack new dwellings from the wilderness, to exult in the freedom they had so recently acquired. Just as they revelled in axes, saws, hammers, and ploughs to help them make their livings, so did they welcome everything which made their undoubted hardships a trifle easier. If some inventor had created a seed-planter to improve corn yield without its purchase being too costly, the thing had to be a blessing. If anyone invented anything which did the job cheaper, faster, easier, it had to be acquired.

And the same was true of better armament, with countless would-be purchasers up and down the land. Richard Gatling's agricultural machinery had scores, hundreds, thousands of potential buyers, yet his rapid-firing, crank-handled, and lethal creation had merely the government (save for the occasional military man, or newspaper editor, with money to spare). His invention was only for decimating armies and, once the War Between the States had been concluded, all urgent need for such a gun had gone. That particular lessening of interest did not mean a reduced desire for more ordinary weapons which could shoot bears, or game, or Indians, or even — from time to time — one's fellow countrymen. Suddenly all sorts of circumstances had begun to coalesce. In the years leading up to the Civil War, the American West had been invaded as never before. Therefore the number of people then wanting, or needing, personal armament had risen tremendously. Production by machinery had begun to prove its worth. Interchangeable parts were becoming a reality. Good percussion caps had already arrived. Cartridges were being manufactured more efficiently. Factories were growing, notably in booming states like Connecticut and Maryland. The old agricultural economy was being up-ended, and a brand new United States was being forged.

On to this stage, so ripe for his performance, stepped a man named Samuel Colt. The world was becoming right for him and, after much trial and error, he was becoming right for it. From being a youngster happy to take pot shots at whales off South Africa, he was very quickly growing, once he had learned to master his trade, into one of the richest individuals of his time. And also one of the most famous, well beyond America. And this all happened — when it did eventually get going — so very speedily. Everything had clicked, or would do so as soon as Sam Colt got his act together.

# Chapter 3

# From Whittling
# to Peacemaking

Samuel Colt must have had great charm, judging by the cooperation he received from all levels. He was also good-looking, being well bearded and with a handsome head. He certainly had drive, never removing his shoulder from the wheel once he had put it there. He could be ruthless with other people, such as creditors, and was devoted to his intimate family. The death of his daughters pole-axed him lengthily. As for more distant relations, such as well-meaning uncles, he could lie to them, cheat them and generally act as conniving trickster. Even his wife said he was high-tempered and impulsive. Nothing was allowed to get in the way of his huge ambition.

He lived his life as if knowing it might be short. At the age of fifteen he conceived the idea of a revolver. At seventeen he set about creating the weapons which would make his name. At twenty-two he received his first patent, and worked more determinedly on his guns, but not until the age of thirty-five did he make his first profit. Previously he had set up business offices in the states of Connecticut, New York, Maryland, and New Jersey. Eventually he would return to his home town of Hartford, but only in 1855, when aged forty-one, did he complete the factory of his dreams. One year later he married as a very wealthy man (and she too had money). Then, less than a year after the outbreak of the U.S. Civil War, he died aged forty-seven. In thirty years he had moved from wanting to make guns into being the most famous gun-maker of them all, his name renowned around the world. In a mere dozen years he had moved from profitability to tremendous wealth, the like of which no gun man (and few others) had ever known. One million Colt weapons, most frequently his patented revolvers, were made during his lifetime.

Samuel Colt had been born in 1814. His father was a go-getting businessman who tended not to get what he was going for. His mother was rich, thanks to the banking activities and West Indian possessions of her father, John Caldwell. The first of many tragedies in young Sam's life occurred with his mother's death when he was seven, this event causing her inherited wealth to vanish simultaneously. The silver spoon with which Sam had been born was therefore swiftly snatched away, but there were other sadnesses. Sam's older sister died in her infancy and his only other sister killed herself at twenty-one. As for his three brothers, they too were variously unfortunate. John was convicted of murder and then died in jail (when Sam was twenty-eight). Christopher died from natural causes when only forty-three, and James, a spendthrift, would spend considerable time attempting to sue his slightly older, and far more prosperous, gun-making sibling. 'A man must learn to paddle his own canoe,' said Sam. His upbringing and all that death had given him much incentive to cater for himself.

In 1829, when Sam was fifteen, he started work in Ware, Massachusetts, where his father had connections. It is said his earlier education ended with expulsion from a Massachusetts private school after he had detonated an underwater explosion. One year later he was at sea, on board the brig *Corlo* bound for India (and enjoying a 'gap year' in modern speak). On this voyage the Colt legends have their initiation. Apparently, while shooting at whales and porpoises when near the Cape of Good Hope, he was frustrated by being unable to fire his weapon with more than one shot at a time. (Many a boy, when simulating gun play, would sympathise with his plight because imaginative fighting with imaginative weaponry never runs short, even momentarily, of ammunition.) There and then, so the Sam Colt story goes, he fashioned a prototype revolver from available materials, such as bits of iron and wood. It is believed that he had been much impressed by the ship's wheel, noting that each position on each spoke passed a particular fixed point however much the wheel was turned. At all events, his design would have the blessing, when properly made, of firing six shots in succession.

After returning home to Hartford, Connecticut, Sam ordered some gunsmiths to create such a weapon from his wood and iron design. Hesitation was never his dominant suit, even at seventeen. He also asked weapon-makers in Albany, New York, to apply his revolver principle to long arms, such as rifles, but nothing was to function properly from all this fabrication, and certainly nothing like money came his way. Youngsters frequently try and fail, and many a youngster then selects some other line of work which actually pays, but Sam

Colt was of a different calibre.

Impulsively, recklessly, disdainfully — in that he knew no one living there — Sam moved to Baltimore at the age of twenty. Perhaps he wished only to leave his home environment, with solo canoes being best paddled without family involvement. His ambition to make guns steadfastly accompanied him, and so did a shortage of funds. In those days of snake-oil salesmen, and four-wheeled loads of merchandise forever ready to be galloped out of town, the impoverished Colt set off south and west, notably down the Mississippi river, to gain some capital as 'Dr Coult, practising chemist from New York, London, and Calcutta'. His money-earning speciality was nitrous oxide, better known as laughing gas. Fly-posters informed passers-by of the treat in store should they part with cash.

### Nitrous Oxide

### GAS

### for Ladies and Gentlemen

Dr S. Coult, respectfully informs
the Ladies and Gentlemen
of this vicinity, that he will
administer the Exhilarating Gas on

MONDAY EVENING AT THE CITY HALL

Sam Colt presumably did return with extra dollars in his pocket, but he assuredly longed to give whiffs of $NO_2$ to his unrelenting creditors. At Baltimore, and in particular, there was John Pearson, loyal employee and noted gunsmith, who was outspokenly miserable at the lack of recompense. 'The manner you are using us in is too Bad,' he wrote; 'Come up with some money . . . In the Devil of a ill humer and not without a cause.' When on the road, and far from Baltimore, Colt had surely learned a thing or two from fellow travelling salesmen about the occasional need to leave town, and back in Maryland that hour had clearly arrived. 'Need money, wood, rent is due, shop is cold,' wrote Pearson finally, but his proprietor had already abandoned him, his colleagues and the Baltimore factory to start all over again in Paterson, New Jersey.

There were good reasons for Sam to choose the Paterson location. It was in another state. It put 170 crow-fly miles between him and Baltimore. The town had a good manufacturing base and was America's first planned industrial city. It also possessed some influential and wealthy relations, such as his cousin, Roswell L. Colt, a prominent citizen, but within a wretchedly short time Sam might have believed himself back in Baltimore. All too soon yet another workforce was wondering when, or if, another pay-packet might ever come its way. Their youthful proprietor was struggling, borrowing, lying, inventing, failing, redesigning, making promises, defaulting on promises, and growing increasingly desperate. Worst of all, his guns were not performing satisfactorily in their tests. The government did purchase some Colt revolvers, but decided their poor quality, rather than poor design, was making them less than adequate. Unfortunately the nation itself was then struggling with a loss of financial confidence. At least Sam Colt's father, the unsuccessful entrepreneur, was still staying faithful to his unsuccessful son. As Colt historian William Hosley has phrased it, this loving parent 'generally covered up for the centrifugal chaos Sam continued to create'. The truth, as Hosley added, is that 'Sam Colt was an abrasive opportunist who lied, cheated, and bluffed his way towards perfecting the first practical repeating firearm.' The Patent Arms Manufacturing Company of Paterson, New Jersey, did make some 3,000 pistols and 1,500 long guns, all using the revolver principle, but the failing company was terminated in 1842, six years after it had been begun with such fresh hope.

Sam Colt went to lick his wounds in New York City. His backers, and that beneficent cousin who had jointly loaned him several million dollars in today's money, also had to lick their very considerable wounds back in Paterson. Not only had the New Jersey experiment proved unprofitable, but the weapons manufactured there, even at the end, were still far from perfect. There was too much 'multiple discharge' when other cartridges fired prematurely. There were too many moveable parts, and the original thirty-six had to be trimmed to seven. A double cocking system made aiming difficult, and accumulated powder from earlier detonations tended to jam further firings. Yet more tediously, the guns would fire themselves even if accidentally hit or dropped. Critics therefore had a point when saying that the Colt long arms, in particular, were 'more dangerous at the breech than at the muzzle'. The short arms, such as hand guns, tended to be less personally damaging because they were fired further from the face, but the situation was far from satisfactory. At least better mousetraps, the traditional fare of inventors, tend not to kill or maim those who purchase them.

New York City was the largest, probably the most exciting, and certainly the most cosmopolitan city in the United States. On his arrival, the failed revolver enthusiast did not sit upon his hands. In that exuberant place he steadily designed, manufactured, acquired patents, met influential people, found new friends (such as Samuel Morse, of the code), caroused merrily, joined clubs, won awards, educated himself in chemistry and engineering, and repeatedly beseeched the U.S. government for assistance. Most notably, he wanted help with an underwater mine he had created. To gain publicity, he not only approached President John Tyler but acquired a derelict 500-ton schooner. When floating this hulk down the Potomac River conveniently near to Capitol Hill, he fired a seventeen-gun salute to encourage his audience, before starting the explosions. (The nitrous oxide salesman, now twenty-seven, was remembering a thing or two concerning showmanship, and how best to stir a crowd.) The first — and more distant — firing did no damage whatsoever, the second splashed the vessel, and the third blew it to smithereens. Everyone was impressed, save for the U.S. War Department. Its nation had been at peace for thirty-five years, and new munitions of any kind were far from high on its priorities.

Then in 1846 war broke out against Mexico. At once, Sam Colt wrote to his father requesting further funds. Colt senior, so helpful during failure, then chose to be unhelpful when light was at last appearing at the tunnel's end. As for Sam, whose prowess with spelling was never strong, he angrily replied: 'A little money invested in mashinery . . . would be dubled every year while the war lasts.' Only Elisha Colt, of all Sam's relations, was still willing to assist, and he did so when wisely appreciating that events were becoming more propitious. Sam's guns from his new designs were now safer and cheaper, and the prospect of U.S. government intervention soon became reality. Revolutions were also simmering all over Europe, leading to further conflict with an accompanying lust for weaponry. Guns were suddenly on everyone's agenda, particularly if they could deliver a more rapid form of fire. And Hartford, Sam's birthplace, was no longer the simple market town it had been for some two centuries. It was high time for the prodigal to return.

When Sam had left for Baltimore thirteen years earlier, Hartford's citizens, steeped in tradition and unwilling to change, had been resisting manufacture. Yet the town's position on the Connecticut River, a major shipping highway, meant the community was well placed to become less conservative, to welcome industry and restrain its young men from heading elsewhere for better pickings. The railway had reached Hartford in 1839, and water power was yielding to steam power, causing broad-based manufacture to be a saner proposition than subservience to the needs of agriculture. Sam had left a place with half a dozen wholesale stores. He returned to find a civic pride in chimneys belching smoke.

The inventive pioneer who proclaimed he was first even to conceive of 'repeating firearms with a rotating chambered-breech' was about to land on his feet. The new war with Mexico was one blessing, as the government now favoured novel weaponry and was making purchases. The change to Hartford itself was another. So too was the advent of better machinery, with its near-perfect production of identical parts. Interchangeability of pieces would soon be arriving, and any new industrialist setting up shop could get practical advice from others along that booming Connecticut

River. Sam Colt could therefore hire individuals who knew about machinery and about quantity production but, most importantly of all for any form of progress, his latest gun designs were much better than their predecessors. That prolonged period of trial and error, however dispiriting, had been most educational.

It is important to recognise the great change in weapon capability which Sam Colt was about to introduce. He had been born one year before the Battle of Waterloo when 73,000 Frenchmen and 67,000 British plus an uncertain number of Prussian soldiers had fought each other a few miles south of Brussels. The style of warfare these antagonists employed had been little altered for many years. Most of the British in that engagement clutched their Brown Bess muskets. These weapons, scarcely changed for a century and a half, fired an iron shot three-quarters of an inch in diameter. The powder to fire it came from a paper cartridge. The soldier bit off the cartridge end, tapped a little of its powder into the firing-pan, poured the remainder down the barrel, and added wadding and ball before pushing everything into place with a ramrod. If the man was skilled, he could do all this, and discharge

84

his weapon, every thirty seconds. Before too long, if he kept on firing, the flint would need replacing, and the barrel would need cleaning. The ball he fired could inflict a fatal injury at several hundred yards but, with accuracy so difficult, its victims would probably be quite distant from the point of aim. At Waterloo there were also Baker's rifles, which were more accurate — they were rifled — but more time-consuming in their loading owing to the tighter fit down the barrel.

There were also cannons at Waterloo, these varying from four-pounders up to twelve. They could fire iron balls (most visible if coming your way), or shells (which exploded when their burning fuses reached the powder), or grape shot (which used almost anything available, such as bits of iron and nails). These three forms of missile were all despatched by applying a 'match', which was kept burning throughout the engagement, to the touch hole, which could be 'spiked' by an enemy merely by hammering a nail into it. Gun barrels had to be sponged clean after every firing, but good teams could match the infantry's rate of detonation, namely twice a minute. After every firing from every kind of weapon there were great quantities of smoke, and this steadily made any aiming of the guns more difficult.

Once again, as with long weapons, the recipients of all these artillery missiles had to stand and wait for whatever came their way. The shot could do fearful damage, removing a leg or a head. If men were closely packed, one ball could kill a dozen or two in quick succession, its momentum not greatly reduced by travelling through the humans in its way. Therefore infantry often stood no more than three men deep or even two, with each rank firing at the enemy in turn. At Waterloo a contingent of Frenchmen was ordered to advance in a massive and terrifying formation, twenty-four ranks deep and 150 men wide. This formidable cohort looked invincible, with 3,600 men marching so stolidly together. It was also frightening, but actually ineffective, with only the outsiders able to shoot and the whole compressed consignment a first-rate target for artillery.

With Sam Colt's birth in 1814, and Richard Gatling's three years after Waterloo, this was the form of fighting which had partnered their arrivals. Hence the revolution these two men emphasised, that firing could be a great deal more rapid than had been customary. Sam Colt was first of the two to have this thought, and first to see a measure of success heading in his direction. In the mid-1840s he could finally afford to smile. He had a good revolver about to be manufactured, and a good understanding of how it should be made. There was a convenient and timely war in progress and, no less importantly, the government was suddenly in favour of novel weaponry.

That smile was then very nearly wiped away when problems surfaced in the customary Colt style. Sam got on well with officialdom at Washington. He had accumulated backing. And he had approached great names in the gun business for manufacturing support, such as Edwin Wesson, Eliphalet Remington, and Eli Whitney Jr., the wealthy son of the more famous Eli Whitney, inventor of the cotton-gin. Colt scored best with Whitney, in whose factory at New Haven the Colt weapons were then created. An exciting order for 1,000 of his revolvers had come from Zachary Taylor, the experienced fighter against Seminole Indians who was then general in command of U.S. forces against Mexico. Colt was still in no position to manufacture his guns himself, hence the Whitney subcontracting to hasten things along.

Unfortunately deliveries were slow and, when the government became unhappy with such relaxed productivity, additional factories at Boston and Windsor Locks were set to work. When these also produced too slowly, both for the government's requirements and Sam's miserable impatience, the Colt-Whitney relationship began to sour and the younger man's cantankerous self rose up once more. He and Eli then parted angrily, leaving litigation in their wake, and they were never friends again. If Sam Colt could not succeed with government assistance, good funding, a war in progress and the gun-happy frontier territory being determinedly invaded, there seemed little hope for him.

At least he managed to remain on reasonable terms with the government and still possessed its contracts. These had been initiated mainly by a Texas Ranger named Samuel Walker. The Republic of Texas had only been admitted into the Union one year earlier, and its assorted residents famously appreciated interesting weaponry as much as anything. The Rangers had been established in 1840 as a new breed of mounted soldier, a kind able to ride seventy or eighty miles without dismounting. Texans had experienced frequent difficulties with Mexico in the recent past, notably with Santa Anna at the Alamo, and there had also been innumerable internal wranglings with Texans fighting each other. The fact that Colt's weapons could be fired eighteen times in fifty-eight seconds had brought them renown, and they had been much used against Mexicans, Indians, fellow countrymen, or indeed anyone meriting speedy reaction, particularly those also Colt-equipped. These guns still had imperfections, but Captain Walker was outspoken in finding more right than wrong with them. He had therefore lent his considerable authority to the Colt application for government assistance. Less happily, he became a thorn in Colt's side when the ordered and contracted guns were not delivered on time, whether from New Haven, Boston or Windsor Locks. After the rift with Whitney, and on abandoning his factories, Sam Colt returned to Hartford much like some injured creature retreating to its lair. 'Civic pride' was the reason he later affirmed. 'Availability of credit' was suggested by others. At all events, he purchased an empty textile mill on Pearl Street, just across the way from Edwin Wesson's establishment (he of the later Smith & Wesson).

Colt moved again in 1849, putting down

ever more permanent roots. Most of us know that year's date, and of the 49ers, such as the father of Clementine (whose shoes were number nine until she tripped into the foaming brine to blow bubbles mighty fine). Everyone knew of the great gold rush to California, and Colt certainly knew about it back in Hartford. At that time he had produced the .31-calibre 1849 revolver, and he would sell 325,000 of them. With all those adventurers heading for the gold fields, each man armed with a shovel, a little capital, much courage, a great deal of hope, and frequently a gun, the Colt factory was turning out precisely the right weapon at precisely the right time. Colt's Patent Fire-Arms Manufacturing Company had at last begun to triumph.

Arguably the most sensible thing Sam Colt ever did was to hire Elisha K. Root. This respected individual had sharpened his manufacturing skills with the Collins Axe Company, an organisation which had also profited from the westward migration of those times. Even if everyone did not want a gun, they almost all needed axes, and Root had developed exciting techniques for their mass production. Sam Colt gave this new arrival twice his Collins salary, making him the highest earner of anyone anywhere in a similar position. Sam thereby plugged a gap in his own abilities. He was a clever designer, and now had a skilled producer as superintendent; the two men's talents were entirely complementary.

In 1849, the year he moved to Colt's, Elisha Root was soon patenting machines for boring and rifling gun barrels, for turning stocks, for splining and making cartridges. He also perfected a drop hammer, and worked with jigs, tools, and gauges to make the Colt weapons as desirable as could be managed during his eight-year stay. All of this work, with machinery increasingly in control, emphasises the distance travelled from Waterloo when craftsmen had been in charge, and when factory production had not yet properly arrived. Root was to retire in 1857, a sick man aged only forty-nine. It is easy to believe he had worn himself out, first for Collins and then for Colt, before choosing to travel far from both of them. (Somewhat inevitably, his retirement present from Colt's was a beautiful box containing an 1855 .44 six-shot sporting rifle, an 1851 .36 Navy revolver, and an assortment of Eley Brothers percussion caps from England. It would seem that Elisha had little need for this donation: the whole package is still in perfect condition and exhibited in Connecticut's State Library.)

Soon after Root's arrival at Hartford, he helped to make the standard revolver price fall to $25, exactly half the Paterson amount. The seventy-strong Colt workforce was then earning, on average, $15 a week and — a fact which would have mightily astonished Pearson and countless former employees — was actually receiving the money when it was due. Only 100 weapons a week were rolling off the production lines, but more would surely follow. By 1851 Colt's 300 workers were creating 20,000 weapons a year, and more men were being recruited. In 1853 Colt ordered work to begin on a new factory. By 1854 the annual production figure was nearer 50,000, and it reached 136,579 in 1863, the central year of the Civil War. Colt's Hartford creation had by then become the world's largest private armoury. It had been founded on the simple notion that a more rapid rate of detonation than single shots was most desirable. The Colt weapons were not yet machine guns, but were mechanically made and undoubtedly promoted the concept of rapid fire.

In any case, one young man's dream, starting with whales and porpoises off South Africa, had finally materialised. As with many an aspiration, it had been premature. Sam Colt's personal shortcomings, plus his treacheries and deceits, had not helped, but his starting year of 1831 had been too early for his wishes to become true at once. Breech-loading, as against time-consuming muzzle-loading, had not then been properly developed. Neither had the expanding oblong bullet, able to take advantage of rifling within barrels. Nor had the metallic cartridge, so much easier to load and unload, particularly in repeating systems. The arrival of these three advantages would mean that soldiers could, at last, lie down before firing, which was better both for aiming and protection. Powder horns, ram-rods, round bullets, problems with dampness, and a discouragingly slow rate of fire, had all gone away. Waterloo was ancient history. Each infantryman in that battle would have given every penny he earned to possess a six-shooter, an accurate and reliable gun capable of firing six bullets in no more time than it took to pull the trigger half a dozen times. Suddenly, for military and civilian alike, such a weapon had become available — for $25 a piece.

Traditionally the military had mainly favoured long guns. Colt's revolving chambers could be universally applied, working for hand guns as well as the lengthier variety. His market was therefore both military and civil, and a low price was equally crucial in each area. Colt was not in the business of selling either expensive devices to a few or cheap ones to many customers; he wished to sell to everyone. Initially there was not much of a market for hand guns, as they were of shorter range than long guns and unconventional (for most forms of warfare and for hunting), but they were lighter. Colt was always trying to reduce weight as much as possible. The Walker .44-calibre dragoon pistol (named for the helpful Texan) was extremely heavy. By 1850 Colt had trimmed his main hand-held weapon to four pounds and two ounces. One year later this .36 model was both smaller and lighter. As for the famous .31-calibre of 1849, that was lighter still, cheaper, and perfectly timed for the westward migration. (It was not withdrawn from production until 1873.)

In 1849, that epochal year, Colt did not travel where his guns were proving so very popular, but he went east to Europe. He never had much use for his guns himself, and did not travel west to test them where they were such a way of life — and death. Instead, savouring another continent, he enjoyed this first foreign trip immensely, and wrote an exuberant Sam-style letter back to his cousin Elisha Colt. It was headed 'Burlin, June 12, 49'.

My dear Sir,
We have been in Paris six days & made a hastey trip by way of Brussels, Cologne, Hanover & Brunswick to this place where we arrived last evening having enjoyed the trip very much. We had from four to twelve hours in each of the principal towns we passed through & imployed it by driving with lightning speed to all the objects of interest. While our time would only permit us to take a bird's eye glimpse of things it was a great gratification to do even that [and] has given us a general idea of the caricter and peculiararites of the cites & people we have seen & I assure you there are wide contrasts between the people and seens here and our side of the Atlantic. I have no time to write to anybody other than yourself by this mail.

When in London, Colt had learned of the 'Great Exhibition for the Industries of All Nations' to be held within a 'Crystal Palace' two years later. He therefore commissioned a huge stand to be erected on his behalf, and returned to England in 1851 to promote this gun display himself. Presentations of cannons and other military hardware formed a major part of that extraordinary exhibition, the first of its kind the world had seen. Sam Colt had immediately realised the benefits such a public demonstration might bring his way. (Reading the Crystal Palace documents in London's Public Record Office is an eye-opener on countless levels. 'Should the working class be admitted?' asked someone. There was agreement, but also realisation that travel would be impossibly expensive unless given freely. Accommodation in London had to be provided within huge halls, where a thousand visitors could sleep on modest mattresses on the floor. Then there was the matter of toilets for the different classes . . .)

At its conclusion, the whole exhibition was adjudged a great success, and it even made a profit of some £350,000. There were thirty categories among the entire display, with the Colt Exhibit, No. 321, being part of 'VIII: Naval Architecture and Military Engineering, Ordnance, Armour and Accoutrements'. Samuel Colt's display was awarded an 'Honourable Mention'. This was not so distinguished as a 'Council Medal', with nine awarded in that category, or even a 'Prize Medal', with seventy-four awarded, but Sam was very gratified to receive his mention. He certainly made much play of it back home, as if he had won the highest prize of all.

Great Britain had frequently advertised itself, with some justification, as the workshop of the world, with Birmingham proudly declaiming that it made everything from drawing pins to steam-rollers, but many of that city's manufacturers were astonished to learn from Colt's exhibit that his pistols had been machine-made rather than by hand. There was so much discussion on this point that Colt was even asked to testify on the matter before a House of Commons select committee. The American visitor assuredly gained much pleasure in these proceedings, at least if judged by its questions and his answers.

'Where were you born?'

'Connecticut.'

'Is that an enterprising state?'

'Yes, it embodies more enterprise than is

contained in Great Britain and France combined.'

'Do you . . . make your pistols better by machinery than by hand labour?'

'Most certainly.'

'And cheaper, also?'

'Much cheaper.'

With Connecticut being no more than two-thirds the size of Wales, and with its population sparse (even today it is only three million), the effect upon the politicians following his answers must have been disturbing at the very least.

Britain's Institution of Civil Engineers, a particularly prestigious organisation when engineers were such public heroes, awarded Colt its Telford medal and elected him to its ranks, the first U.S. citizen to be so honoured. It then, yet more flatteringly, installed a bust of him in its Hall of Honour. Sam Colt was soon suggesting to the British government that he personally should be in charge of its rearmament. He offered to make as many muskets as were required at thirty shillings each, these every bit as good as the costlier hand-crafted weapons then in service. His suggestion was not adopted, but news of it travelled across the Atlantic where it was very well received. How great that an

American, only eight decades after the Declaration of Independence, and only four after the Anglo-American war of 1812, was proposing on behalf of the United States to take care of the British armoury! There was no need of nitrous oxide to put a great smile upon the inventor's face, or on everyone else's back home when they too heard the news.

After his return from Europe, the successful entrepreneur invited local journalism into his premises, and the *Hartford Daily Courant* did him proud. It considered his machines 'of greater curiosity' than the guns they made, and its correspondent was fascinated by their performance of intricate work, their shaping of metal in complex patterns, and their effortless cutting of steel. Perhaps Connecticut was still too agricultural for mechanised factories to be familiar items. In nineteenth-century America, as well as in Britain, there was a prevailing and straightforward astonishment at the abilities of machine production lines, particularly those so efficiently developed in Hartford by the brilliant Elisha Root. Armament production, in particular, was pointing the way to the future.

Sam Colt marketed himself and his philosophy along with his weaponry, even asserting that his weapons were the arbiters of peace. 'God created men; Colonel Colt (which all called him) made them equal,' as they reiterated out west. 'My arms are the best peacemakers,' the inventor proclaimed, and bullets ricocheted all over the new territories while promoting harmony. In 1857 city policemen first carried guns, secretly, as they too tried to keep the peace. Colt promptly designed a .36-calibre, 3.5-inch barrelled weapon specifically for them, notably after the procedure had become legitimate. New York City was earliest (in 1845) to adopt the weapons, with Chicago, New Orleans and Cincinnati following not long afterwards. These guns were first used during the conscription riots of 1863 when so many died in New York City, an unknown proportion succumbing to Colt weaponry. Ordinary city dwellers had also started to want guns, to fire back, to protect the home, to have fun, to make the Fourth of July even rowdier. Colt's pistols no longer fired themselves accidentally but could certainly be fired mistakenly, once killing the daughter of another Hartford resident, Harriet Beecher Stowe, the author of *Uncle Tom's Cabin.*

Along the way Sam changed his logo

from the gentleness of two colt heads to a single rampant colt standing excitedly on its hind legs — and cleverly, even amazingly, balancing two long spears within its jaw and on its forward limbs. As for journalism, he exploited it totally. Give the editor a pistol. Get him to report all problems with other weapons. 'Have his Colums report all the axidents that occur to the Sharps & other humbug arms.' Make him print stories where Colt weapons had been well used 'against bears, Indians, Mexicans, etc'. Foster publicity. Give guns to George Catlin, so famously depicting the wilder world in North and South America. Londoners were told of 'the hordes of aborigines' still inhabiting the United States, making Colt's armament so crucial. 'Conceived in the North, baptized in the South,' as Bill Hosley has phrased it in a terrific book called *Colt, the Making of an American Legend*, 'Colt's arms reached maturity in the unique climate of the American West.'

Sam Colt stayed a bachelor until he was forty-two. He first met Elizabeth Hart Jarvis three years after his turning point of 1849, but he (and she) waited another four years before they married. By then he was enjoying his wealth, taking part in the festivities at Newport on Rhode Island, and the one-time hawker of nitrous oxide was seen by her as an ideal 'of noble manhood', having 'a princely nature' and being 'an honest, true, warm-hearted individual'. Was this person, with 'majesty in his forbearance' and 'gentleness and tenderness', the same person who had 'lied, cheated, and bluffed his way' on the ladder to success?

The couple's honeymoon was lavish, expensive and exciting. Their Fourth of July dinner in London was hosted by George Peabody, the head of America's most powerful bank, which had been founded by fellow Hartford citizen J. Pierpont Morgan. Sam and Elizabeth visited Holland, Germany, Austria, the Alps, and then Russia. As a highlight, they were invited to the formal coronation of Czar Alexander II one year after his accession. Sam Colt promptly hired suitable carriages, clothing, and attendants for this occasion. The Crimean War against the British was about to be concluded, both sides having been equipped, in part, with Colt weaponry. But that sort of fact did not then disturb an armament manufacturer, nor does it now.

Upon their return to Connecticut, the Colts settled into the harmony of a contented marriage. Far from quelling or diminishing the bridegroom's considerable ambition, his new status, embracing wealth and fame, seemed to fan its flames. A successful factory, a good home, a profitable business, and the initiation of a family only caused him to become yet more determined and flamboyant. He decided to construct Coltsville, a rural paradise for workman and employer alike, a place of education and worship, an amalgam of culture and every possible amenity. 'An enterprise of this magnitude . . . carried through by one man is without parallel in this country,' declared the *Hartford Daily Times*, either apprehensively or enthusiastically.

Colt next played what might be called the race card. He welcomed the notion that Germans and Irish, then flooding the nation, should also flood Hartford. Between 1850 and 1860 the town's population doubled, partly due to Colt's recruitment drive, but also because the place had generally accepted that a new kind of day had dawned. Indeed, in 1850 agriculture was toppled from its prime position as the most important section of the town's economy. Sam Colt's apparent benevolence towards immigrants should be taken with some salt; these newcomers were cheaper to employ than home-grown Americans. The German community was particularly strong, with even a *Hartforder Zeitung* on sale for a time. Colt also threatened to quit the city if its fathers proved too difficult, moving his money and prospects elsewhere.

The successful, and triumphant, industrialist found it difficult to restrain himself. He built Alpine-type dwellings to make the Germans feel at home. He grew willow, as the Dutch did, to protect the dike which protected the factory from flood, and the Colt company promptly profited from a willow-ware industry. His guns were selling better than ever, particularly when the War Between the States grew nearer. Workers had to arrive by seven a.m., and not an instant later. In the early 1850s Colt reduced the eleven-hour day to ten hours. His basic wage for males was $2.00 a day. (Farm workers then received $25 a month.) Women were mainly set to work in the cartridge department and earned seventy-five cents. They handled explosive material, their workplace wisely and cynically situated one mile distant from the main armoury. Most favoured for this potentially hazardous task were recent, still unmarried immigrants.

By now Coltsville was flourishing. Its workforce was content, and growing. The boss was boss of everything, of work and home, of body and spirit. Living in Colt dwellings, attending Colt schools, worshipping in Colt churches, and manufacturing Colt armaments does sound neat and tidy, much like the southern plantations, save that Colt's workers were free to leave if, which was improbable, they could find better livings elsewhere. Sam and Elizabeth's huge mansion, Armsmear, looked down upon his empire where (the frequently flooded) South Meadows used to be. He planned to double his factory's output as soon as the looming war became serious, this being a second fortuitous call to arms. His industry would profit the Union, and his commitment to the northern cause would ennoble Hartford. Along the way he would assuredly become richer than ever before, provided that fate chose not to intervene.

# Chapter 4

# Making Hay and
# a Broken Spring

Sam Colt's personal story is not only intriguing in itself, with his struggle against odds becoming such tremendous wealth, but it also helps to explain how one man can shape an industry. Inventions are not inevitable when their time has come; again and again they need the impetus of a single individual. That person is both catalyst and principal ingredient. History is rich with example, and the Sam Colt saga is a prime instance of this drive. Like the first cracks in a dam, their effects can be overwhelming. So too the places where these people choose to work.

During the mid-nineteenth century there were scores of American cities with more residents than Connecticut's capital, Hartford, and its population is still less than 120,000 individuals. In Sam Colt's time

Hartford was even more sparsely populated, and yet it became the spot to be, a silicon valley of its day, the richest small city within the U.S., the first to be fully lit by electricity, the place where gun man Richard Gatling eventually put down roots, the home of many publishing concerns, of Harriet Beecher Stowe (widely popular for her writing), and the site chosen right next to her home in 1871 by Mark Twain for his own dwelling.

Colt's move back to that community, and to the place of his birth, was the fact that put it so positively on the map. However, even before Colt's return, Hartford was a special spot. It had been settled by Puritans in 1636, a mere sixteen years after the Pilgrim Fathers had landed at Cape Cod.

Hartford was therefore an ancient city in which Samuel Colt had been born, and to which he returned after commercial failures elsewhere, but it became even more renowned when his work began to triumph, when everything started to go well for him provided, as already mentioned, that ill fortune did not intervene. Unfortunately it chose to do so.

In 1854, when Sam Colt was only forty, rheumatism began to trouble him. Six years later he was writing from Havana, Cuba, while hoping to benefit from that city's hot sulphur springs. The Civil War was then imminent, and he had no wish to miss out on such a boost to his business and his life:

Run [the factory] night and day with double sets of hands until we get 5,000 or 10,000 ahead of each kind . . . We cannot have too many to meet the exigiences of the times . . . <u>Make hay while the sun shines</u> . . . You must write to me by every steamer, anything of interest, bank balance, no. of arms finished and on hand at armoury . . . News from New Orleans is very warlike, and I am sure of a market for all the arms we can make whether there is a fight or not.

How galling it must have been to be laid physically so low when expectations were suddenly so high. Unfortunately, one year later, he was back in Cuba at the springs — and with his spelling no more improved.

Since my arrival here I have to take a sulpher bath daly and feel much benefitid from that and the delightful warm atmosphere — 80 during the day and 73–74 during the night . . . Was able to walk after the bath some 250 yards without my cruch this morning, and have spent much of the day at the Cock Fite witnessing the famous sport of this country — It is getting too dark to see, and the Flies and Musquitos are biting me horrably, so I must close.

One month later, and a week after the Civil War's opening shots had been fired, Sam Colt was in New York. He could not bear to remain in Cuba, however beneficial its hot waters, during such momentous times. Having hired a stenographer (much altering the spelling), he wrote to the Secretary of War in Washington, wishing to ascertain:

to what extent the Federal Government might desire to employ the forces of our manufactory in Hartford, and am stopped here by sickness . . . We can produce if required one hundred thousand military arms this year which amount may be afterwards increased to an indefinite number. Please bring this subject before the President . . . Until then I shall suspend individual orders.

In another letter to the ordnance chief in Washington, he regretted that he was 'too unwell' to meet him, and stressed that 'new construction etc.' would cost $1,000,000. He needed a contract for 'at least 100,000 rifled muskets to commence with'. He also needed the money to deliver what he presumed would be necessary, and therefore desired the contracts to set everything in train. Above all, he needed good health to make everything coalesce — the war's demands, his ability to satisfy them, and success of a kind beyond his most fervent aspirations. Colt complained, vociferously and most understandably, that it was 'too bad' his illness was striking 'just at harvest time'.

Fate then chose to intervene rather more determinedly. Nine months after those desperate pleas from New York, and six after his visit to further spas in Canada, Colt died at his Hartford home. His young widow was devastated, having already experienced blow after blow to her family. The Colts' first two children had died as infants, with Sam not leaving his room 'for weeks' when first-born Lizzie died, her portrait in his arms. Two more children were subsequently born but the girl, Henrietta, was poorly and also soon to die.

Sam's wife was pregnant with their fifth child when Sam himself expired in January 1862 at the age of forty-seven. 'The main spring is broken, the works must run down,' said the grieving widow, aged only thirty-five. She assuredly had a point.

The Colt labour force must have thought in similar fashion, as the entire armoury ceased work on 14 January 1862, Sam Colt's funeral day. That total closure, with the war at its height and with tremendous demands for more and more weaponry to be used against the South, sternly emphasised the main spring's loss. The one thousand black-arm-banded workmen filed past the body of their dead employer. Their 'colonel' had departed and his Armoury Band, having played so joyously at the Colt marriage less than six years earlier, now sounded melancholy tunes. 'Kindest husband, father, and friend, adieu' had been carved on the casket, but not the word 'employer'. That was surely uppermost in at least one thousand minds.

Elisha Root, one-time superintendent, returned from retirement to serve as pallbearer at his former employer's funeral. With Sam having departed it is easy to imagine pressure, from the widow and the workforce, exerting Elisha to rejoin the firm, whether or not his health had been fully restored. At all events, he agreed to take charge of the company, and to become its president, thirteen days after Sam's interment. Needless to say, his health did suffer but this man's loyalty — to Sam's memory, to the company, and to the Union — was intense, and poor health had to be disregarded, in so far as this was possible. The Civil War, then nine months old, had yet to peak in its casualty figures, in its request for arms, and in its demands upon the factory.

As for Elizabeth Colt, who had inherited a business worth $3.5 million (nearer $200 million in today's money), she may have thought no greater tragedy could come her way than the Colonel's departure but, only two years after that dismal period and on 5 February 1864, the famous and very busy factory was burned to the ground. No one learned the cause, and inevitably there was talk of Confederate arson with the war still raging, but the presence of cotton waste near driving pulleys, and of floorboards deeply soaked in oil, were much more probable. Elizabeth wept as she watched the conflagration from her bedroom window. Not only was her beloved Sam's majestic manufactory disintegrating before her eyes, but hundreds of men would be out of work, and hundreds of Hartford families would therefore be bereft. There was also the matter of cost, the fire destroying property worth $33 million in today's money. Sam Colt had never insured the building; that was not his way. His widow had then done so, but inadequately.

Elizabeth Jarvis Colt, devout Christian, steadily began to show the steel with which she was made. She had married in 1856, and had experienced an astonishing honeymoon. She had then been installed within a tremendous mansion overlooking 200 million dollars-worth of industry. Suddenly, between 1862 and 1865, she had lost her husband, her remaining daughter, her fifth pregnancy (as it did not survive Sam's death), the Armoury, and finally the company's replacement president. Elisha Root died at Hartford one year after the fire, three years after his master, and five months after the Civil War had been officially concluded, this loyal and talented individual having managed to see the Armoury through its most testing time. Elizabeth, as principal stockholder in the company, promptly appointed a major-general, William Buel Franklin, as Elisha Root's replacement. This man had good connections, having been a class-mate at West Point of Ulysses Grant and Thomas (Stonewall) Jackson.

To promote Sam's memory, Elizabeth then turned her full attention towards erecting the Church of the Good Shepherd, a much admired structure in open ground not far from the Armoury. In case any visitor might fail to link this building with the nearby factory, she commissioned innumerable reminders, such as carved revolvers, pistol grips, hammers, moulds, cylinders, and barrels as extra decoration. The font, with its three stone children, honoured the three Colt infants who had led such short lives.

Elizabeth herself did not die until 1903, having been married for six years and then widowed for forty-one. By no means did she forget about the Armoury after she had seen to its rebuilding following the fire. A biographical encyclopedia of 1887 even describes her as a manufacturer of arms. She had made absolutely certain that Colt's Fire-Arms Manufacturing Company continued to grow from strength to strength. That was the least she could do for her husband, the man whose fame, in her opinion, 'won honour and contributed largely to the prosperity of his fellow citizens, and of his native city, which he loved'.

With the Colts both dead and their dynasty extinguished, Armsmear was willed as a home for 'widows or orphans of deceased clergymen of the Protestant Episcopal Church' and 'as many impoverished but refined gentlewomen' as the building could support. Samuel Colt had made a revolution with the design and manufacture of rapid-firing guns. But Richard Gatling's post-war progress with the machine gun, and then the creation of the very first fully automated weapon, were to cause an even greater one.

# Chapter 5

# Guns and Gun Men Multiply

On 9 April 1865 Robert E. Lee surrendered to Ulysses S. Grant at the Appomattox Court House, Virginia. President Abraham Lincoln was shot five days afterwards, and the four-year slaughter of the Civil War was officially concluded during the following month. The need for weaponry might have seemed, along with the killing, to have terminated, but the stimulus of war had altered all manner of industrial development, notably in the North, for ever. And guns, far from having had their heyday, instead became yet more familiar items.

Once the urgencies of war had been removed, the western frontier was pushed forward yet more speedily. Kansas, Nebraska, and Nevada all joined the Union in the 1860s, with many other territories waiting in the wings. The Hollywood picture of gun-toting frontiersmen may not be wholly accurate — where nobody ever leaves home without a broad-rimmed hat, a gun-belt, and at least one gun — but weaponry did undoubtedly play a major part in post-war frontier life. Of today's total of contiguous states within the Union, there were still eleven areas to be absorbed after 1870 before these could form new stars upon the flag, namely Arizona, Colorado, Idaho, Montana, New Mexico, North Dakota, Oklahoma, South Dakota, Utah, Washington, and Wyoming. Guns were involved in every such acquisition, and Colt's six-shot revolver was being famously reported as the Gun that Won the West. Or, as Sam himself had written much earlier: 'The good people of this wirld are very far from being satisfied with each other & my arms are the best peacemakers.'

His works did not run down, as Elizabeth Colt had prophesied when her husband died. Colt's Patent Fire-Arms Manufacturing Company possessed too much momentum for that to happen. In the bleak January of 1862, when Sam's widow could only foresee his works' conclusion, the Civil War was still being fiercely fought. Output was expanding, and it continued to expand with Elisha at the helm. Even when he too departed, shortly after the war had been concluded, the impetus of manufacture was still strong and the booming Colt emporium stayed very much in business. Three years later, this arsenal on the Connecticut River was visited by Mark Twain. He was not yet a Hartford resident, but already a famous journalist, and was most certainly aware both of the city's fame and its prime exhibit:

The Colt's revolver manufactory is a Hartford institution. On every floor is a dense wilderness of strange iron machines that stretches away into remote distances and confusing perspectives — a tangled forest of rods, bars, pulleys, wheels, and all the imaginable and unimaginable forms of mechanism . . . No two machines are alike, or designed to perform the same office. It must have required more brains to invent all these things than would serve to stock fifty Senates like ours.

The factory by the river must indeed have been impressive, particularly when smalltime businesses were still more customary. There were then 1,400 workers in

Colt employment. The building in which they laboured had eight major rooms, each 500 feet long and sixty feet wide, creating the largest workshop — and by far the largest armoury — in the world. There were 400 rifling machines, with each barrel being subjected to forty-five separate operations. The rammers experienced nineteen, the hammers twenty-eight, and the stocks five, and there was a grand operating total of 454 distinct procedures within this single gun-making enterprise. As for the 'manufactory' itself, the place must have been horrendously noisy, with drop hammers hard at work, with 900 horse-power being produced and consumed via belts for the machinery, and the entire works compressed into six and half acres. All of this roaring, clanging, hammering, and screeching was occasionally supplemented by detonations. A proportion of the guns was regularly tested (up in the attic) and, if their firing proved faulty, they were returned for readjustment before being fired again. Did Samuel Colt, when whittling wood off the coast of South Africa, and then desperate to establish himself as a manufacturer of arms, ever imagine for one instant what the fulfilment of his dream might be? Or how the novel and desirable concept of rapid fire might invade the world's consciousness?

After the Civil War, that other major gun man of those times, Richard Gatling, also had a momentum of his own. His original and kind-hearted motivation — for saving lives among the military — had by then been transformed into a desire to perfect the gun he had designed. (There is little further talk from him of philanthropy.) He had missed out on the war, his weapon still too revolutionary and less than perfect in its novelty, but it was steadily being improved. In 1866 his much-amended version of a crank-handled gun was officially adopted by the U.S. Army, the first department of any nation to do so, thus marking the onset of mechanical weaponry. Gatling's gun worked well enough in tests, and he soon received a gratifying order for 100 of his weapons. Although he still lived in Indianapolis, and had his office there, he decided that the Colt factory at Hartford should make these guns for him. Not only was he therefore choosing the world's biggest and most famous armoury, but the forty-eight-year-old medical inventor also plainly considered it most suitable for his purposes. Sam Colt's initiative, and his subsequent determination, were therefore being underlined. The place to go for the manufacture of armaments was Connecticut's capital.

After touring Europe in an attempt to drum up sales, Richard Gatling soon chose actually to live in Hartford, the better to oversee manufacture. In 1870 he purchased a large, two-year-old 'Italianate' house, 27 Charter Oak Place. He too, like the residents of Armsmear not too far away, could gaze upon the factory where so many of the nation's guns, including Gatlings, were being made. There was now the Good Shepherd church to see as well, Elizabeth's imposing structure standing midway between the Gatling home and the Colt armoury. The new gun man could therefore never forget the individual who had brought him to Hartford, even if the two of them never met.

During those post-war years the Colt factory not only created weapons for other individuals and other companies, but spawned an assortment of gun men whose names would become renowned in the business of weaponry. Guns were made upon the premises, and so were gun men. Benjamin Berkeley Hotchkiss, born twelve years later than Sam Colt, learned his trade at Colt's factory before moving in

1867 to France (whose government was more welcoming to his ideas than Washington had been). William Gardner, originally of Ohio and a soldier in the Union army, was yet another to design a rapid-firing and handle-turning gun before — as he had no money of his own — arranging its manufacture by Pratt & Whitney, also of Hartford. Francis Pratt, a great gun designer as well as maker, learned his trade at Colt's. John M. Browning, yet another famous name in guns, produced the first successful gas-operated machine gun. This too was offered for production at Colt's Patent Fire-Arms Manufacturing Company, in 1890.

Sam Colt, if he had lived, might have gained some pleasure from the blatant admiration of his manufacturing techniques, and from their utilisation by other gun designers, but he would probably have preferred that all weapons emerging from his factory were of his design and bore his name. Richard Jordan Gatling was of a wholly different style. He had already achieved success, and money, via his patented corn drill. Just as he had learned about medicine, in case major illness came his way again, he was keen to make, and then sell, his gun. Even so, he did not have the single-minded obsession which had so assaulted Colt. His personal fuse burned more slowly, making it immediately understandable why he lived for a far longer span of time, being born only four years after Colt and dying more than four decades later. Although his gun brought Gatling more renown than his drill had ever done, or would ever do, his creation was principally another invention to be marketed and sold. Colt had hit upon the idea of a revolving chamber, and had then worked defiantly, pig-headedly and single-mindedly, with this fixation. Gatling had straightforwardly presumed, after several other inventions in other areas, that revolving barrels would fire more bullets at an enemy than single barrels could ever do. Excessive barrel heating was a problem which a plethora of barrels would circumvent. He had then devised such a gun, and this was one more patent to his name.

When wealth came their way, the Colts had spent it lavishly and flamboyantly, with their Armsmear mansion reflecting that indulgence. Gatling, on the other hand, had bought a second-hand and comfortable dwelling a few hundred yards nearer Hartford's centre which had no grand estate to partner it. This distinction between the two gun men has been perpetuated in modern times: visitors are currently welcomed at Armsmear's 'public' rooms where there is much to inspect of its former grandeur. Gatling's house is now a few apartments, without even a plaque affirming that he and his family once lived there. (The home was even pronounced 'unfit for habitation' a few years ago before its happy restoration.)

Essentially, as with the inventor himself and his style of life, the Gatling gun was extremely simple. One man fed the hopper with ammunition while another turned the crank and aimed the weapon. There were six barrels (in the first instance) and these were all rotated. One by one the cartridges fell into appropriate grooves, and a cam made certain that each cartridge was pushed in turn within a barrel. The bolt continued to move forward as the crank revolved, thus compressing a spring which, at the correct moment, released the striker pin. The Gatling gun was therefore the sort of creation one might expect from a man accustomed to designing sturdy agricultural implements. It was not a highly refined device any clock-maker might envy or admire, but the sort of thing a farmer's lad (or military recruit) would swiftly comprehend. Its most advanced component, once the gun had been properly improved, was the removal of a primitive percussion nipple and the substitution of a central cap within a brass cartridge.

The army's trials of this weapon were thorough and, or so it would seem, a touch light-hearted. At Fortress Monroe in 1866, for example, Gatling was tested more severely than his gun, as he reported later:

The young officers at the fort tried to play a trick on me. At their old howitzers they had trained artillerists. To me they assigned three old negroes. I saw through their game, and asked [them] to give me an hour in which to instruct my men how to use the gun . . . [They] learned very quickly, and in an hour, I was ready. The firing was a competitive examination and with my three old negroes I fired and made about three hits to [each] one on the target made by the old guns. Colonel Baylor, the officer in charge, was most impressed. I consider it a superior weapon to the twenty-four-pounder Howitzer . . . The moral effect of the Gatling gun would be very great in repelling an assault, as there is not a second of time for the assailants to advance between the discharges.

News that the United States government had purchased this Gatling weapon soon travelled across the Atlantic. Europeans were not only interested in the possible acquisition of whatever had so impressed the U.S. authorities — they had actually bought a new weapon in peacetime — but then asked for rights to manufacture the gun, as with Paget & Co. of Vienna, and W.G. Armstrong & Co. of Newcastle-upon-Tyne. These European versions were made with six or ten barrels, and chambered to accept local cartridge preferences, such as .65, .75, and one-inch calibres. Stringent tests were again conducted, with the guns pitted against the very best riflemen equipped with a similar quantity of ammunition. Colt's company helped with the European salesmanship and was outstandingly welcome to a certain Colonel Gorloff from Russia who visited Hartford to oversee the manufacture of 400 Gatling guns. Since he was under the Czar's direct authority, any failure on the colonel's part would have had — in his proclaimed opinion — to be followed by the personal administration of some weapon upon himself. No other European ever gave the Gatlings such examination and, with justification as well as Russian tradition on his side, Gorloff demanded that each ordered Hartford gun be stamped with his name (properly in Cyrillic). Consequently, when yet another Russo-Turkish war broke out — and Gorloff had happily become a general — the Russians fought with Gorloffs and the Turks with Gatlings. Both weapons were similar, although their calibres were different, being .42 for the Russians and .58 for the Turks.

*The Times* of London somewhat huffily criticised the Russians, the first Europeans to acquire the Gatlings, for 'making haste to adopt American inventions whether good or bad'. Armstrong's company in Newcastle, creators of most things military, had also made haste, receiving a licence to manufacture (and sell) Gatlings within the U.K. from 1869 onwards, later than the Russians but only three years after the U.S. had officially ordered some weapons to be made. Following all this interest, some less powerful nations decided they had no need of Gorloff-type inspection to check on manufacture, and purchased readily, with Egypt, China, and much of South America leading the race to buy. Britain hesitated, and then became most welcoming of all. The Gatling, it had realised, was just the thing to quell unruly natives, and it proceeded to do so, time and time again, in the final thirty years of the nineteenth century.

Meanwhile the Franco-Prussian war broke out. There is nothing quite like a war for adjusting military opinion, but machine guns in action around Paris between 1870 and 1871 did not always impress their observers, their users, or those at the receiving end. In any case 'long guns' had properly arrived, this conflict being the first when each side could load their rifles from the breech rather than the muzzle. And their rifles were accurately named, with the spiral grooves within their barrels ensuring an accuracy much greater than smooth-bored weapons were ever able to achieve. In addition, the Prussians intended to rely heavily upon their advanced artillery, while the French were pinning high hopes upon a secret weapon.

This was so secret that only those manufacturing it knew what the device looked like, and certainly not those who would have to use it. Each of these guns was covered in tarpaulins and accompanied by armed guards when it left the Meudon factory, permitting the story to circulate that foreign powers were better acquainted with the weapon than the French themselves.

(Indeed, a lengthy and illustrated account, 'On Mitrailleurs, and Their Place in the Wars of the Future', had been published one year before the war of 1870 in the British *Journal of the Royal United Service Institution*.) The hard-pressed French government, in making much propaganda about this novel and terrible device, may have bolstered flagging morale, but the actual truth was less exciting.

Called the mitrailleuse, this French 'novelty' was already twenty-five years old before being brought so covertly into action. Captain Fafschamps, of Belgium, had invented what was essentially a battery of guns strapped together (and he had done so some ten years before Gatling initiated his design of several barrels). At first there were thirty-seven fire-pieces in the Belgian weapon, a number later reduced to twenty-five. Two more Belgians, Joseph Montigny and Louis Cristophe, then made improvements to the gun, if not to its title, because the weapon soon became the Fafschamps-Montigny mitrailleuse. Commandant de Reffye, in charge of the Meudon arsenal, also lent his name to the gun assembly, confusing the issue further, but there is one single certainty: the French rank and file were only made aware of it when war with Prussia was imminent (it broke out on 19 July 1870). In theory the twenty-five-gun, 13-mm version could fire 444 'rifle shots' in a minute. In practice the enemy's Krupp guns, with ten times the range, could easily pick out and destroy the mitrailleuses whenever they appeared. Moreover, the gun itself was never so good in its actual use as in theory, with 175 rounds per minute more likely than the claimed 444. (The name mitrailleuse originates from the French for grapeshot, with mitraille being scrap-metal, old iron, etc. The title is somewhat more direct than machine gun, with one dictionary defining a mitrailleur as a 'wholesale slaughterer'.)

Just occasionally the French used the weapon in a manner suited to its capabilities. At Montigny-la-Grange the guns were placed with infantry rather than with field guns, and this new policy made all the difference. Within the war's official German history, one particular action is most significantly recorded:

From this point notably (a cluster of trees west of La Folie), a battery of *mitrailleuses* swept the border northwest of the cluster of trees, and another battery from the south angle of this cluster held under its fire the clearing which separates it from the Bois des Genivaux. In a short time General von Blumenthal saw the impossibility of an attack upon La Folie.

In short, the new gun could, and occasionally did, make its mark. For all those intrigued by coincidences, it is odd that the Montigny gun first did well at a spot named Montigny, and that French tactics — so often called a 'folie' at that time — were actually wise at a location of that name. But the eight-month Franco-Prussian conflict was not a proper test of machine-gun capability. The lesson of Montigny guns at Montigny and at one or two other spots was disregarded, more by the French than by the Prussians. As would happen in many later engagements, the weapons were seen as adjuncts to artillery rather than useful, or even crucial, extensions for the infantry. The mitrailleuses looked like guns, for each weighed two tons even without their ammunition. Therefore, and almost always, they were used like guns and suffered in consequence.

French military competence as a whole was a further issue, and tended to obscure the rapid-fire lessons which should have been learned. One American officer, writing much later about the warnings of that European war, stated that:

> the French were defeated . . . not because they used machine guns, but because they blundered in every other possible way. Their artillery was inefficient, their cavalry worthless, and their generalship conspicuous by its absence. Powerful as the imperfect mitrailleuse was, it was unable to rescue the doomed nation from the fate it had prepared for itself . . .

A war which witnessed the capture of the French Emperor with 100,000 of his troops at Sedan did not encourage others to think well of any of its ingredients, even the first deployment of a machine gun. However, some Prussians had been impressed by the weapon, as at Montigny and at the battle of Mars-le-Tour, when the fire from mitrailleuses increased 'losses almost to annihilation'. British representatives observed the conflict, but were unimpressed, partly because they had never been at the receiving end of such concentrated fire. In December 1871 the British Director of Artillery stated that:

Mitrailleurs, in my opinion, are comparatively feeble weapons, and their sphere of usefulness in war is very limited.

After Sedan, where many mitrailleuses had been captured, some Gatlings were acquired by both sides and introduced into front-line positions. According to a varied assortment of observers, these American weapons won more appreciation than France's ancient novelties. Indeed, even before the Franco-Prussian war, the Gatlings had been earning a better reputation among many nations, save by Prussia whose military hierarchy had thought more highly of the secret 'Montigny' long before they had actually encountered it in action.

After the war ended, the British appointed a committee of seven army officers to report upon the 'Montigny and Gatling Mitrailleurs', having purchased specimens of each type. This group subsequently asserted that 'the Gatling system was the better of the two', and recommended its introduction 'on board ship and in the field'. Britain's Field-Marshal Commander-in-Chief, the Duke of Cambridge (head of the army for an amazing thirty-nine years, holding this post from 1856 to 1895), listened to subordinates, notably those who had been to France as spectators of the war against the Prussians. He then concluded:

I agree with the Director of Artillery so far as to feel satisfied the Mitrailleurs are overrated weapons. I don't think I would take them into the field at all, for they certainly ought not to replace guns, and if they are added to the proper number of field pieces they would add largely to the encumbrances of an army.

Shortly afterwards, Britain ordered some .45- and .65-calibre Gatlings from Sir W. Armstrong and Co., the first of these being delivered in January 1874. They were then issued to the Navy.

Richard Gatling had been encouraged by the favourable comments made about his weapon, certainly in comparison with others. Established by now in Hartford and with the Colt factory nearby, he continued to redesign his gun and make improvements. In particular, he attached a different kind of hopper which accepted drums of ammunition. Twenty rounds could then be fired in quick succession, and the gunner only had to push the drum to fire another twenty, repeating this procedure until all twenty magazines had been emptied of their 400 rounds. An adjustable oscillator was also introduced. This caused the gun to sweep automatically through twelve degrees, thus firing bullets more effectively (against an advancing enemy) than merely killing one man over and over again. This angle of sweep could be altered as need be.

The British, at first laggardly in their approach to the Gatling, then made up for lost time. With imperial tribulations and acquisitions rolling on relentlessly, there was a steady need for superior weaponry — and more so than with other European nations. It is often alleged that most of the second half of the nineteenth century, with Britain's Queen Victoria so comfortably on the throne and with increasing prosperity in her realm, witnessed peace. Between the ending of the Crimean War (in 1856) and the start of the Second Boer War (in 1899) *Pax Britannica* is said to have ruled the world. But during those forty-three years, to name a few of the more notable engagements in which the British were involved, there took place: the Indian Mutiny, of 1857–9; the near permanent fighting in Afghanistan; the China wars of 1859–60;

the Ambeyla expedition (North-West India) of 1863; the New Zealand wars against Maoris, 1863–72; the Abyssinian campaign of 1867–8 (to rescue British hostages); the First Boer war, 1880–1; the West African wars, 1873–4, 1895–6; the Zulu wars, most importantly in 1879; the Sudanese campaign, 1882–5; and the further Sudanese campaign, 1896–8.

With so much combat affecting their overseas territories, it was understandable that the British were the first to become seriously interested in the new and better Gatlings, taking them to the range at Shoeburyness in Essex — where, two generations earlier, Henry Shrapnel had achieved immortality by inventing fragmentation bombs. The Gatling trials experimentally compared this weapon's virulence with muzzle-loading nine-pounders, breech-loading twelve-pounders, Montigny mitrailleuses, and skilled riflemen using Martini-Henry and Snider rifles. After a great quantity of ammunition had been expended, the investigating committee felt 'persuaded that the Gatling Gun is the best adapted to meet all military requirements'.

By 1874 its inventor had produced what has been called his classic weapon, this being lighter, more compact, sturdier and better-looking than its predecessors, with bronze breeches and hoppers in place of iron and steel. There were two types, one with ten thirty-two-inch barrels weighing 200 pounds, and another with ten eighteen-inch barrels totalling 135 pounds. This second category was also known, somewhat quaintly, as the Camel Gun. (It would seem the curious name had been inherited from a famous eighteenth-century occasion when an Afghan army invading Persia encountered a huge defending force near Ishafan. The Afghans then gave way, as if in terror, and the Persians happily advanced, only to be confronted by a hidden line of 100 sitting camels, each with a gun of sorts upon its back. The Afghans won the day, and the notion of gun-equipped, one-humped creatures never went away. The camel is a contrary beast at the best of times, making it hard to believe such animals might ever sit, or stand there, while an assortment of shells and bullets were being launched only a couple of feet distant from their ears. And what about recoil? And aiming? It is therefore good to learn that, although the British made excellent use of camels in their desert expeditions and also welcomed Gatlings, no evidence exists that the animals and guns ever came closer to each other than was absolutely necessary.)

A revolt by the Ashanti kingdom of West Africa gave Britain its first opportunity to demonstrate the Gatling gun in action. In that country, then known as the Gold Coast, there had been little administrative problem with its southern inhabitants living near the ocean, such as the Fanti and Ga people, but the Ashantis living to the north and inland around Kumasi resented what was happening further south. They were a warrior race, and wished to make their presence felt. They did so during the 1870s by attacking and defeating the southerly tribes, who were supposedly safe under British protection. Britain immediately mounted a punitive expedition, and put Garnet Wolseley in command. His force included members of the Black Watch, the Royal Welch Fusiliers, and two battalions of the 1st West India Regiment (from Jamaica).

*The Times* of London quickly offered military advice to Sir Garnet, notably with regard to the .45 Gatlings he would be taking to Africa — along with rifled seven-pounders, a battery of smooth-bore howitzers, and some nine-pound rockets:

For fighting in the bush a Gatling would be as much use as a fire engine, but if by any lucky chance Sir Garnet Wolseley manages to catch a good mob of savages in the open, and at a moderate distance, he cannot do better than to treat them to a little Gatling music . . . It is obvious that it would be absurd constantly to fire a Gatling gun in one direction. A few men immediately in front would be perforated while those on the flanks would escape . . . Altogether, we cannot wish the Ashantees worse luck than to get in the way of a Gatling well served . . .

The newspaper was correct in its concern about Gatlings being deployed in the Gold Coast bush. Although a touch more useful than fire engines, they were still unwieldy and cumbersome along Africa's narrow roads and pathways. These, as like as not, existed solely for the convenience of people on foot, and two-wheeled Gatlings would therefore prove difficult to manoeuvre. The Asian system of slinging everything beneath bamboo poles might have been satisfactory had it been tried. So too might pack transport, with the weapon and its ammunition supported on either side of, say, mules. But in either case, or with any other transport solution which came to mind, there would have been difficulty in operating the gun within a forest. An enemy attack in such an environment would have been successful long before — or even if — the heavy guns could have been brought to bear.

In fact, the only Ashantis to hear Gatling music were a group of envoys arrived to negotiate peace terms on behalf of their ruler. To help them decide upon that war's cessation, one of the rapid-firing guns was made to launch its bullets at a river. The envoys were impressed, with one of them blowing his brains out that night, allegedly for fear of the Gatling's potential. The 'Ashantee Correspondent'(!) of the *New York Herald* wrote that the gun's reputation then spread throughout the kingdom:

It is a terrible gun which shoots all day. Nothing could stand before it; the water [of that nearby river] ran back affrighted . . . The effect of this, combined with many other things, has been to induce the King and his Council to deliberate and reflect on the possibility of peace.

They did deliberate, and soon relinquished all their belligerent demands. Later the Ashanti ruler, the Asantehene, was deposed by his people for having accepted such a humiliating defeat. As for the Gatling weapon, in its first imperial adventure it had helped secure a peace, without firing a shot against any individual. Its repute therefore rose impressively.

However, the gun was not without some rivals. William Gardner, another man with Hartford links, arranged his weapon's two (or five) barrels horizontally. His device could allegedly fire a maximum of 1,200 rounds a minute. Helge Palmcrantz of Sweden, a rarity in that he had not experienced Colt's armoury, invented the 'Nordenfelt machine gun' (named for its financial promoter, Thorsten Nordenfelt). It only fired 200 rounds a minute, but these could be small bore or more than one-inch in calibre, and the weapon was often preferred over Gatling's less wide-ranging device.

With all this competition, it is not surprising that Richard Gatling paid particular attention to the U.S. Centennial Exhibition, held in Philadelphia in 1876. It achieved ten million visitors during slightly more than five months, and they could each examine the Hotchkiss, the Gardner and other weapons on show. Richard Gatling was adamant that he should triumph in his firearm category, and his well-distributed advertising cards were straightforwardly forthright:

> As a practical military machine gun, the GATLING has no equal. It fires from 800 to 1,000 shots per minute, has great accuracy, and the larger calibres have an effective range of over two miles. . . . It has been adopted by nearly all the principal governments of the world.
>
> *Gatling Gun Company,*
> HARTFORD, CONN., U.S.A.

In the end, much to his relief and that of his sales force, he did succeed, gaining the only medal awarded for a machine gun. Interestingly, he considered his weapons to be 'machine guns', even though many historians restrict that name to guns which are fully automatic whereas his needed their handles to be cranked. It is also interesting that he claimed a range of two miles, a formidable distance at the time for a — relatively — lightweight weapon.

Official British War Office reports on rapid-firing guns for the period 1867 to

1886 reflect the fluctuating fortunes of the various weapons, with different officers and committees stating their changing preferences. The Admiralty, after deciding that mitrailleuses (by any name) were no good, compared Nordenfelts with Gatlings at sea. It then requested more of the former and wished to be relieved of the Gatlings in its possession. A further and later trial using the same ship, H.M.S. *Excellent*, contrarily preferred the Gatlings, but yet another committee — set up in 1879 to examine the whole question — suggested a more thorough test with a greater quantity of different weapons, namely three versions of the Gatling, two of the Nordenfelt, one of the Pratt & Whitney, and two of the Gardner. Throwing a spanner into all the earlier preferences, this multi-gun test officially selected the weapon which had done least well on previous examinations, the Gardner, particularly in its five-barrel configuration.

Meanwhile, the British army was preparing for a major Zulu war. It selected four Gatling guns, and these were to prove 'very effective' in engagements with Zulu warriors. Lord Chelmsford, leader of that Zululand campaign, wrote warmly of the weapons:

On the advance to the relief of Ekowe, two Gatling guns accompanied the column, and at the battle of Ginginhlovo did considerable execution among the Zulus *at the opening of their attack* . . . At Ulundi we also had two Gatlings in the centre of the front face of our square. They jammed several times in the action, but when in work proved a very valuable addition . . . Machine guns are, I consider, most valuable weapons . . . where the odds against us must necessarily be great . . .

Five years later, when the army was preparing yet another African expedition, this time within Bechuanaland, the Director of Artillery in London had to borrow four five-barrelled Gardners from the Navy. Despite requests for machine guns from those who would do the fighting, their Commander-in-Chief back home was in less of a haste. He felt 'confident' the weapons would 'ere long' be used generally in all armies, but did not consider it advisable to buy any — just yet.

When we require them we can purchase the most recent patterns, and their manipulation can be learned by intelligent men in a few hours.

In that same year (of 1884) the 'Suakim expedition' was also being prepared, occasioning further requests for machine guns. The Director of Artillery, no doubt harassed by the business of equipping an expanding empire, managed to borrow six two-barrel Gardner guns from the Navy. Contrary advice then came from Garnet Wolseley after his experience with Nordenfelts and Gardners during his unhappy foray to Khartoum from 1884 to 1885. He preferred Nordenfelts because, apparently, Gardners had shown a greater tendency to jam. One way and another, in spots around the globe, Britain was proving to itself — and to others, such as the enemy — that rapid-firing weapons had a positive role to play.

Back in the United States, its military contingents were primarily engaged in further occupation of western territory. Gatling guns accompanied many such forays, but could not keep pace with the cavalry and were therefore often slow in encountering Indians. In the Sioux wars of 1876, made famous by George A. Custer's defeat at the hands of Sitting Bull, the impulsive colonel was offered a detachment of four .50-calibre Gatlings by his commanding general. Custer chose not to take them on his fatal reconnaissance to the Little Big Horn River, believing their wheeled carriages (pulled by retired cavalry horses) could not possibly keep up with his fast-moving column. He knew that speed was essential against such a highly mobile enemy. Perhaps no battle has ever been refought so assiduously as that 'last stand', and today's consensus seems to be that he and his men would have been slaughtered in any case. Paul Wahl and Don Toppel, in describing that engagement, have written that the column of Indians leaving the battleground afterwards was 'three miles long and half a mile wide'. Even if all four Gatlings had been used, they would probably have been unsuccessful against such a quantity of enemy attacking from numerous directions.

In that year and the next, when the Nez Percé Indians were also being engaged, Gatling guns were used with significant effect. The *New York Times*, giving news of the Clearwater River fight only six days after its occurrence, stated that 'the dislodgement of (Chief) Joseph was largely due' to the two Gatlings and one four-inch howitzer used against him. Three months later Chief Joseph and his surviving Nez Percé warriors were again besieged by a Gatling gun and one howitzer. He then surrendered, famously saying: 'From where the sun now stands, I fight no more against the white man.' Nor did he ever do so.

Far from the state of Montana where Custer died and Chief Joseph called a halt to fighting, far from Bechuanaland and Natal where Gatlings were also seeing service, far from the Gold Coast where even the sight of one in action had been sufficient to initiate surrender, and very far from the sites where Russians and Turks were once again embroiled in their ancient war, the mansion known as Armsmear still stood peacefully at the top of its slope looking down upon a factory where so much of this story had begun. Sam Colt had not invented a machine gun, but had fashioned his weapons from machines better than anyone had ever done beforehand. Within his armoury others had learned his trade, had invented different weapons, had seen them manufactured and had then gone their separate ways.

The Colt and Gatling stories do span the gap between Brown Bess muskets and recognisably modern times. Both men were born when Napoleon Bonaparte still lived, and their concepts of rapid fire would have astonished him. Sam Colt had been revolutionary in thinking of six shots, rather than a singleton. He had also tapped a colossal civilian market, bigger by far than the military. As for Richard Gatling, he had created the first workmanlike weapon to make multiple death a practical proposition. In earlier days, when one cannon ball could sometimes kill many of the enemy, few had thought of guns with only that end in view. The thin red line of infantry, shooting at each other rank by rank, had therefore receded into history. New times had arrived and, if attrition was required, it could now be achieved much more easily. Colt had also brought mechanisation and salesmanship into the armaments business, with both him and his factory serving as leaders in this field. No wonder that Gatling had chosen to set up shop in Hartford, and no wonder that other gun men had also learned and profited from Hartford's precedents.

Sam Colt never met the next critical link in the machine-gun chain. He was dead when an aspiring electrician took ship for Europe but, even if a meeting had then been possible, neither would have realised their common ground. No one anywhere knew the importance of that ocean voyage, and what it would mean to guns and warfare. As for Zulus and their kind, they could not possibly have known. European armies did not know, and refused to know even when information came their way that another era had arrived. Nevertheless the forty-one-year-old electrician, cunning about lamps and lighting, did set sail for Liverpool when on his way to Paris. And that, however seemingly irrelevant, is where the most devastating chapter in machinegun history truly has its start.

# Chapter 6

# Chronic Invention and Hatton Garden

Hiram Stevens Maxim was born in the District of Maine (not then a state) on 5 February 1840. In that same year, Sam Colt was failing in Paterson, New Jersey, and was soon to move to New York City. Nine more years had to pass before that consistently failing individual ever made a profit. As for Richard Gatling, then still living at his original home, he had already invented a screw propeller and was working on a seed drill which, in time, would earn him good money. There were another five years ahead before he would take up medicine, and eleven before he would start to contemplate the gun which would make his name. Whereas Sam had been born wealthy, only for this money to vanish when his mother died, the Gatling family was less conspicuously rich, but Richard's father's farm did provide a comfortable living. Hiram Maxim's start in life was quite different, either from Colt's or Gatling's, being on a brand-new farm freshly hacked in Maine by his father from the forest near Sangersville, with only Indians and bears as near neighbours.

Hiram's father was Isaac Weston Maxim, the youngest of seven children. The family was of Huguenot origin, its antecedents first reaching Canterbury in England before sailing to Plymouth County, Massachusetts. There, according to Hiram, 'they could worship God according to the dictates of their own conscience, and prevent others from doing the same'. Maxim senior married Harriet Boston Stevens, born in 1815, and took her to the solitary situation he had created. Life in those remote backcountry woods must have been extremely hard, perhaps too much so, because the family was soon moving into a succession of villages, achieving most of its earnings via the timber business. The young Hiram provides an ebullient picture of himself in his autobiography, stating even on page one: 'I think I am entitled to be recognised as the strong member of the generation in which I was born.' During his early years, when he was not fishing, stealing canoes, catching mink or cheating opponents at cards (with tricks learned from the Indians), he worked as a carpenter, decorator of carriages, mill hand and storekeeper.

At that store, much overrun by mice, Hiram invented a better mousetrap. The traditional traps — then, as now — captured or killed one mouse at a time before permitting every other mouse to finish off the cheese. This inefficiency annoyed Hiram, and he therefore created a system whereby each caught mouse reset the trap for a further victim. The device was extremely successful, and captured five while its inventor was eating lunch after its creation. In essence, although this fact never seemed to cross his mind, he was utilising the fundamental principle of a machine gun. Each bullet, with its detonation, would supply the energy for its successor's positioning, just as each mouse's frustrated antics would do the same for catching further mice. Machine guns would come Maxim's way in time but not, when aged sixteen, he was merely being inventive vis-à-vis the local rodent population.

Young Hiram soon obtained the necessary 'freedom' from any further obligations to his father. This fact was printed as was customary in the local paper, the *Piscataquis Observer*, and he then left home with a few dollars in his pocket. As with Samuel Colt, he was merely wishing to paddle his own canoe, and to create his own life as Gatling had also done when leaving home. The acquisition of certificates of competence was not as commonplace as it is now. As the old saying goes, and was certainly much quoted in the nineteenth century, 'You waste a lot of education by going to college.' There was then more of an informality which plainly suited certain kinds of individual. They could start work somewhat earlier upon whatever took their fancy, and then gather the necessary expertise along the way. Colt had done so via nitrous oxide and failing ventures. Gatling had started to invent while still an adolescent, and Maxim would hone his own development by becoming prize-fighter, creator of blackboards, bar-tender, deviser of the first fire-preventive water sprinklers, and much else while roaming around New England and southern Canada. The course he steered with his canoe was somewhat erratic, but he alone was in charge of it, wherever he made it go.

When the Civil War arrived, so inspirational for Gatling and such a lethal boost for Colt, Maxim was of military age but he stayed distant from any involvement. This reluctance to fight caused retribution to come his way, but friends persuaded him, without excessive difficulty, that he was 'too intelligent' to become cannon-fodder. In fact he did have a legitimate reason for his non-attendance at the war. Two of his brothers, Leander and Henry, were already serving, thus letting him officially off the hook. Peace had been declared by the time this young man's wanderings brought him to New York City. By then he was married to Sarah Haynes, of Boston. His first marriage, to Louisa Budden, had given him three children yet none were to come from Sarah. In his autobiography Hiram Maxim fails to mention Louisa or their children, and also how many brothers and sisters were in his family. As a form of explanation for such deficits, its author gives himself a let-out clause in the book's opening paragraph:

Lawyers see to it that we do not tell the whole truth . . . [so shall I] observe the same rule in preparing this little account . . . It would not be advisable for me to tell the whole truth as it might entangle me in numerous lawsuits.

In New York he founded his first commercial concern, the Maxim Gas Machine Company, with offices at the Equitable Building, 120 Broadway. (For a time he also worked at 264 Broadway.) The company did well, Hiram being both a sound businessman and good inventor. His principal products were gas lights, and these were much used on railway stock and in hotels after he had befriended A.T. Stewart, one of America's wealthiest hotel-owning individuals. Lighting the 1,500-room, Stewart-owned Grand Union hotel at Saratoga was a particular feather in Maxim's cap. So too was sub-patenting his lamps to England, where 80,000 were made. Being a prolific inventor, he frequently diversified — into pumps, valves, paintwork, fire-grates, smokestacks, and boilers. There was still no sign of a gun, but by the mid-1870s he was doing nicely, making money, moving into new areas and inventing all the while. He even owned a steam launch of his design, named *The Flirt*, which was conveniently moored in Brooklyn.

Before long, as he phrased it, 'people were beginning to talk of electric light'. S.D. Schuyler formed the first Electric Lighting Company in the U.S., and Hiram became its chief engineer — at $10 a day, plus 'a quarter interest' in whatever might accrue. No one then knew how a filament might glow without it soon expiring, and arc lighting was more successful. When Thomas Alva Edison began to make incandescent lamps (with internal filaments, much as are used today), Schuyler asked Maxim to follow suit. Very soon, in Maxim's steadfastly forthright opinion, he 'produced the first good incandescent lamps that were ever made'. Edison's early lamps were 'very dim', and only worked at all because they involved a process, concerning irregularity in conductivity, which Maxim had invented. The man from Maine therefore basked a little in his rival's ever-increasing glory, but soon gave up that line of work.

The Maxim autobiography gives no hint of the reason for this abandonment but, as Edward R. Hewitt states in *Those Were The Days*, there was a powerful cause. A consortium of U.S. electrical companies was bribing its inventive fellow countryman to desist. In particular, these companies resented his enthusiasm for patenting ideas. (He took out eighty patents between 1866 and 1884.) Whenever they started work in some novel area, they were immediately confronted by a Maxim patent which served as unwelcome grit in that idea's development. Therefore — so it is said, although not in every version of the Maxim story — they offered him $20,000 a year for ten years on condition that he vanished to Europe and stopped his electrical work. The amount was colossal for those days, but he had been colossally annoying. It was asking a lot to expect a man to leave his native land, although Europe was hardly a penal colony and there may have been further inducement to depart in the alleged confusion of his personal life, with three women involved and even bigamy suspected.

In any case, Maxim was soon to experience a critical moment in his life. He did travel to Europe, and his life was never the same again. He was then forty-one, the year was 1881, and his immediate task (not forbidden by the bribe) was to promote electrical products for the Electric Lighting Co. at a Paris exhibition. The irritating and prolific American inventor sailed from New York on 14 August, enjoyed the *Germanic*'s hospitality, arrived at Liverpool, entrained for London, stayed at the Charing Cross Hotel, ate whitebait for the first time, thought the Thames was very small, and soon reached the capital of

France. This 'chronic inventor' (his phrase) enjoyed living there, and who would not have done so during that city's 'Belle Époque'? As extra gratification, he was made a Chevalier of the Légion d'Honneur for his electrical work. Despite the pleasures which then surrounded him, he was soon on his way back to London.

While still in Paris, according to his personal narrative, he had 'made the first drawing of an automatic gun'. The statement is startling, with weaponry bearing no relation to electrical apparatus, to gas lamps, pumps, fire-grates, boilers or any of his earlier endeavours. If, on the other hand, he had been forbidden to invent anything electrical, with electricity having been his most rewarding occupation, he must have been receptive to novel lines of thought. The gun idea may even have been simmering at the back of his mind as he revealed much later, in a major interview, that his father had been far more than miller and timberman. He too had been an inventor, and had even conceived a machine gun in 1854 (long before Gatling had started on this line of work). As suitable cartridges were not then available, the idea got nowhere. By the 1880s, however, the concept of automatic fire was much more of a practicality. For Hiram Maxim, the idea had apparently been brought from the back to the front of his mind by an individual, described only in his memoirs as American and Jewish. When speaking to *The Times* of London at a later date, Maxim related how this friend, an acquaintance from the U.S., had suggested that he might wish to help Europeans kill each other.

Hang your chemistry and electricity! If you want to make a pile of money, invent something that will enable (them) to cut each other's throats with greater facility.

The United States, with no war on its hands just then, and with anti-Indian skirmishes 'out west' almost ended, was not encouraging inventive minds to think of guns; but Europe was different. It had huge standing armies. Soldiers walked the streets in their resplendent uniforms. And there were so many nations, all looking over their shoulders and across their frontiers, at what might be happening next door. At the time of Maxim's arrival, the Franco-Prussian war had ended ten years earlier, but with neither side content about the outcome. From an American's point of view, fresh from a single nation more united than ever before, Europe was a steaming cauldron of assorted entities. No one knew which ingredient might bring these to the boil, or when or how and why, but Maxim's cynical fellow countryman had been right with his advice. There was a near-universal longing for new and more devastating kinds of weaponry which would be very handy should another war occur.

Making 'the first drawing' before that train journey to London implies a back-of-an-envelope flash of intuition, but it was not quite so straightforward or so simple. Maxim's eventual design makes it plain that he had examined other weapons and had incorporated some of their ideas. Moreover, he had long been interested in recoil, certainly after using guns in his childhood and then, as an adult, having once made his shoulder 'black and blue' by firing the .45-calibre Springfield rifle when on a visit to Savannah, Georgia. Could this force be used purposefully, he reasoned to himself, instead of being no more than a bruising inconvenience? The first problem was to discover if this backlash was sufficiently powerful to do what he had in mind.

In London there was already an office owned by the company he served at 47 Cannon Street, and it had 'works' on Bankside across the Thames. This branch of the New York company was not doing well (any more than Colt's company had done well when he too had set up shop in Britain's capital) and Maxim was appalled by what he saw. The all-pervading filth and grime was leading to enormous gas bills as so little natural illumination was able to enter through the windows. Maxim ordered the place to be cleaned at once. He himself dusted off a bench, acquired a draughtsman and set to work. Before long the American inventor needed a workshop of his own in which to install the lathes, presses, planers, and milling machines which would enable him to manufacture the weapon he had designed. Soon he encountered 57D Hatton Garden, just round the corner in London from St Peter's Church and at a junction with Clerkenwell Road. These manufacturing premises were to serve him well.

His first task was to discover the actual recoil force involved in a single firing. He wished to know how far a gun's bolt could be safely driven back before the bullet, with all its pursuing gases, had left the barrel. Only then could his gun be un-locked and the next cartridge inserted. Im-mediate encouragement came from the first six bullets he ever despatched; they all departed in what he estimated was less than half a second. Prompt discourage-ment came from the superintendent of the Henry Rifle Barrel Co., from whom Maxim had requested barrels:

Don't do it. Thousands . . . have been working on guns. There are many hun-dred failures every year . . . You don't stand a ghost of a chance in competi-tion with regular gun-makers. You are not a gun man; stick to electricity.

For the ebullient, determined and cocky Maxim, this was fighting talk. 'I am a to-tally different mechanic from any you have seen before, a different breed,' he asserted. The abashed superintendent, after giving 'a deep sigh in reply', meekly consented to deliver the barrels. Quite what Maxim's head office back in New York thought about its European representative going off at such a tangent, and one so far from elec-tricity, is not known. Perhaps its inventor-in-chief had been permitted to be aberrant from time to time, or perhaps not. Perhaps it knew of Edison's demand, or not. Hiram himself makes no mention of their possible anxieties and anyway, he could afford to be casual about their interests, supported as he allegedly was by those 20,000 annual dollars.

At all events, energetically and whole-heartedly, he devoted himself to creating the world's very first automatic gun. He certainly knew of his rivals in the business of rapid fire, considering the workmanship of their products to be 'exquisite'. Of these guns, the Hotchkiss, the Gatling, and the Gardner were each worked by a crank, whereas the Nordenfelt was operated by a lever (like any village's conventional water pump). These guns' speed of action was limited, not so much by the operator's cranking abilities, as by the time taken for the slowest cartridge to fire. In those days cartridges were unevenly manufactured, and too slow an explosion (detonation) could mean the premature arrival of the next cartridge. And that would mean a jammed and useless weapon. No 'rapid-firing gun has yet been made', said the military of those days, 'without a tendency to jam', particularly at awkward moments. Plainly the situation could be improved. Get rid of the cranks and levers. Use a better class of cartridge. Circumvent the readiness to jam. And create the first truly automatic weapon which, once a finger had been put to its trigger, would fire by itself.

The 'totally different mechanic', the 'different breed', had evidence to partner his optimism ever since he had fired those first six bullets and noted the speed with which they had left the gun. Admittedly he was never short of enthusiasm concerning his personal creations, but he saw 'certain success' ahead. If half a dozen cartridges could be detonated so very hastily, there was no knowing how many might be fired in, say, half a minute, and there was, of course, only one way to discover.

As he worked, he patented, and he took out his first for a gun on 26 June 1883. Only two months later, on 16 July 1883, he took out a second, calling his new design the 'Forerunner'. In this amended version the bolt of his single-barrel gun was permitted to travel back three-quarters of an inch before it became unlocked. Recoil continued to push back the bolt, which then not only extracted the empty cartridge case from the chamber but, after compressing a spring, was soon accelerating forward to bring a new round into position for insertion and firing. Maxim was particularly fortunate in the timing of this work. Cartridge manufacture had been vastly improved, and there were — in general — no problems on that score. Maxim's single gun barrel was cooled by a water jacket, and he thus avoided the multiplicity of barrels which all earlier rapid-firing guns had used.

The Maxim Gun Company was officially incorporated on 5 November 1884. As ever, the Hiram Maxim autobiography is eager to promote its author and his expertise. Within this book his English workers are 'amazed' at his skill. He takes delight in 'knowing more chemistry' than neighbouring chemist shops. His new American tools, brought over at his request, were incomprehensible to those working for him in London, and the clever designer also had to become a machinist. He then did a little glass-blowing, there being need for some glassware and with none of his employees so capable. One Maxim worker, astonished by such wide-ranging expertise, threw his cap upon the floor, and stamped on it, while proclaiming, 'There's nothing that the old man can't do.' What the old man (who was then in his early forties) had to do was work 'day and night' until he had a proper drawing of a prototype on his hands which then had to be turned into reality. When it was finished, he tried it out with a lengthy belt of cartridges instead of a mere half dozen. 'I found that it fired rather more than ten a second' was his exultant conclusion.

The 'certain success' was now yet more of a certainty, and this fact soon spread — or was spread by the inventor himself — around the Hatton Garden area. News in that locality tended to involve diamonds, it being (then as now) a centre of this trade, but in 1885 there was sudden excitement of quite a different kind. A local newspaper printed that the 'well-known American electrician', previously mentioned in its columns under that description, had made 'an automatic machine gun with a single barrel, using service cartridges, that would load and fire itself by energy derived from the recoil over 600 rounds in a minute'. As a piece of journalism, it was succinct, informative and entirely accurate. There was immediate talk about 'Yankee brag', but also curiosity. The reported gun was much lighter than any Gatling. And faster. And British-made.

As an extra blessing, the weapon even had a rate of fire selector, this controlling the number of bullets to be despatched per minute. Any number between one and that awesome figure of 600 could be chosen. On one occasion a French observer asked to see the gun working. 'It is working,' said its inventor proudly, just before — automatically — it fired off one more round. The Frenchman is then said to have kissed the weapon, so great was his astonishment and delight. Plainly the new device was revolutionary, with the gun itself performing all the action, and all the charging and recharging. No one was needed to turn a handle or keep a hopper full of rounds. One man with his finger on the trigger was entirely adequate, with assistants only required to bring forward additional ammunition belts, as and when these became crucial to satisfy the gun's incredible demand. Hiram Maxim was overjoyed with his new invention, and cared not at all that it had been produced by someone who, in theory, should have been promoting electrical goods in Paris.

Disagreeable telegrams would occasionally arrive, reminding him of his 'huge' salary ($5,000 a year) and of a considerable obligation to the U.S. Electric Lighting Company. But each reminder from New York earned short shrift, and this became shorter still when high-ranking British dignitaries started to arrive, so excitingly and flatteringly, at the Hatton Garden works. Commendably quick off the mark, having been encouraged to visit by a Hatton Garden dealer, was the Duke of Cambridge, long-time Commander-in-Chief of the British Army. He was delighted by the weapon, and promptly recommended a Harton tour of inspection to other members of his royal family (he being a cousin of Queen Victoria). The Duke of Edinburgh soon arrived plus the Dukes of Devonshire, Sutherland, and Kent, but these prestigious arrivals were then eclipsed by the Prince of Wales. They all, notably the Prince, wished to squat upon the ground, aim the gun, pull its trigger, hear the roar, and watch 600 bullets vanish to the range's other end. Maxim must have beamed with pride, and smirked contentedly, but did have 'to work at night and on Sundays' to keep the invention ready for further assortments of trigger-enthusiasts from Britain's aristocracy. They were to consume a total of 200,000 rounds as they revelled in the weapon. Hatton Garden, with its fashionable clientele and eager traders, had never known anything quite like this attendance of well-heeled and exuberant visitors. Diamonds, for all their value, had never held the attractive power of such an amazing gun.

Hiram Maxim did once find time to return to France and fulfil some electrical obligations, but then had to hurry back to London on hearing that Garnet Wolseley proposed a visit to Number 57D. This most famous of British soldiers had been victorious in the Ashanti war when the exhibition firing of a single Gatling had been so overwhelming. He had more recently returned from the less glorious, but more famous, expedition to north-east Africa when a huge force under his command had failed to reach General 'Chinese' Gordon in time to prevent that man's slaughter at Khartoum. From Paris, Maxim caught the night train, hurried to his workshop and prepared everything for this crucial new arrival who would inevitably be accompanied by a high-ranking entourage. All went well. 'Some hundreds of cartridges' were fired before the most appreciative and distinguished audience. Wolseley himself was particularly laudatory, saying that 'You Yankees beat all creation'. Thereafter Maxim considered Wolseley 'one of the cleverest and brightest of military men'. The general had, in effect, only been reiterating the sentiment so frequently expressed after Sam Colt's visit to London thirty-four years beforehand. Americans were particularly good at mechanical manufacture, most importantly of guns.

In the following year, when the War Office was producing yet another 'Précis' of rapid firing guns, 'more particularly for land service', most of the discussion concerned Gardner guns and Nordenfelts. Wolseley, when writing earlier from Egypt, had 'advocated the attachment of two Nordenfelt guns to each Infantry Brigade', having already expressed his 'decided preference' for Nordenfelts over excessively jam-prone Gardners. In this 'land service' report every weapon mentioned was weighty, with the general opinion formed that 'such guns . . . should be transported on carriages, with limbers, each with a track of five feet two inches and a load of one ton'. The 'latest proposition . . . of attaching galloper guns to Cavalry regiments is now engaging attention'. Then, before its date of 6 July 1886, a final paragraph promotes yet another possibility.

A gun, by Mr. Maxim, was tried by order of the Director of Artillery last month, which promises to outrun all rivals. Its weight is only fifty-six pounds, and its ascertained rate of firing is 500 rounds per minute and 1,000 rounds in three and a half minutes, including shifting of ammunition boxes. Further trials with weapons by the same Maker will shortly take place.

Hiram Maxim had arrived, together with his gun. The government had already specified that it would greatly favour a machine gun weighing less than 100 pounds. This should fire 400 rounds a minute and 600 rounds in two minutes. The guns that Maxim had taken to Enfield for appraisal weighed a mere forty-two pounds each and despatched 670 rounds in a single minute. No wonder the appraisers thought the Maxim weapons looked set to outrun their rivals. They would be vanquished most decisively if the inventive Hiram had his way. The gun was powerful; that was a fact. The man behind it, Hiram Stevens Maxim, was of a similar calibre. That fact too, in its fashion, was just as positive and significant. Everything was set for a bright future, for both the inventor and his gun.

# Chapter 7

# One More 'Yankee' Beats All Creation

It must have been quite difficult, or even very difficult, liking the man called Hiram Maxim. It is certainly hard to welcome the picture he draws of himself in his autobiography, with so much arrogance, self-esteem and brazen confidence peppering its paragraphs. On the other hand, there is no doubt that he had talent. When young, and catching 'all' the mink, understanding longitude, and drawing recognisable likenesses of visitors, why should he not say so? Friends in those Maine backwoods, presumably all short on literacy and education, were possibly incapable of creating mousetraps, winning at cards or understanding geography. They too, had they been able to put pen to paper, might have conceded that their clever companion continued to exceed them, in fighting, in woodwork, in decorating carriages, and making better bedsteads even than old hands. 'That young man has broken all previous records,' exulted one employer — or so Maxim would write with unremitting and self-rewarding praise.

Sam Colt had fallen on his feet when he returned to Hartford, found financial backers, took advantage of a war and received government contracts supplying him with all the work he could handle at that time. Hiram Maxim also fell on his feet after travelling to Europe. In New York City he had done well, had earned good money, and had enjoyed 'glorious days', with all hours 'given to hard work and to study', but in Paris and London he was able to blossom as never before. Perhaps he liked being more of a rarity than had been possible in the United States. He no longer had to compete against Thomas Edison, or others, in a booming community so capable of invention, and so famously eager to accept every form of novelty. In Europe his accent marked him out, and so did his style. He had a fine beard, thick hair, forceful eyes, a strong physique, and must have been difficult to miss. Apart from all of that, he was a New Englander who welcomed the renown afforded him for being another of that tribe.

'You Yankees beat all creation,' Wolseley had said, and it is almost possible to hear the inventor purring softly in reply.

His preference for Europe was then augmented by a lack of enthusiasm back in his homeland for the Maxim gun. In his opinion he had 'perfected' it. He considered that its automated arrangement, properly patented as was his way, would have to be applied to 'firearms of all sizes'. He therefore wrote to 'every prominent gun and pistol-maker' in the U.S.A., advising them of this fact. Not only did he never receive a single favourable reply, but the answers which did reach him were often scurrilous. They 'ridiculed' his idea and 'detected no merit' in it whatsoever. Such ripostes may have been genuine opinions, or their senders may have resented this inventor's abdication from his native land, it being a form of treachery. Or maybe mere distance got in the way, with misunderstandings so much easier when there is an ocean in between.

A further reason for Maxim's appreciation of Great Britain was the matter of his upbringing. He had not been born into a distinguished family, as had the famous and prosperous citizens within Connecticut whom Sam Colt had numbered among his kin. Hiram's father had first tried farming, had failed, and then had worked in mills of various kinds to feed his family. For his children there was never the hint of a silver spoon, nor was there among any of his acquaintances. No prestige existed, no status, no inherited wealth to foster admiration. Hiram did not, and could not, attend the parties, the junketings and revelries at Newport on Rhode Island as Sam and Elizabeth Colt had both done. Hiram Maxim was no more than a self-made man who had managed to do well, most notably after abandoning the country of his birth and then becoming so famously inventive in another land. (Even today, however much the names of Colt and Maxim each represent a considerable measure of armament success, for every hundred Americans who have heard of Colt there is only one who knows of Maxim. He had left America.) But now this boy from the backwoods of one of America's least developed eastern areas was suddenly at the heart of London and being fêted by British nobility. Generals, dukes, and even a prince sought his company. They all revelled in his weapon, applauded its inventor, fired off rounds enthusiastically, and took their top hats with them when they departed, no doubt laughing merrily, to find their broughams and other carriages waiting in the street. What a gun and what a man!

A thought which never seems to have troubled Hiram Maxim, at least in print either then or later, is that he was in the killing business. His weapons had no other ability than to shoot more men per minute than had previously been possible. These guns would kill many hundreds of thousands, if not millions, before their time was up, and Maxim would be knighted for these pains. It was not patriotism, for another country than his own, that served as his impetus and inspiration — his guns were sold to any nation which would buy. Being applauded by the high and mighty was one reward. Others were a bulging order book and the prizes to be won, such as the personal Grand Prix in Artillery he achieved at the Paris Exhibition of 1887. Both commercially and socially, Hiram Maxim was therefore doing very well, with his reputation soaring in leaps and bounds. Nothing like this had ever happened back in the U.S.A.

The great advantage of Europe for a gun man, already mentioned, was its multiplicity of nations. The three million square miles of the United States formed but one. The four million square miles of Europe possessed a score or so, each fiercely independent, all jealous of their neighbours, and each more likely to buy a weapon if rivals had already done so. After the Civil War, the U.S. had hugely reduced its numbers of men in uniform. Over in Europe, such numbers were steadily increasing as the nineteenth century progressed towards its end. There were empires to run, most notably by France, Germany, Portugal, Holland, Belgium, and Great Britain. There were sabres to be rattled, and then used, as with Russia against Japan. And there were huge internal empires, such as Austro-Hungary, which not only needed stern control but caused others, most jealously, to begrudge their power. That turn-of-the-century period may have been the beautiful epoch, and thoroughly stimulating almost everywhere, but there must also have been — as with youth — a feeling that it could not last. Therefore threaten rivals into acquiescence. Launch more dreadnoughts. Have bigger military parades. Stir up patriotism. Make treaties of mutual defence. Learn to distinguish likely friend from possible foe. And forever acquire new weapons to keep at least abreast, or better still ahead, of the other nations, however amicable they might appear to be.

Hiram Maxim was never a man to sit on his hands. Having invented successfully he did not wait for others to 'make a beaten path to his door' (as Ralph Waldo Emerson is reputed to have said, believing good inventors with good inventions to have no trouble whatsoever in marketing their goods). Even if Maxim accepted this general truth, he would have been out there, busily smoothing the path, putting up helpful signposts, labelling his door. He certainly did everything possible in Britain to promote his gun, firing variations of it at Whale Island near Portsmouth, at Shoeburyness in Essex where the Gatlings had been fired, at Pirbright in Surrey where the target was a cast-iron gong, at Enfield in outer London, and at the Inventions Exhibition in Kensington.

It so happened that Francis Pratt of Hartford, a former employee at Colt's Armoury and distinguished partner of Pratt & Whitney, was in London when Maxim was merrily enjoying his new-found fame with the 'perfect' gun. This visitor, an old friend and 'one of the finest mechanicians in the world', was asked to give his opinion. He did so handsomely:

If anyone had told me that it would be possible to make a gun that would pull a cartridge belt into position, pull a loaded cartridge out of it, move it in front of the barrel, close the breech in a proper manner, cock the hammer, pull the trigger, fire off the cartridge, extract the empty shell and throw it out of the mechanism, feed a new cartridge into position, and do all these things in the tenth part of a second, I would not have believed it. I would not have believed it if Mr Whitney had told me — no, I would not have believed it if my wife had told me. But now I have seen it done with my own eyes.

By now Maxim had secured good orders from the British military, but there was still the continent to be won. First stop, somewhat oddly, bearing in mind its long-standing and respected neutrality, was Switzerland. The inventor had learned of some recent trials in that country between Gatlings, Gardners, and Nordenfelts, with the two-barrelled Gardners winning the prize. Maxim promptly decided to offer his services and travelled to Thun — beneath 'the snow-clad Jungfrau' — with Albert Vickers, whose name was to reoccur most importantly in machine gun history. The winning Gardner gun was fired first, earning — inevitably — scathing comments from the Anglo-American gun man. It was four times heavier than his own weapon. With one man sighting it, another turning its crank, and two more filling its hopper with cartridges, it managed to blast off 333 rounds in slightly longer than one minute. Worse still, or better still from Maxim's point of view, the bullets arriving at the target were widely scattered whereas Maxim's gun, launching its 333 rounds in half a minute, shot out 'a big hole' in the target's centre.

After the Gardner had dropped out of the competition, having experienced too much jamming and general difficulty, Maxim was asked to fire at a target — a dummy battery of artillery — which he could barely see, the distance being 1,200 metres and the light very hazy. Nevertheless he fired, and afterwards a telephone announced that three-quarters of the images of men and horses had been 'technically killed'. The Swiss officer in charge was particularly enthusiastic: 'No gun has ever been made in the world that could kill so many men and horses in so short a time.' Knowing a good investment when they saw one, the Swiss authorities promptly placed an order for the Hiram Maxim gun.

The inventor's next stop was Italy. The Duke of Genoa, Admiral of the Fleet, wished to see the now famous gun in action. His stipulations were different from those of the Swiss: the exciting weapon had first to be immersed in sea water for three days. Then, without any subsequent cleaning, it had to be fired from one moving battleship at another such battleship near La Spezia. Maxim's two assistants, savouring Italy more assiduously than Switzerland, chose to immerse themselves in alcohol for those three days, causing a minor but tedious postponement for the Duke's battleships, but all eventually went well. The gun's inventor does not relate whether his task was solely to hit the other ship, or what range was thought suitable, or why machine guns were contemplated for such enormous and well-armed craft, but he soon 'received a large order from the Italian government'. And that, if you are in the gun-selling business, is what counts over any actual logic behind the purchase.

News from Italy spread to Vienna. Once again Maxim was greeting royalty, with the

Archduke William, a field-marshal in the Austrian service, wishing to see both the man and his device. The inventor instantly took time not only to praise his weapon but also to criticise the opposition, as the Austrians then favoured the Nordenfelt. The testing day at the Steinfeld range was extremely hot, enabling Maxim to show his disdain for such a trifling inconvenience, the heat having 'no effect' upon him. After firing his gun, he even ran the 600 metres to the target and then, 'to the astonishment of everybody', ran back. With the day's conclusion, after firing his gun at various distances, Hiram asked 'His Royal Highness' if the gun's speed of action had been sufficient. 'Too fast,' said the man; 'It is the most dreadful instrument that I have ever seen or imagined.' Once more Maxim can be presumed to have purred with pleasure at the accolade, however sharp-edged the compliment.

There had been some trouble with cartridges, the Austrians preferring an Austrian variety. Maxim therefore had to return to England and make adjustments. Once again, of course, it was necessary to cross the Channel, which he labelled 'dreadful', causing readers of his book to wonder if a weakness is being revealed.

Could it be that the 'strong one' of his family, the 'cleverest mechanician in the world', the confidant of admirals and royalty, was prone to sea-sickness? Readers of his autobiography may even welcome this admission, since defects about his character and constitution are such a rarity within it.

On his return to Vienna, following yet another 'dreadful' crossing, 'everyone was amazed at the pace' of the modified weapon. It was also accurate, with Maxim cutting out the letters F and J on the target. As the Emperor Franz Josef was present at the firing, this was a sound move, impressing all those not yet committed. A 'comic paper' then illustrated this demonstration in telling fashion. Maxim's gun was drawn as coffin-shaped and, while drilling 'F.J.' on the target, was being witnessed by Death holding a crown over Maxim's head. The terrible truth of this cartoon did not apparently concern its subject. He thought one other fact far more significant: Austria's prompt presentation to him of 'an order for one hundred and sixty guns'. (Although 160 was a sizeable figure, it would have been far greater but for unscrupulous machinations by Nordenfelt's salesman, about whom much more later.)

The most disastrous truth of all, however, was Maxim's sale of his gun to Germany. The nation with the world's largest standing army had naturally heard of Maxim's weapon. It even possessed some but thought them less than satisfactory. One trouble, as Maxim learned, was the German use of German ammunition for their firing. No one could believe that German industry, so highly regarded, might have been dilatory in its manufacture of cartridges, but all became clear — to Maxim at any rate — when he learned that preparation of his guns for firing was a form of punishment inflicted upon recalcitrant military personnel.

Years passed. Then Germany's Prince Wilhelm, grandson of Britain's Queen Victoria, visited England in 1887 during celebrations for the fiftieth anniversary of her reign. He took time to inspect sections of the British Army, notably the 10th Hussars at Hounslow, expressing particular interest in their weaponry, and was greatly impressed by Maxim's gun. The Prince of Wales, by now a stalwart Maxim supporter, therefore decided to take the matter in hand, feeling that a family's close relations should behave in kindly fashion towards each other by passing on advice. Besides, any subsequent deal would profit one man's country financially and the other's by improving its military strength. This was the sort of thing that an uncle should do for a nephew, prince to prince, man to man, and gun enthusiast to another of the breed.

A Maxim weapon already existed at Spandau, the Berlin district famous for its armaments production. During the 1890s, with the German prince now Kaiser Wilhelm II, Emperor of Germany, he and the future Edward VII travelled there to witness a trial of strength. Arraigned against Maxim's weapon were the three familiar rivals, a Gatling, a Nordenfelt, and a Gardner. Once again, Maxim is happy to relate their poor showing in the trials. The Gatling gun, with its four operators, got through its cartridge allocation in slightly less than a minute. The Nordenfelt took a similar time, the Gardner slightly longer, but the fact that their handles had to be cranked meant that they were less accurate. Maxim's gun not only fired faster, but all its bullets — from 200 metres — landed in the bull.

Wilhelm II was much more of a soldier than his British counterpart. He had been educated, following the insistence of his father, the seventh King of Prussia and first

German Emperor, in a strictly martial fashion at the Kassel Gymnasium. Despite his deformed left arm — or perhaps because of both it and his shortness in height — the man had become an enthusiast for all things military. When he looked at Maxim's weapon and said, 'That is the gun — there is no other,' his approval went deeper than the then Prince of Wales's. The future King of England probably admired Maxim's gun more for its raucous and invigorating qualities, much like the shot-gun banging he so enjoyed against his nation's driven game. His German nephew was pondering its potential in a future war and considering its awesome credentials as an instrument of death. These, he realised critically, were quite considerable. Even at the Spandau demonstration, it proved this point almost too precisely. The gun had been arranged to traverse an arc, one of its abilities. The Kaiser then 'inadvertently' started this mechanism. According to the author Edward Hewitt, it 'would have mown down the entire German General Staff and spectators' had not Maxim jumped in swiftly and stopped the thing.

As Germany's Kaiser was, no less than Maxim, so responsible for the dreadfulness of 1914–18, it is important to reflect upon this powerful individual. Winston Churchill, always so intriguingly readable, asks the question (in his *Great Contemporaries*): 'What should I have done in his position?' With the prince brought up from childhood to believe he had been appointed by God to rule a mighty nation, to be called the All-Highest, to lead the finest army in the world, to name the chiefs of army and navy plus those of government, and to be granted every desire, it is easy to understand that he might wish to exercise such authority. (He was even a British field-marshal, as well as being a colonel of the Royal Dragoons.) 'Limitless wealth and splendour attend your every step,' adds Churchill; 'Sixty palaces and castles await their owner; hundreds of glittering uniforms fill your wardrobes.' But there were also, on occasion, some discordant notes from others: 'We have a weakling on the throne; Our War lord is a pacifist; Was it for this that the immortal Frederick and the great Bismarck schemed and conquered; Are we to be denied our place in the sun?' The man himself then meets Hiram Maxim, and encounters Maxim's gun. He is confronted by a weapon, also all-highest as a killing machine, and the two of them — man and gun — are promptly at one with each other.

After the Spandau exhibition, so clearly applauded by Germany's emperor, Maxim was happy to record: 'Since which time vast numbers of Maxim guns have been acquired by the German Military and Naval Services.' Kaiser Wilhelm's enthusiasm for the weapon was not immediately endorsed by his general staff, but he continued to advocate its blessings and they, in time, acceded to his wishes (and certainly far more so than their British equivalents). The British did all they could to cause this change of heart. They even sent a machine gunner (of the 10th Hussars) to Potsdam to train the Germans concerning the best use of their 'vast number' of the new weapon.

As the Maxim gun was a British invention, every weapon subsequently made under licence in Germany, following the joint accord, led to royalties being paid to Britain. The British therefore relaxed contentedly. Not only were they receiving handsome revenues, but knew to the nearest gun how many of the weapons were being constructed and deployed by a possible enemy. In practice, of course, the truth about numbers was concealed. What else could be expected of a nation preparing for war, desperately trying to match — dreadnought for dreadnought — Britain's naval strength, and making its army yet bigger every single year? (This point about inadequate royalties was taken up after the war. Germany argued that, if such payments were insufficient, they should be set beside the failure by Vickers to pay Krupp for royalties on the patented fuses it manufactured so liberally during the hostilities.)

In time, the Kaiser's generals so welcomed the new machine gun, particularly after the Russo-Japanese war had been closely observed, that he and they gave special prizes for soldiers most skilled in its use. Each company of infantry was provided with the weapons, enabling everyone to understand their awesome power. The British had handed Germany a splendid instrument, as well as a supreme opportunity for advancement. The Kaiser could not have been more grateful — to a fellow member of Queen Victoria's wide-ranging family, and also to the man this prince had brought with him in order to demonstrate the invention's excellence. The emperor even purchased some of the guns out of his own pocket, once they had been adjusted for 11-mm Mauser calibre, and gave one personally to each of his Dragoon Guards Regiments. The German weapons were initially manufactured by the Ludwig Loewe company, but anti-Semitism caused this name to be changed to Deutsche Waffen und Munition Fabrik, with D.W.M. becoming the favoured — and famous — abbreviation.

Just as Sam Colt's most exciting European venture had been his Russian visit, so did Hiram Maxim rate his experience there extremely highly. It nearly did not happen for there was inevitable suspicion that Hiram, the son of Isaac Maxim, and grandchild (on his mother's side) of Levi Stevens, had to be a Jew, and such foreign individuals were disallowed on Russian soil. The Maxim gun's inventor promptly stressed his Puritan origins and a personal lack of enthusiasm for, or interest in, any religion. This too was considered unacceptable, and Hiram naturally protested. In consequence, following a modern interpretation of protesters (Martin Luther having been the first), he was accepted as a Protestant and permitted to remain.

Other problems in St Petersburg were more to his taste. One officer, having inspected the weapon with its crank, asserted loudly that no one could pull such a handle 600 times a minute. The automatic nature of Maxim's gun had not been fully appreciated and, with the gun demonstrating its customary and devastating rattle, that officer was quickly put to rights about his error. The Czar himself then wished to see the gun. Therefore Hiram Maxim, as with Colt before him, dressed himself most grandly, his clothes befitting such an audience. But as guns were never allowed in his majesty's presence (understandably, with assassination such a pastime in Russia), the inquisitive host had to be satisfied with photographs. Later, with a group of Russian officers in charge, the Czar did manage to see it fired in the St Petersburg riding school and, before long, 'vast numbers of machine guns' were being ordered by the Russian authorities. Beating a path to other people's doors was paying off extremely handsomely. (The Russian visit proved to be the most rewarding of them all: more of Maxim's weapons were manufactured in that one country than in all others combined. The final total was in excess of 600,000.)

It is almost a relief to learn that Maxim was not successful everywhere. Li Hung

Chang, the most influential Chinese states-
man of the time, visited England. After
stepping off the boat at Dover, he almost
immediately asked to see the Maxim gun.
At Eynsford in Kent he was given a demonstration, with three guns making an impressive clatter — and swiftly felling a fair-
sized tree. On being told that each cartridge (of the 1,800 the three guns had
fired per minute) cost 6s 6d, he considered
the firing 'altogether too fast for China'.
The King of Denmark reached a similar
conclusion: 'That gun would bankrupt my
little kingdom in about two hours.' The
Shah of Persia, given an exhibition within
the prestigious grounds of Buckingham
Palace, assumed he would be presented
with whatever he required. He was not,
and therefore left Britain empty-handed.
Turkey welcomed the inventor, offering
him 'one of the rarest gems' in the Sultan's
harem. 'The State of Maine Yankee with
no civilised vice', as Constantinople called
him, would not accept the gem and did not
receive an order. 'Invent a new vice for us,'
said one official blithely, 'and we will welcome you with open arms.' The inventor
could not oblige, and Maxim's order book
suffered accordingly.

Hiram Maxim's various successes, with

the nobility in England, and during his travelling around Europe, had not been in isolation. Sam Colt, rapid-firing pioneer, was long since dead, but Richard Gatling and his gun were still very active. In time he would be eclipsed by Maxim, but when the inventor of the Maxim gun was establishing himself in London, patenting his new ideas, selling guns wherever possible, and forging ahead with his automatic weapon, Gatling was still very much in business. Maxim was a pioneer, but was firmly treading in the footsteps of others.

Gatling, whose initial thinking of rapid-firing weaponry had occurred twenty-three years before Maxim's, certainly helped to pave the way for his successor. His multi-barrelled weapon had encouraged military and naval authorities to think more about a speedy rate of fire. The single-barrelled Hiram Maxim never gave credit to his predecessor, but he should have been grateful. Gatling's own travelling, much of it within Europe, had been considerable. His determination to gain foreign patents had certainly served as a precedent. He too had displayed his wares at major exhibitions. And he too had courted royalty, as with Napoleon III, nephew of Bonaparte, at the Paris Universal Exhibition of 1867. The

French emperor had asked for a Gatling to be tested at Versailles, causing its delighted inventor to telegraph the old Colt factory at Hartford that 'a respectable order' would soon be forthcoming. Trials at Versailles were successful but, save for two additional weapons requested for further testing, no big order surfaced.

Gatling wrote to William Franklin that the French government would, if rumours were correct, make more guns from the samples he had donated 'without leave or license from me'. Americans resident in Paris alleged that such perfidy was customary, but a French preference for things French was yet more customary. The 'secret' Montigny mitrailleuse was being preferred over the better, newer and more respected but American device. One final ingredient, also promoting France's weapon over its competition, was Prussia's interest in the Gatling gun. It had purchased three and was intent on ordering a further ninety-seven if trials proved satisfactory. With the Franco-Prussian conflict looming, causing inevitable resentment of all things Prussian, France was additionally loath to mimic the impending enemy. It therefore stuck, as it were, to its guns, losing interest in the Gatlings. And so, as it happened, did Prussia.

Gatling's salesmanship on behalf of his weapons was impressive, but nothing sold them so well as yet another war. Six years after the end of the Franco-Prussian conflict, the Russians and Turks were attacking each other once again. Both sides possessed Gatlings and each scored victories with them, Russia at the siege of Plevna, and Turkey at Shipka Pass. At Plevna the guns were used most effectively at night, spraying the area held by the Turkish troops, thus providing good protection. At Shipka, according to the distant *Hartford Daily Courant*, patriotically keeping in touch with local produce, the Gatlings did 'exactly what has been claimed for them — they effectively defended the pass against the advance of the Russians'. In short, the guns were good for the Russians, good for the Turks, and could therefore be good for other nationalities in other skirmishes.

They could also be good at sea. While the Russians and Turks were fighting each other in Bulgaria, there was a strange but convincing engagement which made use of a Gatling in the Pacific. Two British warships and a Peruvian vessel were involved, with the enemy being a British-built ironclad named the *Huáscar*. This craft was in rebel hands and had evaded the Peruvian government squadron. Britain's Royal Navy, notably the unarmoured wooden corvette H.M.S. *Shah*, then went to the government's assistance near the port of Ilo in southern Peru. The *Huáscar* was attacked, both by guns and torpedoes. Unfortunately, the torpedoes were not as speedy as their quarry and the gunfire was not lethal. Therefore a British victory did not occur, but the single Gatling had performed useful service by 'sweeping the enemy's decks' clear of personnel when firing from the *Shah*'s tops. This assault, according to a Peruvian report, 'seriously incommoded the combatants', and helped Peru to recapture the vessel later on.

Once returned to Peruvian employment, the *Huáscar* was thenceforth equipped with Gatling guns. A lesson had been learned and it soon earned dividends. When a war between Chile and Peru broke out not long afterwards, an attempt at boarding the *Huáscar* by Chilean sailors was thwarted when 'all' were killed by Gatlings and muskets. The iron-clad survived for four more months, but was eventually shot to pieces by the Chileans, with only eighty-three of the complement of 210 surviving the engagement. It is thought that most of the Peruvian sailors were in fact killed by Gatlings, the Chilean navy having also equipped itself with these new guns. That fighting may have been in a distant land, but news of it, and further renown for the Gatling gun, quickly travelled around the world.

Gradually, throughout the 1870s, more and more nations acquired Gatlings. Simultaneously these guns were being improved, becoming lighter, better-looking, more adapted to their wheeled carriages, more able to cope with different calibres, and forever benefiting from actual experience in warfare, whether on land or sea. Their tripods also became more suited to the task but, as must be the experience of every novelty, the accumulating fame not only profited production but also boosted rivalry. The Gardners, the Nordenfelts and those guns promoted by Hotchkiss were all snapping at Gatling's heels. Although the U.S. Army found Gatlings useful in clearing the West of its former inhabitants, it was Hotchkiss weaponry which proved particularly damaging at the Battle of Wounded Knee, the final and most tragic major encounter between invaders and invaded which saw the death of Sitting Bull.

Even before then, Richard Gatling, the one-time philanthropist, had been stung by growing competition. In 1881 he published a forthright challenge in the *Army & Navy Journal.*

## THE GATLING GUN

Many articles have recently appeared in the press, claiming the superior advantages of the Gardner and other machine guns over the Gatling gun.
In order to decide which is the best gun, the undersigned offers to fire his gun against any other gun, on the following wagers, viz.:
First, $500 that the Gatling can fire more shots in a given time, say one minute.
Second, $500 that the Gatling can give more hits on a target, firing, say one minute — at a range of 800 or 1,000 yards.
The winner to contribute the money won to some charitable object.
The time and place for the trials to be mutually agreed upon.

R. J. GATLING, OF HARTFORD, CONN.

No one took up the challenge, possibly because the various purchasers of these guns had made up their own minds about the merits of the rival weapons. Nevertheless, of all the rapid-firing guns in business at the time, the Gatling had pride of place. It was seeing service all over the world, and perhaps Gatling should not have bothered to express such apparent nervousness. What he did not know, and could not then know, was that an electrician working out of New York City would soon serve as the greatest rival of them all. Three years after that gamble had been published in the *Journal*, Hiram Stevens Maxim would be travelling to Europe. There he would appreciate quite how many nations were rattling sabres at each other, and hear his friend's advice that, if he wished to make money, he should help their citizens kill each other. And that is what he did. The 'greatest mechanician of them all' would change warfare dramatically, and the first fully automatic machine gun would eclipse all others.

# Chapter 8

# 'I Never Dreamed Such Things Could Be'

The Britisth welcomed jingoistic verse in the nineteenth century, particularly during its latter half. This partnered the growth of the British Empire and the spirited resolve with which much of it was embraced. There was also an emotional blending of sport with warfare, of boyhood days with adult life, and of the simple heroism involved in either sphere. Sir Henry Newbolt's epic poem makes the comparison as blatant as could be, starting off as it does at school.

*There's a breathless hush in the Close*
*tonight —*
*Ten to make and the match to win —*
*A bumping pitch and a blinding light,*
*An hour to play and the last man in.*
*And it's not for the sake of a ribboned coat,*
*Or the selfish hope of a season's fame,*

*But his Captain's hand on his shoulder*
  *smote —*
*'Play up! play up! and play the game!'*

Then, with no change in style, or in attitude, the cricketing skirmish becomes a bloody engagement with rather more to lose.

*The sand of the desert is sodden red —*
*Red with the wreck of a square that*
  *broke; —*
*The Gatling jammed and the Colonel*
  *dead,*
*and the regiment blind with dust and*
  *smoke.*
*The river of death has brimmed his banks,*
*and England's far, and Honour a name,*
*But the voice of a schoolboy rallies the*
  *ranks:*
*'Play up! play up! and play the game!'*

For Hiram Maxim, or any other inventor of rapid-firing guns, such a sentiment must have been difficult to absorb. They had to learn that wars should be fought according to rules, just as games are fought, and just as life is lived. Nothing dishonourable should ever occur. There was no glory in machine guns. Where was the valour, the élan, or the pluck, in mowing down an enemy? The better man could not win in a machine-gun kind of war. Therefore, if there was no other course, keep the man and get rid of the gun.

There was one important exception to this rule. If the enemy was an unruly mob, yelling and fanatical, that was occasion to use the fire-power of a Gatling, a Maxim, or a Nordenfelt. British colonisers faced with such belligerence would be particularly grateful for machine-gun power, time and time again. Corpses then lay, as the reports described them, in heaps, in piles, in throngs and pyramids, while vultures circled in the sky. The victims were often said to have been naked, as if that made any material difference to a speeding bullet. The enemy's courage was never denied, but considered to be senseless, despotic, tyrannical. These other kinds of people had not been thinking of the last man in, with no more wickets in hand. They had been howling, rabid, rabble, riffraff, alien. How else to deal with them, save by the superior technology of a machine gun from a superior force? Hilaire Belloc told it so succinctly:

> 'Whatever happens we have got
> The Maxim gun, and they have not.'

Again and again, the enemy possessed courage, desperation, hate and fury, but did not have advanced technology and therefore paid the price.

Wolseley's visit to Maxim's workshop was of particular significance. His failed foray to relieve Charles Gordon, who had bottled himself up in Khartoum, could have much benefited from Maxim guns. As for Gordon, his perilous position would have been considerably altered had he possessed a single rapid-firing weapon. His enemy did not have any, but neither did he when overrun by a force some eight times greater than his own. Nor did Gordon or Wolseley mention machine guns, and their desirability, in each man's very considerable personal diaries. Gordon writes of ten field guns when describing the 'Defences of Khartoum', but is not explicit about their type or calibre. Similarly Wolseley gives details of 'one Camel Battn (six guns) R.A.; two Guns of Native Battery' when giving facts about his battalions, his mounted infantry, a camel corps, and marines, but again there is no specific reference to rapid-firing weapons. Historians have suggested that there were mountain guns and machine guns accompanying his 7,000 men, but without emphasis.

'Gardiners' are casually referred to late in the campaign records, but without suggestion that they were hugely relevant — being not even spelt correctly. It is therefore easy to assume they were unimportant in the fighting which ensued. Neither Wolseley nor Gordon worried about the lack of guns (much as Shakespeare's Westmoreland bemoaned the lack of Englishmen before the fight at Agincourt, and was then chided by Henry V for his concern).

Wolseley certainly worried, but more about the accompanying journalists than his lack of armament.

> Our press is a monstrous humbug, unbridled and uncurbed as it is. Who can gauge the amount of evil done . . . to our people? But because we have silly notions about liberty we do not think licences should be checked, & the propagation of infamous heresies, foul untruths, and bestial immorality interfered with.

The *Illustrated News* and *Daily Telegraph* had hired some boats, but three of these would come to grief, causing Wolseley to comment, of course adversely:

Our soldiers can now not only manage their boats, but many could give these goose-quill fellows some good advice . . . What an ass Willy Russell was to commit himself to the opinions he expressed in the *Army & Navy Gazette* against our boats and the boat scheme. I wonder if there is any man (connected with the *Gazette*) who knows the difference between Strategy and Tactics. Willy Russell does not certainly, or he would not write the nonsense he does.

This is the same William Russell, founder of the *Gazette*, who had so upset almost everyone back home when writing during the mid-1850s of the mismanagement, horrors and sickness he personally witnessed during the Crimean campaign. He had certainly antagonised military officialdom in various other wars, and was doing it all over again in 1884. Wolseley therefore fought

the unscrupulous lying set of vagabonds . . . the creatures that John Bull pays to supply him with news, . . . the best of whom are weak about their H's, who are mostly cowards, and who do not in the least care how they lie as long as they can furnish their employers daily with a certain amount of sensational rumours reported by them to be facts.

The journalists could well have been annoying, whether or not they dropped their Hs, but it might have been presumed that a general about to be engulfed in war would be more preoccupied with guns than emissaries from Fleet Street.

The other foe Wolseley fought, and attacked most ferociously, was William Ewart Gladstone. It is true this prime minister had vacillated before being persuaded to send an army to rescue Gordon. But it is also true that Wolseley's foray could have been speedier in bringing its 10,000 men over 1,500 miles of difficult terrain, of desert and heat, of flies and dust. Wolseley is weak on self-blame and forever vigorous in attacking the Grand Old Man, as Gladstone was known. No doubt the antagonistic general received some comfort later on when the G.O.M. became widely known as M.O.G., the murderer of Gordon.

These personal and abusive battles, against press and politics, received far more attention in Wolseley's journals than the approaching fight against the Mahdi's men. What was his thinking, for example, about possible troop deployment against this violent enemy? And what were his thoughts about machine guns when approaching an opposition far superior in numbers? As he came nearer and nearer to his destination, there was some warfare and this is only briefly mentioned in the diary. At the Abu Klea wells there was a fierce engagement when a British square was broken — with, no doubt, much of the sand then sodden red. Over a thousand Arabs died in that battle, and so did 200 of Wolseley's men. A further attack on the following day killed and wounded 111 more British soldiery, including Herbert Stewart, the man in charge of them. Some of the survivors embarked on two steamers, earlier sent by Gordon from Khartoum, but they fared badly, and were much shot at, before reaching the outskirts of Khartoum. From their river situation it was then possible for them to see that no flag flew above Government House. Gordon had been killed two days earlier, and the city was in the Mahdi's hands. What a difference machine guns would have made, either in defending Khartoum or in the mixed fortunes of the relieving force. Neither of the men in charge made this point, before death on one hand, and dejection on the other, engulfed the two of them. Machine guns were not thought relevant.

The diaries written by the expedition's two most famous individuals reveal more about themselves than any shortcomings in the weaponry with which they had to fight. Their personal confessions go some way towards explaining why rapid-firing guns, when they did arrive in later years as extra armament, were not welcomed as enthusiastically as might have been expected. The wars the generals fought were, in part, conquests of an enemy but were also conflicts about themselves, their fears, their attitude when confronting death, their spirituality. The besieged Gordon took time to write:

For my part I am always frightened, and very much so . . . It is not the fear of death, that is past, thank God; but I fear defeat, and its consequences.

His fellow countryman, when endeavouring to reach Khartoum, was equally busy with his own diary after some soldiers had been drowned in a Nile cataract.

I hate men dying so. How much better

to die nobly fighting with all one's nerves strung up & full of that sentiment of loyalty to Queen and of patriotism which fills me with a sort of pride in myself when I am being shot at and fighting for my country.

How much better to die nobly in the service of one's Queen when gaining prestige for the regiment. Sitting behind a machine gun, and loosing off hundreds of rounds per minute at an advancing enemy, could contribute little to one's personal pride, to strung up nerves, to an individual's banishment of fear. This sentiment was widespread and important. Machine guns were lengthily regarded, notably by the British, as improper instruments of war, save for quelling unruly mobs, the yelling and fanatical forms of enemy who had to be suppressed. That was not proper warfare. It was bringing into line some awkward enemies who needed to be taught some rules. The Mahdi's men were exactly in that category, but the failed relief expedition of 1884–5 on behalf of Gordon was a touch too early for the development of rapid fire to play a major part in it. Hiram Maxim had only started on his gun in the early 1880s, and the 'Machine Gun Précis', which expected his weapon to 'outrun all rivals', was not to be written until July 1886. There were Gatlings, which had been tested in Britain since 1867, and there were the Gardners developed not long after. These had seen service in, for example, the Ashanti war, when Wolseley had also been the man in charge. Russians had used the Gatling Gorloffs against the Turks, and the Turks had used their near-identical Gatlings against the Russians. Word should therefore have spread that, if killing large numbers of an enemy was important, machine guns could do the job efficiently. Against straw-filled dummies at Shoeburyness they had been effective, and in action elsewhere they had shown their power, but there was not yet a general acceptance that very rapid-firing weapons were as much an adjunct to modern war as corned beef, dry biscuits and heavy hob-nailed boots.

It took further time for the distinctive rattle of Maxim's gun, officially applauded in 1886, to be heard by friend and foe alike. The inventor himself, a great salesman for his weapon, distributed samples to distinguished individuals, much as Samuel Colt had done half a century earlier. Maxim gave one to Henry Morton

Stanley before that man's third expedition into Africa — the first having found the apparently lost David Livingstone. Maxim even asked the brash explorer why, having found him, he had not brought back the famous missionary. 'He had no wish to leave,' said Stanley; 'He was well satisfied where he was, and was having a thoroughly good time.' (In fact, he was to die less than two years later.) Stanley's third foray was, in part, intended to save Emin Pasha, Britain's Governor of Equatoria in the southern Sudan who, much like Gordon further north, had been cut off by the Mahdists. The gun cannot have been much use to Stanley, the leader of a small band occasionally fighting within the bush rather than against an army in open ground, and it ended its days with Frederick Lugard in Uganda. Lugard, who had served with Wolseley in the Sudan, and who later played a dominant role in Uganda's story, also had little use for this bizarre weapon with its unhelpful appetite for weighty ammunition.

As it was, the first significant use of Maxim's machinery by British adventurers of any kind occurred in Matabeleland, which lies in present-day Zimbabwe. One side had now got the Maxim gun, and the other side had not. The African territory was largely occupied by Ndebele people, an expansionist Zulu offshoot pushed north from the 1830s by Boer trekkers advancing from the south. Lobengula, the Ndebele king from 1870, was fat, multi-married and ruler of a hundred thousand square miles of territory, a region twice the size of England. South Africa's millionaire politician Cecil Rhodes coveted this land, primarily for its mineral possessions. He and the buccaneers of his Chartered Company had already occupied Mashonaland further to the east. Before long the wealthy British imperialist met the powerful Ndebele ruler and acquired the rights he desired. In exchange Lobengula received £100 a month, 1,000 rifles (which, at first, he refused to accept) and the promise of a gunboat (which never materialised).

There was then peace of a sort. Lobengula was reluctant to confront his white neighbours, who were largely congregated around a fort they called Victoria. He knew of their power from earlier Zulu-British confrontations, but his warriors were impatient to 'wash their spears' once more, not having done so against advancing white men since fights against the Boers. Rhodes's followers, growing in strength but modest in number, could not hope to defeat a disciplined impi, several thousand strong. Rhodes was also reluctant to spend the money such an attack would entail, but the imperialist invaders were too hungry, and the aggrieved warriors too eager, for the uneasy tranquillity to survive. Something would surely happen to break the calm.

A word first about the Zulus. They were not a rabble of undisciplined warriors but one of the most formidable fighting units the world had ever known. The great King Shaka had forged their empire early in the nineteenth century, and had transformed a small pastoral nation into one of military might. Discipline was intense, and loyalty was total. He forced his warriors to travel barefoot, knowing that sandals would slow them down. They ran tremendous distances, arriving at an enemy's position hours before they were expected. Shaka favoured the short stabbing weapon, somewhat akin to the Roman broad-sword, and could see no point in throwing a spear at opponents: it might kill one man at the most, but might then be returned no less fatally. It was ironic that such a formidable fighting machine should be first to encounter the world's most lethal killing device.

Missionaries entering Shaka's region of Natal would sometimes be made to witness terrifying shows of strength. Author Stuart Cloete tells the story of a Zulu regiment being ordered, barehanded, to pull a hippopotamus from the river. The warriors did so, leaving many of their number dead, before their leader saluted his obedience of the command with the remainder of his arm. He was thanked, and told to end his life. After Shaka's mother Nandi died, her son felt insufficient grief was being displayed and paraded regiments to check their melancholy. Sexual intercourse had long been forbidden, and young Zulu girls were instructed to dance before the warriors. Their Great Elephant, as Shaka was known, walked among them with half a dozen slayers armed with clubs. Any man visibly moved by the undulating forms was promptly put to death. As one near-victim recounted afterwards: 'The platoon immediately in front of the Great Elephant went to the birds to the last man, but even that did not seem to dampen our manhood.' It was the girls themselves who managed to halt the slaughter, by telling the men to hit themselves as hard as possible. 'It is better to be a live ox than a dead bull,' reported the survivor, 'particularly if the disability is but temporary.'

Shaka was long dead in Cecil Rhodes's time, but the discipline he had instilled still earned his Zulus and their war-cries great respect wherever they fought and raided. Hence the perverse situation of effective machine guns first encountering — of all possible enemies — some Zulu regiments. The impis, the crescent shapes with which the charging warriors attacked so ferociously, were rightly feared. Nine years after Maxim had started work in London, and seven after the Précis had so commended his machine gun, South Africa's Chartered Company had acquired some of his weapons. Rhodes and his associates were wanting more of Lobengula's land than its minerals; they wanted the land itself. But they needed a pretext for its acquisition, and this arrived, along with the guns, in 1893.

The Ndebele nation had been maddened that certain Shona, their traditional and generally less aggressive enemy, had had the impudence to steal some cattle. Lobengula was forced to abandon his cautious policy of restraint. He sent a raiding party to exact revenge, with the proviso that all white property should be respected. Unfortunately the temptation to wreak havoc, after so many years of abstinence, proved too strong. Several hundred Mashona were killed on the very outskirts of Fort Victoria. Worse still, and making it difficult for the British to turn a blind eye, many 'houseboys' were murdered in white homes, and some Mashona women and children were abducted. Even a few horses and cattle belonging to British residents were also taken. Cecil Rhodes was uncertain about a raid to punish the wrongdoers, mainly because he knew it would be costly. But one of his friends, Leander Starr Jameson, who later achieved fame as the prime culprit for the outbreak of the Boer War, was hot-headed and determined. He was eager to quash the Ndebele, once and for all, by occupying their capital, Bulawayo, and then of course the land around it. The pretext awarded by Lobengula was, in his immediate opinion, too good to miss.

Rhodes eventually consented to the plan and Jameson set off from Fort Victoria with 700 volunteers, each to be paid with 6,000 acres of the new land after their victory. It was a small force to be pitted against an impi numbered in thousands but, along with a couple of seven-pounder field guns, it possessed six machine guns, mainly Maxims, plus an appropriate quantity of ammunition. By the Shangani river, deep in Ndebele territory, an impi of 6,000 warriors chose to attack at night, although this made little difference to the stream of bullets which promptly came their way. Hundreds of the Ndebele died, with the whites losing one killed and half a dozen wounded. One week later, when the warriors had regrouped only twenty miles from Bulawayo, they launched a second assault, no less courageously than the first and no less devastatingly. This time the engagement was even fiercer. The Ndebele lost over a thousand of their number, while the whites suffered four dead and seven wounded. The victorious owners of the Maxim guns then rode into a deserted Bulawayo, not long after Lobengula and all his people had abandoned it.

The Ndebele chief then wrote to Queen Victoria, as one ruler to another. 'Why do your people kill me? Do you kill me for following my stolen cattle which are seen in the possession of the Mashonas?' The British queen replied, somewhat enigmatically, stating as one chief to another that

It is not wise to put too much power into the hands of men who come first, and to exclude other deserving men. A King gives a stranger an ox, not his whole herd of cattle, otherwise what would other strangers have to eat?

The poor recipient of this letter, both misunderstood and misunderstanding, knew only that he was being terribly assaulted. To his own people he proclaimed:

Matabele! The white men will never cease following us while we have gold in our possession, for gold is what the white men prize above all things. Collect now all my gold . . . and carry it to the white men. Tell them they have beaten my regiments, killed my people, burnt my kraals, captured my cattle, and that I want peace.

He did not get peace, any more than the Incas of Peru had received it when, almost four centuries earlier, their chief Atahualpa had used nearly identical words and soon been strangled by the Spanish. Or when other people in other areas were invaded, for gold or merely for the land itself, by foreigners whose armament was superior and whose greed was paramount. For some of Rhodes's men, it was insufficient that they had defeated the Ndebele impis, humiliated Lobengula and acquired his land and capital. This group therefore set off to capture the man himself. They assumed, with the arrogance of victors, there would be no fight left among the opposition, but they were wholly wrong. There were only thirty-five in this cocky band, and they were without machine guns. All were to be stabbed to death in the fight which followed.

Lobengula nevertheless retreated into the bush and soon died. Some say that smallpox was the cause, others that he poisoned himself. It does not really matter which, since machine guns had destroyed his impis and had been the true deciders of his fate. The British did at least admit and accept how their victory had been achieved. After the slaughter, one man wrote to what was now the Maxim-Nordenfelt Guns and Ammunition Company:

The Matabele never got nearer than a hundred yards . . . the Maxims far exceeded all expectations and mowed them down like grass. I never saw anything like these Maxim guns, nor dreamed that such things could be.

219

The *Daily News* of London, on 3 November 1893, also gave credit where it was most deserved, the guns on one hand, and Zulu courage on the other.

Their trust was in their [stabbing] spears, for in all their rude experience of warfare they had never known an enemy able to withstand them. Even when they found their mistake, they had the heroism to regard it as only a momentary error in their calculations. They retired in perfect order and re-formed for a second rush . . . Once more, the Maxims swept them down in the dense masses of their concentration. It seems incredible that they should have mustered for still another attack, yet this actually happened. But by this time they had reached the limits of human endurance. They came as men fore-doomed for failure, and those who were left of them went back a mere rabble rout.

Or, as Roger Ford wrote in *The Grim Reaper*, when quoting a Matabele's story:

The white man came again with his guns that spat bullets as the heavens sometimes spit hail, and who were the naked Matabele to stand up against these guns?

And who also were the fearsome mountain people, living near the Khyber Pass (then between British India and independent Afghanistan) when they too encountered heavens spitting hail? Shortly after the subjugation of the Ndebele, the Maxim gun was first used formally in action by British troops rather than by the British irregulars, police and volunteers who had used them in Rhodesia. Six .303 Maxims had arrived a few weeks before operations began against the Ghazis at the Malakand Pass, slightly to the east of the Khyber. The guns arrived slung in unwieldy fashion between large wheels, as if they were artillery. This arrangement was promptly modified so that mules could carry them, a more convenient arrangement for mountainous territory.

The Ghazis had protected themselves within sangars, or rocky breastworks, but then charged against the British — and against the British rapid-firing guns. These proved 'very useful', as various reports proclaimed, and the lightness of the Maxims — some forty pounds each — was much appreciated by their users in that difficult neighbourhood. The London *Globe*'s military correspondent summed up the experience.

[The] military authorities were enabled to issue three Maxims to the troops, and to send up an unlimited supply of cordite ammunition of the same kind as that used in the Lee-Metford rifle . . . Sangar after sangar was obstinately held . . . and here I may note the admirable service done by the artillery and Maxim guns . . . [They] will probably be used in all future expeditions, and will, I trust, be taken up with increased interest at home . . . In regard to rapidity of fire and accuracy, the Maxim has much the best of it [over the rival Gardners], and is in all respects a far superior weapon.

Maxims were certainly 'taken up'. In 1898, thirteen years after the humiliating failure to rescue Gordon, twelve after Wolseley (now Commander-in-Chief of the British Army) had visited the Hatton Garden workshop, five after the conquest of Mashona and Matabeleland formed these territories into Southern Rhodesia, and three after British regulars had found the gun so 'useful' up by Afghanistan, the British had occasion to enter the Sudan once again. The plan was to settle a matter that had never gone away. Gordon's enemy, the Mahdi, had died five months after his fallen adversary, but the Mahdists had grown even stronger. No one knew the cause of the Mahdi's death, with smallpox, typhus, or poison from an outraged woman all put forward as possibilities, but a life — well recorded by his European prisoners — of considerable debauchery in an unsanitary spot like Omdurman, which was across the Nile from Khartoum, would probably have been sufficient.

The Mahdi's successor was the Khalifa Abdullah, preferred by his predecessor over the other khalifas (lieutenants) or any of the Mahdi's own family. The newcomer was reputedly cunning, charming (if need be), cruel, vain, energetic, and as courageous as his men. He lived modestly in Omdurman's only two-storey house. He had worshipped the Mahdi, and then his memory, since reaching the age of thirty-five. He was equally fanatical for the holy war against the infidel, claiming that vengeful exhortations from the Mahdi were reaching him in dreams. In fact, out of reverence for that individual, Abdullah had built in Omdurman a major shrine surmounted by a dome. For a while this became, for some, a worthier place to visit than the Kaaba at Mecca. Pilgrims even arrived there from that other and most sacred place of all.

The Sudan had been a problem ever since 1819, when Mohammed Ali of Egypt had sent his forces to conquer it. His subsequent rule was so corrupt and loathsome that it became entirely comprehensible why the Mahdi, rebelling against such despotism and evil, had risen to fame and power quite so speedily. The British, along with almost everyone else, had aligned themselves against Egypt, but the building of the Suez Canal in 1869, and then the British acquisition of it in 1875, meant that the country had to become an ally. The Mahdi's revolt, although initially praised, came to be viewed as an anti-British insurrection. Virtually all of Gordon's defending troops were Egyptian soldiers, the hated representatives of a hated government, and they too had been slaughtered during the assault upon Khartoum. That Mahdi victory of 1885 greatly encouraged his followers, and a further fight between Britain and the Mahdists therefore became inevitable. Preparations were made for it during the 1890s, with a massive expedition eventually setting forth in 1896.

Emotionally the most powerful reason for this further assault upon the Sudan was one of revenge for Gordon's death. Politically there was also concern, supported only by rumour, that the Belgians were planning an expansion of their huge Congo territory towards the Nile. And so, most incongruously, were the French, with a small contingent known to be intent on annexing the southern Sudan. This was the end of the scramble for Africa, a last bid to gather what remained of the continent not yet in European hands. The Sudan was one such entity but, yet more importantly for the British, it posed a threat to Egypt, and therefore to the Suez Canal, and therefore to India. In fact, there was no knowing what the belligerent and numerous Mahdists might do next by way of inconvenience. They had already invaded Egypt in 1889. Although repulsed on that occasion, they might try again. In consequence, it was time to end their aggressive fanaticism, once and for all. Or, in Gordon's well-remembered words:

The Mahdi must be smashed up . . .

225

Once Khartoum belongs to Mahdi the task will be far more difficult; yet you will, for the sake of Egypt, execute it . . .

In command of the new and avenging army was the forty-six-year-old Herbert Kitchener. As a major, he had accompanied Wolseley on the earlier Nile foray which had failed to rescue Gordon. On that trip Kitchener had not been just one more middle-ranking officer among many within the force. Gordon had been his hero, and he had also admired Colonel Stewart, the man Gordon had sent at the eleventh hour to liaise with Britain's army, then still heading south. The fact that both Stewart and, a few days later, Gordon, died at the hands of the Mahdi's men had profoundly influenced the young major. No one wished to avenge those deaths more than him.

During the earlier invasion, Kitchener had been appointed 'Special Commissioner for the Arabs'. His task had been to travel ahead of Wolseley's relieving army, collect intelligence, secure the loyalty of influential tribesmen (by subsidies), and be 'charmingly independent', as Kitchener phrased it, with 1,500 men under his command. He himself, like some early Lawrence of Arabia, dressed in a turban with Arab robes and possessed a devout following of 'blood brothers' as an escort. He had therefore been at the forefront of the invading force and had been first to hear of Stewart's and Gordon's deaths. Earlier he had warned headquarters that, unless more haste was deployed in efforts to reach Gordon, 'the day would come when 20,000 men would be needed' to reconquer the Sudan. As general in charge of that reconquest (with, it so happened, about 20,000 men), he was as intent as anyone that it should succeed.

This time there was to be no ignominious repulse. This time, also, there was no need for haste, and Kitchener ordered a railway to be constructed for 230 miles south from Wadi Halfa. The line would take him, his men and his river-boat sections over the Nubian desert by making a direct short-cut to Abu Hamed, thus eliminating the long loop taken by the Nile with its several cataracts. And finally, the most crucial ingredients on this second foray into the Sudan were many Maxim guns, and a general more determined than ever to 'smash up' the Mahdists.

But other engagements occurred before

the decisive battle of Omdurman, some taking place on the journey south. Also, and rather bizarrely, the French had a battle with the Dervishes in southern Sudan. After reaching the Nile (near modern-day Juba), and numbering only a hundred without any artillery, they were abruptly confronted, not by the British but by 'at least 1,200 dervishes' on river gunboats. Without too much trouble, mainly because they possessed the latest magazine rifles and the sense to fire from concealed positions, the French routed their attackers and so the first retaliation for Gordon's death was inflicted by Britain's arch-rivals in the slicing up of Africa. Yet this small French contingent would inevitably be mopped up and slaughtered by further Dervishes unless their prime antagonist, Great Britain, succeeded in the north.

Kitchener had every intention of succeeding in the north (and then the south), but was outnumbered. He had 8,000 British troops, and almost double that number of Egyptian and Sudanese military. The Khalifa had some 40,000 followers, or possibly 50,000, but they were ill-equipped, save in their terrible courage. Most were armed with spears, and with swords or daggers, but a few possessed obsolete, and relatively short-range, Remington rifles. Kitchener's men had magazine Lee-Metfords of much greater range and power. They also, according to the battle's fulsome account by Edward Spiers, had eighty guns, mostly twelve-pounders, and forty-four machine guns distributed almost equally among the land forces and those on river boats. Kitchener had so much respect for the Maxims' effectiveness, and their value in the approaching conflict, that he had them carefully wrapped in silk to prevent dust from infiltrating their mechanisms. Each day the guns were carefully removed from this protection and cleaned, but oil was never used, save just before the fight. Kitchener's progress towards Khartoum must have appeared extraordinarily impressive. Apart from all the men, and their guns, and their hundreds of camp followers, the formidable force was accompanied by 2,469 horses, 896 mules, 3,524 camels, and 229 donkeys, as it headed south to meet the Khalifa's men. Everything possible had been arranged to settle the Sudan — for good.

It was a powerful contingent, but was also far from home and in unfamiliar territory. The enemy, so hugely superior in numbers, could have overwhelmed the invaders — if it had attacked at night, had used stealth and had rendered the artillery and machine guns impotent by engaging at close range among the scrub. The Dervishes were highly skilled in hand-to-hand fighting, and their spears and daggers would then have been more effective than magazine rifles or guns of any kind. Furthermore, every successful engagement would almost certainly have brought greater recruitment, with more and more Sudanese flocking to join the Mahdi's victorious regiments, whereas Kitchener had no reserves whatsoever. In many ways he ought to have been intimidated by the situation, and so should his men, but there was an arrogance which gave them confidence. The enemy was adjudged inferior, being a rabble, a mob, a chaotic assembly of yelling savages who were not an army. Gordon would be avenged; of that there was no doubt.

Winston Churchill, a twenty-three-year-old lieutenant who had previously served with the 4th Hussars on the Afghan border, had bullied his mother to use her influence after he had learned of his country's preparations for war in Africa. Could she not have him transferred to Egypt so that he might see something of the fight? According to young Winston, she left no stone unturned, no cutlet uncooked, to get him there. In a commendably short time she succeeded, but at the expense of angering Kitchener. He suspected (rightly) that Churchill was thus hoping to further a political career. Worse still, the ambitious lieutenant was combining his military service with journalism, having received a commission to report on the River War (as he later called it) for the *Morning Post.* Kitchener did not welcome newspapermen any more than Wolseley had done, but was polite to them, although regretting their fondness for drink (on a drink-free expedition), their excessive use of the telegraph lines and their perpetual presence: there were fifteen full-timers following his campaign. As for Churchill, it had been Lord Salisbury, then Prime Minister (and perhaps one recipient of cutlets), who had sanctioned the soldier-journalist's transfer to the 21st Lancers. Therefore Kitchener had to yield to this higher authority, and to Jennie Churchill's connivance on her ambitious son's behalf.

In any case the Sirdar, as all called him (the title being Urdu for military leader), had much else to concern him as he travelled south. His huge army of men, animals, guns, and camp followers (women and children of the Egyptian and Sudanese troops), had to be disembarked and organised. The soldiers had to be made ready, inspected and prepared for the conflict. They were well armed in comparison with the opposition, but a victory was not inevitable. The enemy's numbers were impressive, as were their fanaticism and readiness to die. They might choose to attack at night. Their knowledge of the terrain was plainly superior. Much of the land was covered in zeriba, a form of scrub ideal for surprise attacks. The British troops were better disciplined, but each man knew that Gordon, within the well-prepared fortifications of Khartoum, had been swiftly overrun. By no means was the result assured, despite the presence on one side of Maxim's formidable invention. Either side could win, and the losers would die horribly.

The Sirdar was apparently cheery, and in great fettle, after a final inspection of his troops. To be in charge of such a cohort must have been exhilarating as well as intimidating. The total invading force of men and animals marched in ranks almost three miles wide and one mile deep, while the river gunboats travelled upstream to keep pace with them. The hilly country through which this army marched was thick with bushy vegetation sometimes twelve feet high. Everywhere seemed ripe for a sudden attack, but nothing happened, either by night or day, before the open plain by the mud-walled city of Omdurman became clearly visible. There, in the haze ahead of the British force, was the dome of the Mahdi's tomb. And there was Khartoum on the Nile's other side, with Gordon's palace still standing close by the river bank. The date was 1 September 1898.

After lunch, the Sirdar rode to the top of a nearby hill for a better view. What he saw, among much else, was an officer of the 21st Lancers galloping his way and then slowing down in order not to imply any form of panic. This was Lieutenant Churchill, meeting his C.-in-C. for the very first time and with important news to tell. The enemy, out of sight from Kitchener's hilltop, was only five miles away and 50,000 strong. Expecting an immediate attack, the Sirdar ordered the Egyptians and Sudanese to the right and the British to the left. A thorn hedge and hastily dug trenches would serve as protection, but astonishingly the huge horde of advancing enemy then halted when only three miles distant from the invaders.

It was presumed by the British that there

would be a night attack. Similarly, it was presumed by the Dervishes that the British might do something of the sort themselves. Therefore both sides slept uneasily. What was not known were the contents of yet another of the Khalifa's dreams arriving from the Mahdi, whose mystical instructions had been to fight in daylight. This meant the Khalifa's followers would have to gallop and run across the open plain; rifles and Maxims would be at their most destructive after day had dawned.

Churchill, back with his fellow Lancers, was no less astounded than everyone else at the sight which unfolded on the plain.

Suddenly, the whole black line which seemed to be the *zeriba* began to move. It was made of men, not bushes. Behind it other immense masses and lines of men appeared over the crest; and while we watched, amazed by the wonder of the sight, the whole face of the slope beneath became black with swarming savages. Four miles from end to end and, as it seemed, in five great divisions, this mighty army advanced — swiftly.

At a range of 2,700 yards, the Sirdar ordered his field guns to start their firing, both from their land positions and on the boats. Their shrapnel shells burst above the enemy, but without appreciable effect. Meanwhile the 'wild brave savages', as one officer described them, advanced 'to their destruction', with the emirs on horseback yelling at their white-robed warriors. Maxims and rifles then opened fire at 800 yards, and the attackers fell in droves. 'One's feelings,' wrote an observer, 'went over to the enemy — they just struggled on . . . All the pluck was displayed by the Dervishes, our side had no chance of showing anything but discipline.'

Within two hours Kitchener's guns, which had already shelled the famous tomb in Omdurman, had wrought havoc among the advancing men. So had the several thousand Lee-Metfords. And, crucially, so had the six Maxims of the 1st Brigade, firing 4,000 rounds each, and the four of the 2nd Brigade, each firing 2,500 rounds. Only a few of the enemy got within 300 yards of the merciless weapons. The slaughter was more or less over in fifteen minutes, with 'Sir H. Kitchener', according to Churchill, 'shutting up his glasses' before saying to the officers around him that the opposition had received 'a good dusting'. 'It was not a

235

battle,' wrote a war correspondent afterwards, 'but an execution.' Or, as an officer wrote, with somewhat different emphasis and appreciating the courage displayed by his enemy, it was 'a fine performance truly for any race of man'. Or as another officer recalled: 'It was *picturesque and safe*, which is my idea of what a battle should be.'

As during the U.S. Civil War, and as with the French and Prussian armies fighting near Paris, there were observers come to see the fight. One such with Kitchener was Baron Adolf von Tiedemann, German military attaché and always splendidly attired. When the Dervishes started their assault, he rode away from the headquarters' hill-top position in order to watch the Maxims in action. He then noted that, at first, the gunners did not find the range but, having done so, caused the enemy to fall in heaps. The Maxims, in his opinion, did a large share of the work of repelling the Dervish rush. Without doubt his thoughts on the matter influenced those back home — and therefore caused British soldiers to fall in similar heaps when their time came in France.

A curious sideline to the battle was the charge of the 21st Lancers, an unnecessary move against the Khalifa's right flank (possibly explained, it is said, by the fact this regiment did not have a single battle honour to its name and, frequently teased about this lack, longed to put the matter right). At all events, the headlong rush was no less idiotic than the famous foray of the Light Brigade forty-two years earlier. The galloping 21st Lancers were soon surprised by some previously unseen and hidden Dervishes and suffered half the casualties of the British in the battle as a whole. Twenty Lancers were killed, including Robin Grenfell, a Kitchener relation. Rather more of the Lancers' 400 horses were killed or wounded, and two V.C.s were subsequently awarded.

The young Winston, who seems to have been everywhere that day, was also in the charge. He savoured the experience and was astonished by the quantity of corpses to be seen lying on the ground. Kitchener ordered a count and learned that 10,883 of the enemy had died that day — and in such a small portion of it. The wounded were estimated at 16,000, with some of their number despatched by looters and, allegedly, some others bayoneted to death. 'Remember Gordon' is said to have been muttered by those who carried out this task. No one knew with any accuracy by what method most of the dead had been killed in action, but it was thought — officially — that the chattering Maxims had claimed three-quarters of the total.

Two hours after the fight had begun, despite thousands of the enemy still nearby, Kitchener sounded the advance towards Omdurman. Two journalists were slightly too far ahead when a single Dervish suddenly sprang from among the dead. They were about to be speared by him when a British major, Neville Smyth, intercepted the attack, was wounded and earned a V.C. Within the narrow twisting streets of Omdurman, rich with corpses from all the shelling, Kitchener himself nearly came to grief. Some British artillery had loosed off their guns, perhaps because they had seen the Khalifa's flag being carried proudly by the victors, perhaps entirely by mistake. This friendly fire, in modern terminology, added to the British losses, also killing a journalist, Hubert Howard, who had been writing for *The Times* (and who also, much like Churchill, blended journalism with action by galloping with the 21st Lancers in their attack). The total of British, Egyptian, and Sudanese dead was less than fifty, or one two-hundredth of the enemy's losses. Had the Lancers not charged, and had the artillery not erred, these casualties would have been even fewer.

The battle had been won emphatically, but the Khalifa had escaped. Rather more importantly, he was thought to be organising yet another army. Therefore a British contingent, armed with Maxims, went to look for him, and for whatever forces he still possessed. Once again, there was formidable courage from the Dervishes and, once again, the chattering machine guns were totally triumphant. They opened fire at 800 yards, and no white-robed tribesman got 'nearer than ninety-four paces', according to the official report. As one observer of the campaign wrote afterwards with telling brevity:

To the Maxim Gun primarily belongs the victory which stamped out Dervish rule in the Soudan.

Yet there was no comprehension among those in authority that Maxim weaponry had altered all the rules. It had undoubtedly changed them for savages, naked warriors, infidels, and others of their kind, but not — as many men believed — for any wars which Europeans might fight against each other. Africans were different. Whether Zulus or Dervishes, Ashanti or Ndebele, they were not as those who lived in Europe. Instead they were regarded as if alien, as if comparisons were quite impossible. They could never become equals, however hard they might try in years to come. As for becoming civilised, they would surely fail. They were savages, and would remain so. They were wholly different, and might have been raised on another planet rather than another land. (Charles Darwin even wrote to a friend about to leave for China: 'Find out if the gestures & expression of countenance under various emotions with real savages [are] the same as with us'.)

As a result of this fundamental feeling, the battles against different kinds of people were not seen as relevant to warfare among equals. Few military officials appreciated that this new and mechanical technology might engulf them too. Among them was Sir Edward Arnold, historian of the 1898 campaign, who later wrote:

In most of our wars it has been the dash, the skill, and the bravery of our officers and men that have won the day, but in this case the battle was won by a quiet scientific gentleman living down in Kent.

What, after all, was the point of warfare if dash, skill and bravery were no longer fundamental? Let us have nothing to do with these machine guns if they are so destructive of tradition. Let us pretend they have never been invented, and let us put them to one side. Or so said many after Omdurman, and continued to say, steadfastly, in the years to come. That slaughter of 10,000 courageous men in the desert had been terrible, and afterwards Kitchener was criticised by some outspoken individuals for overseeing such devastation. Much worse was to come.

Almost twice that number of British soldiers were to die on the first day of the Battle of the Somme as had perished in the first few hours of Omdurman. Most of the victims on 1 July 1916 were men who had answered Kitchener's call, responding to his gloved and pointed finger, for volunteers to fight. The various descendants of Maxim's gun were once again victorious, uncaring whether the recipients of their bullets were white-robed tribesmen yelling frantically or quieter soldiers dressed in khaki. Omdurman had provided one example of what such guns could do. Eighteen years later there was this other rendering, and the only difference was that these new heaps, piles, and pyramids were of equally brave men whose generals had learned nothing from the earlier exercise.

Hilaire Belloc's famous verse about the Maxim gun's possession, included in *The Modern Traveller*, was written when this unilateral advantage was in full swing. He knew about military matters, having served in the French army (before becoming a British citizen in 1902), and could therefore appreciate the weapon's value. He did not write an equivalent verse for World War One when the enemy did have the Maxim gun and we, in the main, did not.

> *I shall never forget the way*
> *that Blood stood upon this awful day*
> *Preserved us all from death.*
> *He stood upon a little mound*
> *Cast his lethargic eyes around*
> *and said beneath his breath:*
> *'Whatever happens we have got*
> *The Maxim Gun, and they have not.'*

The galling fact, for all those cut down near the River Somme and elsewhere, was our making certain that the enemy had got what we did not, Britain's Prince of Wales having helped to clinch the deal.

# Chapter 9

# Fire Without Smoke

The British machine-gunners at Omdurman were not only able to slaughter the advancing hordes, but had no difficulty in seeing them. Such visibility had by no means always been the rule. In former days, when standing lines of infantry had fired at one another as and when their weapons were ready to do so, smoke was an immediate accompaniment of every fusillade. All the descriptions of battle in which early firearms were involved tell of clouds quickly enshrouding the men involved, of the problem even in seeing the opposition after the first shots had been fired, and then of yet more smoke and yet more problems as the fighting grew severe. The resulting lack of visibility was as certain as misfirings, as damp powder, and as noise and death. Gunpowder made smoke when it was ignited. That was a fact of life.

After guns had been created to fire more

rapidly, such as the Colts and Gatlings, they undoubtedly despatched more bullets towards an enemy. Therefore they made more smoke. Very frequently, if the air was calm and several guns in line were firing, the difficulty of seeing an enemy became immediately acute, if not impossible. No wonder that Garnet Wolseley, the 'brightest and cleverest of military men', not only saw the great quantities of Maxim smoke in Hatton Garden and elsewhere, but suggested that some kind of smokeless cartridge ought to be created, if this were possible. For Maxim the challenge was both welcome and enticing. As a draughtsman turned electrician turned gun man, he needed to turn again and sort out some of gunpowder's basic chemistry.

Wolseley's comment that Yankees beat all creation, coming after his visit to 57D Hatton Garden, was a general statement. Americans were known to be adept at making things. Much earlier, and also with weaponry, Sam Colt had taught Britons a thing or two. Richard Gatling had done likewise, and then so did Hiram Maxim. They were an inventive lot, these one-time colonials, and they could surely devise a smokeless cartridge. The same thought about American inventiveness had also struck Andrew Clark following his own visit to the Maxim workshop. He, as Surveyor-General of Fortifications of the British Empire, had taken the inventor aside after witnessing the gun in action because he too had a powder problem. For its solution he considered that Maxim, 'being an American', would swiftly find an answer.

Clark's quandary concerned a slow-burning German mixture. This was known to give high velocities to bullets but did so with low pressure, and British gun-makers were intrigued. High velocity (better for bullets) and low pressure (better for barrels) were both advantageous, but the British ordnance men did not understand the German secret. Chemically, the German powder proved to be identical to the British kind, and yet there was this difference in the manner of its explosion. Could the inventive Maxim please use his American ability, and thereby solve the problem? The Germans were asking £35,000 for their secret, a sum the British were prepared to pay if Maxim could not oblige.

The enthusiastic Anglo-Yankee set to work, promising in his cocksure fashion to provide an answer by the following day. Earlier he had read of Chinese powders which were the converse of the German kind in that they were chemically identical but burned violently. He also knew of the Chinese procedure for making such powders, with the same old ingredients of charcoal, sulphur, and nitre (saltpetre) being ground most finely before their use. Therefore, after making his promise to the Surveyor-General, Maxim bought a microscope. Through this he examined the German powder, soon discovering that its sulphur and charcoal were finely ground, but not its nitre, which was much more granular. As nitre contains all the oxygen necessary for the explosive combustion, its granular form made it less immediately accessible to the other two components. Hence a slower burning. And hence the greater bullet velocity with a more prolonged acceleration up the barrel, a better procedure than a single violent kick. Therefore game, set and yet more fame to Maxim. He earned not a penny piece for his revelation to the Surveyor-General, but acquired still more respect for his overall ability. No wonder that Wolseley was encouraged to presume that every kind of difficulty, even that of gun smoke, could be solved in the twinkling of an eye.

Indeed, in Maxim's memory, that particular problem did not take him long to solve. Its solution apparently occupied no more time than one train journey to Vienna. During this trip he concluded that nitroglycerine coupled with gun-cotton might do the trick. Both these substances were well known, and both had to be handled with appropriate concern for their extreme explosiveness. As a result, after he had made known his recommendations following this journey, he was informed that no one would welcome such a mixture, however smokeless it might prove to be. Maxim disregarded this advice, of course, and persisted with his thinking. After adding some castor oil to prevent the mixture drying excessively, he produced a powder which, according to his ebullient memoirs, 'has never been surpassed in efficiency'. For good measure he then spent a few happy hours making a hundred varieties of powder, these differing only in the amount of time their nitre had been milled. The less granular this became, and the more accessible its oxygen, the faster was the chemical reaction. Therefore, and henceforth, the right powder could be selected for any kind of weapon. Its speed of explosion would govern the quantity of smoke. The more complete the combustion, the less there would be of this visible and unwelcome residue.

The Surveyor-General of imperial fortifications was naturally delighted. He had saved £35,000, and had learned how to make the desirable German powder. As a modest but important reward, he gave Maxim some sound advice concerning the new gun and the possibility of its acceptance by the military:

Do not give up until you make it so simple that it can all be taken apart, examined, and cleaned, with no other instruments than the hands.

Maxim wholeheartedly accepted this counsel and in the Maxim gun's early years was forever amending, improving, and adjusting his invention. No sooner had others approved of his creation than it was altered. Maxim was not a man for giving up just because an invention was good enough. Instead he reinvented, again and again. That was his way. Clark's recommendation had merely underlined and emphasised his personal attitude.

In the current encyclopaedic descriptions of smokeless powders rather less credit is given to Maxim's inventiveness than he gave himself. Indeed, his name is scarcely mentioned, if at all, but he was on the right track while he journeyed to Vienna. In order to achieve smokelessness, it is necessary not only to have the right ingredients but also for them to be in the right state. Most smokeless powders tend to be colloidal, these substances being noncrystalline and semi-solid within a medium. In this condition the materials appear to be dissolved but, being colloids, they cannot pass through a membrane. Most importantly for gunners, whether with artillery, with rifles, or rapid-firers such as Maxims, the explosions which follow from their shell or cartridge detonations create hardly any smoke, or even none that is visible. There were two important merits in this advance. The enemy could not see where shells or bullets were coming from, and those despatching them could still observe the targets which they wished to hit.

Who was actually first to create a smokeless powder, as with so many initiations, is a matter for dispute. Captain E. Schultze of the Prussian artillery is said to have done the trick in 1864. So, more famously, did the French chemist Paul Vieille who produced the so-called B powders twenty years later. Contrarily, many Germans favour Max von Duttenhofer, who allegedly beat Vieille by one year. The problem with all such 'smokeless' powders was twofold: how to retain the explosive energy and yet make the explosive reaction less speedy. If it was achieved too slowly, the bullet or shell would do no more than drop out of the barrel's end. If too quickly, it would probably leave behind an incomplete transformation — and therefore smoke. When assessing the priority of invention, there is also the tricky matter of smokelessness itself. Just how little smoke must be produced to count as smokelessness?

By the end of the 1880s, when Maxim was working (so briefly) on the problem, Alfred Bernhard Nobel was also entering the fray. The Swedish chemist, famous and wealthy for creating dynamite in 1866 (this being a manageable form of nitroglycerine), produced in 1888 a superior form of smokeless powder which he called ballistite. It was also based on nitroglycerine. So was cordite, a much-used mixture created in 1889 by Frederick Abel, the 'ordnance chemist' who had been attached to Britain's War Department since 1858. Intriguingly, in this late nineteenth-century proliferation of novel powders, there is an unexpected link. Before settling down in Sweden, his native land, Alfred Nobel had worked with John Ericsson in the U.S.A. This other inventor, also Swedish-born, had been the individual who had pipped Richard Gatling to the post with his invention of a screw propeller. Gatling's gun would, towards the end of its reign, use smokeless powders based on Swedish ingenuity, and the curious connection is then complete.

Whatever each explosive's actual chemical composition, and whatever the physical status of its chemicals, the military's wish for smokelessness had been granted by the start of the 1890s. By that all-important decade the mixture called gunpowder had been violently exploded in warfare for some five and a half centuries, in fact ever since stampede cannon had been used at Crécy in 1346. Only after all that span of years did smoke cease to be a certain consequence of every detonation. Guns therefore suddenly became yet more significant, and much more deadly, since the individuals who were being attacked were no longer able to pinpoint their attackers. This was not important in engagements such as Omdurman, where the precise gun positions of their opponents were irrelevant to the charging Dervishes, but in most later battles the matter of concealment became extremely pertinent. How could an enemy be fought when, despite his firing and all his bullets, he was invisible?

Hiram Maxim's interest in the Maxim weapon did not diminish because he had been temporarily side-tracked into worrying about explosive powders and their smokelessness. Manufacture of his guns certainly did not stop. Nevertheless Maxim preferred to invent rather than to manufacture. In time he chose to hand over the creation of his weapons to the Vickers Company. He might have chosen Armstrongs, Britain's major armaments manufacturer, but that company was then busy with Gatling guns and was therefore not an option. Following the amalgamation with Vickers, although Maxim was one of that company's directors, the organisation itself became increasingly influential over the Maxim gun's development. Its original inventor was not so much being disregarded as losing interest.

By the time of World War One, the old weapon became known as the Vickers rather than the Maxim. The Maxim gun, whatever its actual name, had gained substantial ground over its rivals as the nineteenth century had yielded to the twentieth. The Gatling gun had been incorporated within the British army in 1875, the Nordenfelt in 1878 and the Gardner in 1882. For Maxim guns, the crucial decision was made in 1887, and they began their work officially in 1890, with the first training manual specifically for Maxims being published in 1893. Despite this greater favour for Maxim's gun, the numbers required for the British armed services stayed modest for many years. Every cavalry regiment, for example, was provided with one Maxim on a wheeled carriage. A second gun was 'put in store' but 'could be used' for training purposes. In other words, the gun's existence was not welcomed with anything approaching open arms.

During the years of his energetic salesmanship, notably around Europe, Hiram Maxim had been particularly plagued by an individual named Basil Zaharoff. Often described as 'Eastern European', this man was actually born as Basileios Zacharias of Greek parents within Turkish Anatolia and educated in Istanbul and England. Earlier, and even afterwards, he was widely engaged as 'a vagrant in the purlieus of Constantinople', according to one biographer, and a man whose 'early days passed through various vicissitudes in the less reputable walks of commerce'. As it was, his name was put forward as a possible agent for Thorsten Nordenfelt's company. For Zaharoff, this was a breakthrough, even though the descriptive labelling applied to him had by now become even sharper — a 'shadowy figure', the 'mystery man of Europe', and 'unscrupulous'. Zaharoff certainly did everything he could to promote Nordenfelt weapons over those of rival companies, and he was undoubtedly a prime salesman of arms.

Apparently, after realising that Maxims were superior, Zaharoff advised Austria's Emperor Franz Josef not to attend the Maxim trials, with 'the weather too hot, and the results (unlikely to be) rewarding'. When Maxim duly scored his triumph, one that was witnessed by the Emperor, the wily Basil switched his tack and claimed that Nordenfelt guns had, in truth, been the weapons which were employed. He also, it is said, bribed Maxim's workers in London to despatch deficient guns: some Austrian officers — and money — were said to be involved in this duplicity. Nowhere is this salesman, who was undoubtedly trickier than most, given any credit in Maxim's autobiography, save implicitly when the Maxim company welcomed its amalgamation with Nordenfelt in 1887. There must have been a grudging respect for the mystery man's devious techniques. The Maxim-Nordenfelt Gun and Ammunition Company was formally established in 1888 and Zaharoff formed an obligatory part of the incorporated package. His reputation therefore became attached to the Maxim business, but before long Zaharoff's energetic salesmanship paid off. Later still, he became a French citizen and, much later, was even knighted by the British 'for services to the armaments business' during World War One. Along the way he had acquired great wealth and even became a considerable philanthropist. By the time he died in 1936, he was being called 'legendary' and a 'grand old man' of the armaments industry. Gone were all the less congenial epithets which had previously come his way in such abundance.

Nordenfelt's association with Maxim had been engineered by Zaharoff, presumably because the fact could no longer be denied that Maxim weaponry was superior. The deal had been welcomed by Maxim, partly for the manufacturing facilities the company possessed in Britain and also, one assumes, because it meant that he would no longer have to contend with Zaharoff. In any case, it did not last. The united company did produce some new weapons, such as the 37-mm pom-pom, but was abandoned when Maxim preferred an alliance with Vickers. This liaison was to be far more fruitful, and very much longer-lasting. In 1904 a gun was even labelled the Vickers Maxim, and thereafter the new name steadily overtook the old. The Vickers .303-inch Mark 1 machine gun was officially accepted into service in November 1912. Its changes from the Mark IV Maxim were sufficiently different, notably in connection with its mounting, for the new name to be valid. As a result, British gunners in World War One fought with Vickers machine guns (and Hotchkiss and Lewis guns) rather than Maxims. Nevertheless, in all but name and a few modifications, they were Maxim's weapon. So too were those used by the Germans and the Russians in the conflict.

The Vickers organisation had started life as a steel firm with no interest whatsoever in armaments. A blending of steel manufacture with the creation of guns and ships became almost inevitable during the 1890s, when sea power became so favoured. Dreadnoughts and other warships were constantly needing thicker protection, as well as more powerful guns. These two aspects of the arms race were each complementary. To help with its expansion, Vickers purchased the Naval Construction and Armaments Co. at Barrow. It then acquired the Maxim-Nordenfelt Guns and Ammunition Company, with factories in the south-east of England. The new name of Vickers Sons & Maxim Ltd. was revealing. Hiram Maxim, so much his own man, was prepared to become secondary, but his name (and his fame) were thereby associated with a colossal company, far bigger than his own had ever been. At the same time, Maxim was synonymous with weapons, and therefore everyone now knew that the Vickers Company was in the armaments business.

Maxim's weapons formed only a minute part of the overall Vickers production — of warships, armour plate, etc. Similarly Hiram Maxim was no longer the gun man he once had been. He liked the prestige of being part of Vickers and welcomed his director's salary, but he was more of a sleeping partner. The Vickers organisation enjoyed his name, but did not involve the famous man in its deliberations. In any case, Hiram Maxim was never a team player or a committee man, and in 1911 he officially resigned his directorship from a company thenceforth known as Vickers Limited. The Maxim guns, much amended by their new constructors, became Vickers guns and were to have an extraordinarily lengthy career. Hiram Maxim's willingness to distance himself yet further from machine guns is understandable. He had taken out his first patent on them in 1883 and was abdicating twenty-eight years later. Nothing in his life had kept him so fully occupied, in designing, promoting and litigating. Now, though, he was in his seventies, when many an individual retires from previous employment.

The new Vickers weapons did become much more powerful than the Maxim brands, and had an extraordinarily lengthy career. The inventor himself could never have imagined, even during his final year of life, that his fundamental design would not be withdrawn from service until the 1960s. During that prolonged period the weapon had switched back and forth from being considered an artillery weapon, and then an infantry device, and then back again to the artillery. Crucial to all this was the increase in its range. Even in World War One its effective firing distance tripled from little more than 1,000 yards to 3,000. Yet the problem had been to persuade those in authority that the new gun was not an inefficient form of artillery but a useful addition for the infantry. As that First World War progressed and the gun's range steadily lengthened, the Vickers weapons were increasingly used for 'indirect fire', as it was termed. This caused the enemy's support areas to be harassed, with machine-gun barrages being laid down to supplement artillery. No longer was the gun seen simply as a slaughterer of men. At the war's end, according to the General H.Q. of the British Expeditionary Force:

> The machine gun must be regarded as a distinctive weapon with tactics of its own, which are neither those of the infantry nor the artillery . . . Next to the artillery the machine gun is the most effective weapon in modern war, and against troops in the open at suitable ranges it is proportionately more effective than artillery.

David Lloyd George, even before he became prime minister, was to say — which had to be extreme guesswork with so little known about so many deaths — that machine guns had caused 80 per cent of the casualties. By that time the inventor was no longer interested in his guns, either because Vickers (and other nations) were in charge of them or because his enthusiasm for them had finally expired.

In his autobiography, Hiram Maxim has labelled one photograph 'My favourite occupation'. It shows him at his drawing-board. Indeed that was the activity which pleased him most, and at which he was most adept. This interest persevered even longer than his enthusiasm for guns had done, and led him into innumerable alleyways, such as flight. He claimed, for example, to have been personally responsible, with him at the controls, for 'the first time in the history of the world [when] a flying machine actually lifted itself and a man into the air'. It was hardly airborne travel, as the Wright brothers (or indeed anybody) would merit the term, but Hiram Maxim did, however inadvertently, leave the ground under his own steam, quite literally.

The craft he had developed was awesome in its dimensions, being 105 feet wide and having 4,500 square feet of wing surface. It was propelled by two airscrews, each eighteen feet in diameter and weighing 135 pounds. The screws were in turn powered by two gas-fired steam engines, each weighing 300 pounds and creating 150 horse-power. Astonishingly, these units could reach a steam pressure of 600 pounds per square inch three minutes after being fired. The runway for this device was a nine-foot-wide railway track constructed within Baldwyn's Park, near Bexley Heath on the Kentish border. (Maxim's impressive home at the time lay within five acres of this park, its entrance corridor flanked by two machine guns.) Along the 1,800 feet of railway track there were guard-rails to prevent the machine from 'flying' higher than a couple of feet once its wheels had left the ground. The whole construction looked as solid and airworthy as a house of cards but, much to its creator's delight, it did manage to lift itself after 300 feet of travel and reaching a speed of forty m.p.h. There was a complex system of windlasses, ropes and fans at the track's furthest end, thoughtfully provided should braking be necessary, although in fact the machine never managed to proceed that far. As it was, the first manned flight in aviation history was claimed after the guard-rail snagged the machine's undercarriage, leaving the inventor temporarily 'floating in the air with the feeling of being in a boat'.

Once again, the Prince of Wales attended to witness yet another form of Maxim wizardry. As Maxim's aerial pioneering occurred a little before, as well as a little after, the turn of the century, and as Queen Victoria died in January 1901, the Prince therefore became Edward VII during these endeavours. It was also at this time that the inventor became a British citizen, and very soon afterwards was dubbed a Knight of the British Empire, this honour no doubt facilitated by his long-standing friendship with the new monarch. Not everyone was impressed by Maxim's aerial experiments. On his seventy-first birthday the weekly magazine *John Bull* published a curious piece, which leaves one perplexed about its author's actual thoughts.

*By increasing the horrors of war, maybe,*
*You have carried us nearer to peace*
*So feel no remorse*
*That so fearful a force*
*As your gun has caused thousands'*
*    decease.*
*I don't really see why the world should*
*    complain*
*If they hadn't died thus they'd have died*
*    all the same.*

*Therefore on your birthday be merry and*
    *bright,*
*But please drop the problem of aerial flight.*

Maxim nonetheless foresaw a great future for aviation. Only a few individuals in those early days of the twentieth century believed that aerial adventuring would lead to anything, beyond a death or two from time to time, but Maxim had an exuberant vision about its possibilities:

When the flying machine is perfected the whole world will be changed. In one year . . . there will be no more ironclads, no more guns, no more fortifications, no more armies. There will be no way of guarding against what this machine will do.

Maxim's ultimate creation, which rounded off his life, had even less to do with machine guns than his flying machine. It was a breathing device to soothe his personal bronchitis. By then his hair was snowy white, he had a massive paunch, and his deafness (perhaps caused by all the detonations) had been extreme for many years. His new invention permitted 'the vapours (to be) introduced directly into the throat, instead of medicating the inside of the mouth'. According to its proud developer, 'hundreds of thousands' of this apparatus were then made and sold, with Maxim himself earning nothing save for rebukes from gun enthusiasts. 'You have ruined your reputation absolutely', said one outspoken friend, who deplored that a man 'so eminent in science should descend to prostituting his talents on quack nostrums'.

Sir Hiram Maxim, inventor of the world's first fully automatic rapid-firing weapon, permitted himself towards the end of his autobiography a certain introspection, the first time in his life he had come anywhere near expressing doubt over the nature of his principal creation. Even so, it is difficult to know how that concern is placed. Did he truly have remorse about the machine-gun portion of his life? And did he really worry whether his reputation had been damaged, or enhanced, by relieving a human ailment instead of causing human death?

> It will be seen [he wrote] that it is a very creditable thing to invent a killing machine, and nothing less than a disgrace to invent an apparatus to prevent human suffering.

His own bronchitic troubles ended on 24 November 1916, and he was buried in West Norwood cemetery. Maxim's book finishes with a sentence which reads as if inverted, but the writer is thinking of his inhaler rather than those millions whose own breathing had been stopped so suddenly when a machine gun's bullet came their way.

I suppose I shall have to stand the disgrace which is said to be sufficiently great to wipe out all the credit that I might have had for inventing killing machines.

His use of the words credit and disgrace are mystifying. So too his true thoughts about the most famous portion of his life's work. He had come a long way since inventing a better mousetrap. That creation was never taken up by the world at large, but much of the world had fallen over itself to get hold of the Maxim gun. And much of the world then fell, most dreadfully, when the gun proved so terrifyingly what it could do. As to his reputation, a useful summation was made by a grand-daughter, Mrs Percy Maxim Lee. She never met her grandfather, but wrote:

It seems to be generally accepted that the Maxim gun revolutionised warfare. And yet, it is fair to say that Hiram Stevens Maxim's purpose was not the destruction of mankind; it was rather his irresistible impulse to invent and perfect a mechanical device.

Maxim even took out two fresh patents during the very year he died, the last in August 1916. The grand-daughter was correct. His name may be inextricably linked with machine guns, but invention was his trade. Apart from all those patented devices already mentioned, such as the lamps and electrical fittings, and those considered bizarre, such as his flying machine and bronchial breather, he also put his mind to chandeliers, hair-curling irons, silencers, governors, batteries, a merry-go-round, a water heater, and many chemical procedures. It would seem that he could never see anything without wondering how it might be improved. He was not just curious how that something might be bettered; he then acted upon his curiosity. It so happened that, along the way, he had wondered about machine guns.

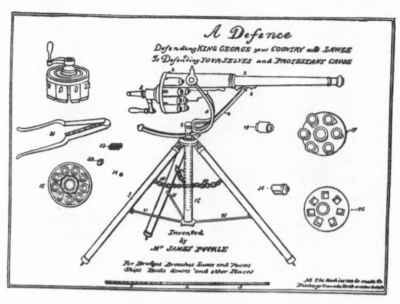

A Defence

Defending KING GEORGE your COUNTRY and LAWES
Is Defending YOUR SELVES and PROTESTANT CAUSE

Invented
by
Mr JAMES PUCKLE

For Bridges Breaches Lines and Passes
Ships Boats Houses and other Places

It looked workmanlike, but it may never have worked. James Puckle's patent of 1718.

As a boy Sam Colt made a model of his 6-shooter idea. As a man he became the world's wealthiest

Dr. Richard Gatling invented his weapon during the American Civil War in order 'to save lives.' He steadily improved this gun, and was photographed in 1893 with the latest version, the Bulldog.

The United States was slow to adopt Gatling's weapon, and was also slow to phase it out. A Gatling Battery at Fort McKean, Dakota Territory, during the 1880s.

Hiram Maxim was the first inventor to create a truly automatic gun.

Rival machinery at the end of the nineteenth century: a twin-barrelled Gardner *(left)*, a .303 Maxim *(centre)*, and a multi-barrelled Nordenfelt *(right)*.

The British encountered many uses for Maxim's gun across the Empire, as in North-West India with the King's Royal Rifle Corps in 1895. *(National Army Museum)*

Both sides possessed machine guns during the Boer War of 1899–1902, but neither found much use for them in a conflict where the rifle was pre-eminent. Boer fighters at Mafeking with a Nordenfelt-Maxim. *(Imperial War Museum)*

A recruiting poster of 1916. The Machine Gun Corps, initiated one year earlier, took time to get going before being accepted as a crucial arm.

Maxim's gun was water-cooled, consuming a pint and a half every 1,000 rounds. *(Imperial War Museum)*

Arrival of the relatively light-weight Lewis gun, with its drum of ammunition, was particularly welcomed by the infantry. *(Imperial War Museum)*

The Lewis weapon was most adaptable, as with this wheel-mounted arrangement for firing at enemy aircraft. *(Imperial War Museum)*

*(Left)* Stripped-down versions of the Lewis gun were the weapon of choice for the Royal Flying Corps. One pilot of 22 Squadron is holding an example. *(Right)* Russia manufactured more Maxim guns than any other nation, and depicted one on this fund-raising poster. *(Imperial War Museum)*

Americans of the 77th Division being instructed about Vickers guns by a British sergeant in May 1918. *(Imperial War Museum)*

An American Hotchkiss seen in action in 1918.
*(Imperial War Museum)*

'The Boy David', official monument to the Machine Gun Corps, was erected in the 1920s, removed shortly afterwards, and then resurrected in the 1960s within the grounds of London's Hyde Park Corner. Underneath is the chilling biblical inscription: 'Saul hath slain his thousands but David his tens of thousands.'

# Chapter 10

# Lessons Learned and Unlearned

The naval engagement at Tsushima is defined by the *Collins Encyclopaedia of Military History* as the 'greatest battle of annihilation since Trafalgar', marking 'a turning point' in world history. Many a current reader might now be at a disadvantage, unaware even of Tsushima's location, let alone the battle's significance. It occurred as the final encounter in the Russo-Japanese war of 1904–5, an important and violent conflict which should have opened the eyes of its numerous observers to the many changes it involved. It taught, for example, that the concept of 'white supremacy' was a shibboleth, with 10,000 Russian sailors dying off Tsushima as against 1,000 Japanese. The continent of Asia promptly realised that Europe need not always be invincible. As for the land battles between Russia and Japan, they amply dem-

275

onstrated the modern machine gun's destructive capabilities.

Prejudice, of course, dies hard. Opinion against rapid-firing weapons had first been formed by the failure of Gatling's weapons to play an important role in the U.S. Civil War. Such views had then been strengthened by the Franco-Prussian conflict of 1870–1, in which the much-lauded mitrailleuses failed to fulfil expectations. Confusion still reigned about the machine gun's actual status. Was it a weaker member of the artillery, nothing like as good as real guns, or an additional and unhelpful burden for the infantry? Colonial disturbances, notably those affecting Britain, had proved the weapon 'useful', but such contests against hordes of nakedness were considered fringe activities, not strictly relevant to true warfare as discussed and detailed by influential strategists, such as Karl von Clausewitz and his military successors. In many areas, an anti-machine-gun conviction was firmly in place when Russia and Japan, each hungry for Manchuria and Korea, chose to go to war — until Japan's victory in the waters by Tsushima Island caused Russia to sue for peace.

At the start of the twentieth century,

over forty years after Richard Gatling had tried to sell his novel weapon, the machine guns on offer were no longer the cumbersome, heavy and unreliable objects they had once been. Maxim's guns had, during the twenty years since their inception, been much improved. They had seen service, particularly violently with Kitchener at Khartoum, and their role as effective slaughterers ought to have been realised in every military academy. Yet Japan had initiated that war of 1904–5 without a single machine gun in its armoury, save for a few with the cavalry, and this despite a massive military commitment.

The war Japan started (without a declaration) was to be no trifling confrontation. Five Japanese armies opposed the Russians in the Manchurian theatre at the beginning of May 1905, these consisting of 276 battalions totalling 387,000 men. At least as many Russians were to be ranged against them. If killing the enemy is a prerequisite of war, it seems astonishing that machine guns were not considered by the Japanese, right from the start, as essential ingredients for their campaign. All manner of articles, lectures and pamphlets had publicly extolled their chilling virtues.

Back in 1885, at the United Service Institution in London, Garnet Wolseley had made some pithy comments. Fresh from the Sudan, and soon to become Commander-in-Chief, he said that

the English army has now most certainly arrived at the conclusion that we must have machine guns, and I am very glad to say the authorities have at last decided upon their being introduced . . . I feel convinced the fire of this small arm, an infantry arm — it is not an artillery arm . . . will be most effective.

During the following year *The Times* was commending the use of this new weapon in two closely printed columns 'from a correspondent'.

Whatever the defects of the earlier patterns of machine guns, the principle of these weapons was sound, and so powerful a man-killer cannot safely be left out of account.

In 1886 machine guns were still in their relative infancy. The newspaper's correspondent was therefore being perceptive about the principle involved, rather than criticising the actual machines. He had based his arguments upon the weapons then readily available, such as 'the one-barrel gun which, with ammunition, weighed 200 pounds; the three-barrel gun of 210 pounds; and the five-barrel gun which, with 400 rounds, weighed 465 pounds'. These three kinds, stated the journalist, could be carried by 'one mule, two mules and three mules' respectively. Even so, and despite their weight and certain awkward extras such as forage for the animals, *The Times* correspondent (soon after interviewing Wolseley, and no doubt greatly influenced by him) was in favour of them.

It is now recognised that the machine gun is no rival of field guns. There is, in fact, no comparison between the two, the machine gun being only a contrivance for procuring accelerated, multiplied and concentrated infantry fire . . . By employing machine guns you can dispense with a certain number of infantry, and thus diminish the transport of food. You also diminish the number of men exposed to the enemy's fire, and thus lessen the number of casualties. As to the tactical uses and advantages, they are so obvious . . . that nothing further need be said on the subject.

The middle part is pure Richard Gatling, his original and philanthropic motive being that fewer men would need to be sent to war if machine guns were employed. The article is also sound foresight, outlining uses and advantages of the gun that were not to be understood by many tacticians for another thirty years. As Wolseley himself had said, on another occasion than the United Service meeting:

The machine gun will take the place of considerable bodies of men . . . I believe there is a very great future for [it], and that that general or that nation which knows how to develop or make use of it will in the future have very great opportunity — an opportunity that has never been made use of by any one before.

Wolseley too felt that nothing further need be said on the subject, the advantages being so obvious, but almost two decades later the Japanese went to war against the Russians and sent company after company of their infantry over open ground towards well-prepared Russian positions and Maxim machine guns. Japan may not have learned from other fights elsewhere which had involved machine guns, but direct experience is always influential. When Japan did encounter Maxims on the field of battle, its military authorities quickly remedied the situation and, instead of Maxims, acquired many of the lighter Hotchkiss weapons. They had appreciated not only that all such rapid-firing guns were deadly but also that they needed to be up there with the infantry to serve most usefully.

It might be argued that events on the far side of Asia could not interest Western Europeans, but there were many foreign witnesses, notably from Britain. They described the battles from suitably safe vantage points, and then published their accounts. (The London Library possesses several shelves of volumes dedicated solely to that distant war.) It was indeed no trifling engagement, however far away. Almost a million men were to be involved, and many tens of thousands were to die. As a dress rehearsal for the European war of ten years later, it could not have been better timed, save that the lessons it should have taught were not absorbed. The observers' accounts make vivid reading, with soldiers' lives seemingly of little account to those in charge (a state of affairs that would be mirrored so precisely in northern France).

At the battle of Mukden, fought from 19 February 1905, the men from Europe saw that certain Russian fortifications had to be attacked.

> The intrenchments [were] as impregnable as the art and science of military engineering would allow . . . [with] barbed-wire entanglements, the endless rows of spiked pitfalls, and the many open patches [creating] the suspicion of contact mine and other diabolical contrivance. But, grisly as they were, these works had to be carried; and it is curious that a nation so young in the arts of modern warfare should have been able to produce an infantry so dogged, so steadfast, and so persevering, that it was able, by sheer recuperative insistence, to carry obstacles such as infantry had never before been called upon to face.

An observer with the Russian forces, serving as a special correspondent for the *Kölnische Zeitung*, is equally blunt about the tremendous loss of life. Near Lin-chin-pu on 28 January 1905 he saw a Russian stronghold being attacked by 200 Japanese who were only armed with rifles. The Russians, with two machine guns, did not open fire until their enemy were within 300 yards. They then fired 1,000 cartridges in a couple of minutes and the Japanese were no more. That German observer, together with some fellow countrymen, took the news back home of the machine gun's capability. They had been far more impressed with the weapon than either France or Britain. George M. Chinn, former lieutenant-colonel in the U.S. Army, wrote in his monumental book on this weapon:

True to the German military tradition, they sought to build tomorrow's weapons today. In contrast, it has always been our custom to build yesterday's weapons soon.

As it was, all the observers expressed great admiration for the men going to their doom, and scarcely any concern for the travesty causing them to face such odds.

In Manchuria and Korea the Japanese, whose fighting was frequently called 'Homeric', took 'their cover with them'. Each man carried a sandbag and then 'grovelled' behind 'such scant shelter' when need be. Meanwhile 'they were swept by a hail of shrapnel which seemed ceaseless'. A subsequent and macabre advantage of this barrage was the great number of corpses it made available behind which men could shelter. The dead bodies formed 'stepping stones' in the attack and served the next battalions, with Japan's infantry 'leaping forward in waves', before lying down in similar waves, hiding where it could, and drawing steadfastly nearer to an all-important objective. In the end, at Mukden the soldiers' obstinacy, courage, madness and sacrifice paid off, with some 200,000 Russians being eventually routed from their well-entrenched positions. On the battlefield lay a similar number of dead from both sides, the Japanese and Russians having contributed equally to the grisly total. If ever there was a battle where machine guns in very large numbers could have prevented the Japanese assault, and then given overwhelming victory to the Russian defenders, it was Mukden, but rifles, artillery, and bayonets had in the main to take their place.

Afterwards Aleksei Kuropatkin, the Russian general in charge, wrote his own account of that 'Campaign in the Far East'. He thought highly of machine guns, and of the few which he possessed, but less enthusiastically of his nation's ability to supply its army. In 1904, according to his official memorandum, he had requested 246 'pack machine guns' but 'only sixteen' were completed. 'Machine guns on wheels' did slightly better, with fifty-six completed out of the 411 orders made. The reasons for these deficiencies were all too blatant, and involved both the brand new Siberian railway and countless strikes at home. That 4,607-mile rail link from west to east, begun in 1891, had only been completed in July 1904, finally linking all the 1,000 stations on its route.

This period of Russia's history was one of turmoil, with 500 workers being shot dead by troops in January 1905, and the battleship *Potemkin*'s mutineers killing their officers later on that same year. It is therefore easy to understand why the eastern campaign did not receive the attention or support it needed, quite apart from the sorry state of the soldiers sent to fight. Russian armies were to be defeated at Telissu in June 1904, at Liao-Yang in August, at Port Arthur in January 1905, at Mukden in March, and then, no less devastatingly, Russian naval forces in the naval engagement at Tsushima. In May 1905, after they had sailed half way round the world to get there, thirty-five of the thirty-eight vessels of the Baltic Fleet were sunk, disabled, or captured. European observers of these terrible failures seem to have been most struck by the élan, the dash, and the determination of the Japanese fighting man. Nowhere is there criticism of frontal assaults against well-entrenched positions, or of the certain loss of life. Instead there is only admiration for the zeal involved.

The first line leaps from the trenches . . . the dots dash forward . . . A man falls, gets up, staggers a pace or two, and then falls again . . . When the first line was half-way to the obstacles, a second line leapt from the trenches . . . and then a third . . . volunteers rush out by twos and threes to cut the wire of the entanglements . . . Seldom did these heroes get back unscathed . . . Now the fire on either side is getting hotter and hotter, and men on both sides are falling fast . . . Whole parties are wiped out, they are replaced by others; the flood abates momentarily, but always advances.

This particular spectator was clearly consumed by excitement, and he does not bemoan the slaughter, or argue that there had to be a better way. Instead, following his description of line upon line of soldiers leaping from their trenches, and of men on both sides falling fast, the British observer writes:

The form of attack thus graphically described resembles that now in force in our own Army most closely. Our Army is recently experienced in war against a people armed with modern weapons of precision, and has very little to learn in actual minor tactics from this war. Probably, as far as technical training of the lower ranks goes, no army in the world is superior of our own.

The recent experience had been the Boer War of 1899–1902. It ought not to have cost so many lives. It ought not to have been so expensive, or so time-consuming, or even to have been fought in the first place, and it was hardly a victory. Its outstanding difficulties — a highly mobile and motivated enemy, one well equipped with accurate rifles and skilled at using cover — were not especially relevant to the problems of any European war. The Russo-Japanese experience ought to have been a terrible warning — for everyone — of future possibilities. Instead, there was 'little to learn'. The observed tactics 'resembled' those already planned, and no army in the world was 'superior' to the British.

Not everyone in Britain reacted in similar style to the news from Manchuria. Aylmer Haldane, a future general, stated in 1909 that it was 'impossible to take a position which is well defended by machine-guns until these guns have been put out of action'. It would seem that people saw in that distant battle what they wished to see, with one British general considering it demonstrated 'over and over again that the bayonet was in no sense an obsolete weapon'. (Official reports of the Boer War stated that less than 100 of the enemy were killed by British bayonets in four separate charges.) Only Germany, of all the European nations, fully realised how machine guns could dominate the field of battle. Six hundred rounds per minute, the figure which Hiram Maxim had achieved so proudly, had stepped up the killing business with great simplicity. It had caused other orders of magnitude to be introduced. As for the inventor himself, it was all a vindication of his earlier pronouncements. Back in England, he was 'pleased to learn' that more than half of the Japanese who died 'were killed with the little Maxim gun'.

It may seem disruptive to mention the Dardanelles campaign of 1915 when describing the Manchurian battles taking place ten years earlier, but the comparisons are there, even if separated by a decade. Remember those Japanese, so bravely leaping from their trenches, and then encounter John Masefield in his book *Gallipoli.*

The [Allied] invaders may see . . . no sign of the enemy, only the crash of guns and the pipe and croon and spurt of bullets. Gathering themselves together, their brave men dash out to cut the wire, and are killed; others take their place, and are killed; others step out with too great a pride even to stoop, and pull up the supports of the wires and fling them down, and fall dead on top of them, having perhaps cleared a couple of yards. Then a couple of machine guns open on the survivors, and kill them all in thirty seconds, with the concentrated fire of a battalion.

Edmund Blunden uses almost identical words when describing his experience on the Western Front.

I go forward with them . . . up and down across ground like a huge ruined honeycomb, and my wave melts away, and the second wave comes up, and also melts away, and then the third wave merges into the ruins of the first and second, and after a while the fourth blunders into the remnants of the others, and we begin to run forward to catch up with the barrage, gasping and sweating, in bunches, anyhow, every bit of the months of drill and rehearsal forgotten.

Nothing, it would seem, had been learned from Manchuria, or indeed from anywhere else, where men on open ground had proved their courage and their vulnerability when confronted, as *The Times* had phrased it so much earlier, by the 'accelerated, multiplied, and concentrated' fire from infantry equipped with rapid-firing guns. Garnet Wolseley, who would die one year before World War One began, was surely astounded by the British lack of interest in machine guns. He had been advocating their use since 1885, a mere twenty-nine years before the outbreak of hostilities in which these weapons were to play such a devastating role. Instead, had he lived two more years, he would have been able to read fervent admiration from John Masefield rather than heartfelt condemnation of the one-sided carnage. The (later) Poet Laureate had apparently been as stimulated, or even as excited, by machine-gun fire as he was so frequently by storm and gale at sea.

> One speaks of a hail of bullets, but no hail is like fire, no hail is a form of death crying aloud a note of death, no hail screams as it strikes a stone, or stops a strong man in his stride.

There had been other battles before World War One which could, and should, have been educational concerning the effect of rapid fire. Most notable were those of the Spanish-American war in Cuba. Machine guns were involved, teaching different lessons, but teaching them nonetheless for those prepared to learn. Cuba, unlike most of Latin America by then, was still under Spanish rule in 1895, but only just. In that year Spain sent 150,000 troops to quell the insurrection, and did so both violently and ruthlessly, using concentration camps to corral civilians. Americans became increasingly sympathetic to the cause of 'Cuba Libre', and were then further stirred when the battleship U.S.S. *Maine* blew up and promptly sank in Havana harbour with the loss of 260 sailors. The cause of the explosion was never established, but there was widespread conviction within the U.S. that Spain was somehow guilty. Congress promptly authorised the use of troops to help the 'Cuban patriots'. Accompanying the first wave of 17,000 men were some Gatling guns. The man in charge of them, Lieutenant John Parker, later wrote about his detachment's success in *Tactical Organization and Uses of Machine Guns in the Field.* (One wonders at once how many European strategists read, or even knew of, such pertinent advice concerning modern war. It could be that Americans attacking Spaniards was not considered relevant, particularly when a prominent politician such as Theodore Roosevelt could roughride his way into the fight. What kind of a war was that?)

The guns were pushed right up in the

hottest place there was in the battle-field, at 'the bloody ford' of the San Juan, and put into action at the most critical moment of the battle, after part of the troops had already been forced back by the strong fire of the defenders, and so successfully subdued the Spanish fire that from that time to the capture of this practically impregnable position was only eight and a half minutes.

Roosevelt himself, famously involved in this war with his 'Rough Riders' (and soon to be U.S. President), was thoroughly impressed by the weapon.

If I were to command either a regiment or a brigade, whether of cavalry or infantry, I would try to get a Gatling battery with me . . . I feel sure that the greatest possible assistance would be rendered, under almost all circumstances, by such a Gatling battery, if well handled; for I believe that it could be pushed fairly to the front of the firing-line.

He was also lavish with praise for Lieutenant Parker who, 'by his own exertions, got [his battery] to the front and proved that it could do invaluable work on the field of battle, as much in attack as in defense'. Yet Parker's recommendations for more reliance upon machine guns, despite having Roosevelt's support, were given short shrift by the U.S. government: only Spanish troops had experienced the Gatling fire, and perhaps only the bitterness of personal experience enables lessons to be learned. Parker continued to hammer away about the use of machine guns, but neither of his books on the subject were much appreciated. (He chose to stay in the army, rising to colonel, and receiving the Distinguished Service Cross with three oak leaf clusters for heroism in World War One. He had earned nothing for his advice and leadership back in Cuba.)

The trial of modern weaponry afforded by the Boer War of 1899–1902 was certainly personal, so far as Britons were concerned, and extremely bitter. In some ways it was a precursor to the Great War which followed. In others its battles and lessons were quite irrelevant. It was certainly up to date, with efficient new weapons, and was also a European war, despite being fought in Africa. No charging hordes of nakedness were involved, no fanatical assemblages of spear-laden warriors. Instead, it was like against like, both sides having much to lose, and both disdainful of the local population, of the Africans who lived there.

Its roots of enmity lay in the past, but the abortive 'raid' by Leander Starr Jameson over three years earlier had united and stirred the Afrikaners. That failed attempt to seize Johannesburg, and then to annex the surrounding Transvaal, had served as a wake-up call. The Afrikaners had promptly equipped themselves with suitable armament, ordering 42,000 single-shot rifles from Europe, as well as 37,000 of the more proficient Mausers. Twenty-two major pieces of artillery — 75-mm up to 155-mm — were also ordered, along with twenty Maxim-Nordenfelt one-pound machine guns, later to be known as pom-poms. (This was the 1.457-inch/37-mm large-calibre Maxim, developed in 1898. The shells it fired were the lightest weight for explosive projectiles permitted by the Geneva Convention. Those intrigued by warfare's rules may be further amazed by this particular piece of legislation.) Furthermore, the Afrikaners were able to put 40,000 well-armed men into the field when the war began, a force four times greater than the British contingents then in southern Africa.

Although the British were now less conspicuous in khaki, having finally abandoned their bright red uniforms, they were taken aback by the enemy's ability to do rather better, to 'use ground', to hide behind rocks, to fire invisibly, and then to gallop elsewhere as soon as need be. On occasion there were large-scale battles when the British were fired at by several thousand Mausers. As one witness wrote, this was like 'the perpetual frying of fat, like the ripping of air, like the tearing of some part of nature'. As for the machine guns, according to Thomas Pakenham in *The Boer War*: 'Pom-pom-pom-pom went the Boers' spiteful little one-pounder Maxim, squirting across the sand like a fire-hose'. The weapon did little serious damage but, according to one gun historian, 'the succession of sharp explosions of ten shells bursting one after another on nearly the same spot got on men's nerves even more seriously than rifle or artillery fire'. Hiding from gunfire, of whatever kind, became a major activity for everyone when the enemy came near. 'Now the cry is to get in some sort of cover, but there is not much of that,' wrote one Englishman in his diary; 'The Maxims kept us here [so] that we cannot move . . . the fire is incessant . . . For two hours I lie on my stomach making myself as small as possible.'

Maxim himself wrote of his gun's service in that war.

It often happened that one pom-pom, manned by four Boers secreted behind stones, and under brush, would put a whole battery of British artillery out of action in a very short time.

The Boers did not fire long bursts which might, either by sound or sight, have given away their position. The pom-poms could therefore damage the British artillery before that artillery could damage them, but such incidents were rare. The fight against the Afrikaners was not really a machine-gun war. There were not the massive charges which the Zulus and others had made over similar ground a few years earlier. There were offensives from both sides, but these were more piecemeal, with only a few hundreds involved. Riflemen were then in their element, aiming accurately from concealment and picking off targeted men as and when these showed themselves. Spion Kop, one of the fiercest engagements, is also one of the best remembered. By the standards of World War One, its casualties were minimal. The British lost 243 dead, with 1,000 wounded, and the Boers suffered 1,500 killed, wounded, and captured, but the defeat — for both sides — seared itself into military minds. Within an acre of trampled grass, as Thomas Pakenham has phrased it, the fight was 'the precursor, . . . this Armageddon in the trenches under the African sun, of a greater one, fifteen years later, in the mud of Flanders'. The 'central paradox of the new smokeless warfare,' added Pakenham, meant 'that ignorance hung over the battlefield, ignorance deeper than any battle smoke.'

The British achieved the summit of this kopje, a significant hilltop near beleaguered Ladysmith, but were not ready for the aftermath. Crouching within inadequate trenches, they were subjected to Boer shells, these arriving at a rate of seven a minute, as well as machine-gun and rifle fire. The spade had become an important weapon of war, a fact the British had not yet understood. 'Dig your own trench now,' as one man wrote, 'or they'll dig you a grave later.' Most of the British dead were indeed buried, following the battle, within that inadequate shelter which had been the death of so many of them. This lesson had been cruelly learned. Take a spade, dig deep, escape the enemy's fire, be reasonably safe from its artillery, and absolutely safe from its bullets, however numerous these were.

The Boer War was won, in the end, not by conventional battles, with consignments of men firing at each other. Instead the Afrikaner opponents were prevented from carrying on as they had begun, skilfully using their mobility, striking at will, vanishing no less speedily, and then refreshing themselves with supplies from their compatriots' isolated homesteads. To counter these tactics, the British built blockhouses and erected barbed wire to serve as barriers. They herded the Boer families from their homes into concentration camps. They hindered and generally demoralised their enemy. Britain's imperial and colonial force grew larger, with almost 450,000 men becoming engaged, while the Afrikaner total of less than 90,000 gradually grew smaller. It proved to be the most costly British war, in lives and expenditure, since Waterloo, with 5,774 British killed and almost three times that number perishing from disease or wounds. For the Boers there were 7,000 deaths among the fighting men out of the 90,000 who took part. As for the concentration camps, they caused a further '18,000 to 28,000 deaths', the vagueness of this official estimate an additional indictment of that aspect of the war.

As machine guns played a lesser role to rifles in the Boer War, their status remained vague. Their relative failure in South Africa was put down to low training standards, to want of knowledge of tactical handling, and to poor targets. For this combination of reasons the weapons therefore fell further into disrepute. It was not appreciated how, in terms of fire-power during a more conventional war, they had tilted the odds greatly in favour of defence. The glory of war, still actively promoted, lay in attack, in dash and enterprise. It was hard to win a medal and promote heroism when sitting behind a machine gun casually spewing forth its unpleasant brand of death.

Those individuals who were unfavourably disposed towards these rapid-firing guns had their opinions boosted by Africa's brand of a European war. The spade was what mattered, and artillery, and accurate rifle fire (from .303 Short Magazine Lee-Enfields): thousands of men each despatching at least fifteen accurate rounds a minute was preferable to a more mechanical delivery. The machine-gun promoters, unable to convince others of this weapon's virtues, had to accept that speedy riflemen were the next best alternative. They spoke of human machine guns, and of a rate of fire superior to that of every other army. Soldiers who could not perform well in the 'mad minute' against targets 300 yards distant were likely to be discharged. Those who could be accurate with twenty or more shots in those same sixty seconds were specially commended. This ability of the regular army held up the Germans near Mons in 1914 more than any single other factor, and helped prevent that invasive rush from reaching Paris during the war's earliest days. The rifles in such skilled hands had done well, but machine guns would have done so much better when the famous grey wave of Germany infantry assaulted Belgium.

John French and Douglas Haig, who were each to lead the British Expeditionary Force, had both served in southern Africa. They had learned much during that war, about the need for better organisation, more artillery and bigger shells, but neither man had appreciated the merits of defence. If attrition was involved, and the need to halt enemies in their tracks, it was better to sit tight within a trench, permitting rifles and machine guns to do their job when the need arose. Unfortunately, attack gave the opportunity for dash and enterprise, and could therefore lead to promotion, award, fame and honour. Defence usually gave nothing of the sort, even if it was less costly in terms of casualties.

As for Kitchener, the First World War's great recruiting agent, he had only become Earl Kitchener of Khartoum because of his resounding victory at Omdurman. That triumph had been largely due, if not almost wholly, to machine-gun fire. Although the Somme offensive would start a few days after his death, he, as Secretary for War, had surely known about it and its planned procedure for attack. Could he not remember how the Dervishes had fallen eighteen years earlier? Were men in khaki on no man's land any different from those white-robed tribesmen rushing at the guns? Similarly, Ian Hamilton, in charge of the disastrous Gallipoli expedition, had seen service in Afghanistan and with Kitchener during the Boer War. Did these two men never discuss modern rifle fire, and how its virulence could be assisted by machine guns? Had French, Haig,

Kitchener, and Hamilton read any of those volumes about the Russo-Japanese war, in which mechanical rapid fire had proved so terribly destructive?

Europe's Armageddon still lay ahead, with attack after attack by infantry gaining yard after yard of ground, and leaving in their wake a corpse or two, or more, for every inch of mud thus gained. The machine gun, waiting patiently, would have its field day. It had already slaughtered naked savages. It had done well, but only modestly, against Spaniards in Cuba. It had killed a few of those who had died upon the veldt of southern Africa. Later it had flexed its muscles much more determinedly, first against the Japanese and then against the Russians, in a very distant but very awful war. Its triumphant staccato stammering would soon resound as never before, while killing and killing millions as awesome proof of its dreadful capability.

# Chapter 11

# The Bonds
# of Attachment

For the military man, despite his business being conquest and death, there can — or could — be occasions of supreme magnificence: the famously serried ranks, the cavalry charge, and the cry of victory. There was, of course, a price to be paid, of injury, mayhem and slaughter, but this could paradoxically highlight the wonder. In time, the disagreeable memories might outweigh the excellence, the savagery having been so great, the loss of friendship so overwhelming, the vanishing of youth so unforgettable, but glory had lasted for a while. The Duke of Wellington preferred to win, of course, but did concede (rather more than once) that 'Next to a battle lost, the greatest misery is a battle gained'. Nevertheless the military life has consistently appealed at various levels in society. Its likely danger has formed one attraction. So too, when these were dashing and outstanding, have its uniforms. The various regiments created a singular fervour that, for outsiders, can make little sense. Fathers were overjoyed when sons took up the cause, the same old cause they had themselves revered. Sentiments of pageantry and splendour, of honour and duty, could bind men and generations together with hoops of steel. Such professionals fought, partly for sovereign and country, but mainly for their corps, their particular detachment, their close-knit brotherhood. Each man and every unit had a reputation to maintain, a particular lustre which needed polishing whenever there was the opportunity. The backdrop was always of war and death, but at its front were honour and self-sacrifice, glory and fulfilment, each earning further laurel wreaths to go with all the rest.

William Cobbett, famous for his *Rural Rides* (published in 1830), had his political radicalism honed in the army. After promotion to sergeant-major, and encountering the 'epaulet gentry', he discovered their 'profound and surprising ignorance . . . in a twinkling'. He considered the officers to be, 'in everything except authority, [his] inferiors'. Later he was even imprisoned for campaigning against flogging, but he was devoted to the comradeship he had encountered, and to the organisation he had supported for seven years.

To the army, to every soldier in it, I have a bond of attachment quite independent of any political reasonings . . . 'Once a soldier, always a soldier' is a maxim, the truth of which I need not insist on to anyone who has ever served in the army for any length of time.

This bond certainly existed among the brand-new soldiers of the First World War. Despite the killing, or perhaps in part because of it, the fetters could become extremely strong. 'We were banded together,' wrote Charles Carrington, an infantry officer, 'by a unity of experience that had shaken off every kind of illusion, and which was utterly unpretentious.' 'To be perfectly fit, to live among pleasant companions, to have responsibility and a clearly defined job — these are great compensations when one is very young,' wrote another such officer, Graham Greenwell, (and quoted by Richard Holmes in *The Western Front*). 'I look upon the years 1914–1918 as among the happiest I have ever spent,' added Greenwell, no doubt mystifying many of those unacquainted with such camaraderie. 'They never can sever the bonds that unite us now,' as certain schoolboys can sing with similar feeling.

This attitude of loyalty and tradition must be appreciated if there is to be any comprehension why the machine gun's arrival was not immediately, and gratefully, welcomed by the military. The new weapon was so unfortunate, merely killing for the sake of killing. Where was the lustre in merely mowing down an enemy? This was no more glorious than scything through a field of corn or knocking down skittles. Where was the excitement and the honour one might gain in a fight which was man to man? The new device might be welcomed by a dastardly enemy, but it deserved no space where honour made the rules. It could kill, but was not a proper instrument of war, being unworthy and unacceptable. 'Put that thing to one side,' said officers during pre-1914 manoeuvres; 'Lose it somewhere; do anything with it save involve it in the action.' The thing was as wrongful in its status as turning up at Agincourt with rifles or grenades. It might win the day, but without a trace of glory.

A similar attitude was displayed towards submarines when they made their first appearance and subsequent disappearance beneath the waves. Such despicable and shameful practice should be banned, said numerous naval authorities. The underhand creations should be outlawed: they violated all notions of a proper fight. Their only and most wretched purpose was to hit below the belt, quite literally, and they should be disallowed. They were even worse than machine guns, for they hit and then they hid as cowards do. In time, of course, they found their way into the navies of the world, and were unpleasantly effective, but their arrival had certainly not been greeted with acclaim.

The machine gun did have one acceptable virtue; it was most handy against kaffirs and their kind. The rabbles had already broken convention, by ludicrous displays of insane courage, by deploying in massive numbers against small contingents, and by yelling uncontrollably when leaping to their deaths. They did not wait for the whites of anyone's eyes, nor hold their fire, nor play the game as it should be played. Their rules were alien — if they had anything of the kind. Only certain groups of Earth's inhabitants knew what should be done and, equally, what should never be allowed. In southern Africa, Boer residents and colonial Britons had disagreed violently, both before and during the two South African wars, but these two sets of people were united concerning the use of blacks. These other kinds of African might serve as carriers, as beasts of burden, or as cooks and labourers, but should be distanced from the war itself. They could not form part of a proper conflict between Europeans. Already, as Zulus, Swazis, and Matabele had demonstrated, they had proved themselves incapable of fighting a proper war. They should therefore be relegated to less worthy roles.

Nevertheless the dilemma continued in military minds concerning chivalry. On one hand were valiant concepts — grandeur, nobility, fame, honour, status, élite, élan, and glory. These permitted palms to be gained and spurs to be won, *sans peur et sans reproche*. On the other hand, as absolute certainties, there was injury, pain, blood, sepsis, tetanus, amputation, misery, dismemberment, and death. No kind of renown could ever be accrued without the ravaging, but killing was only a consequence and not the purpose of a fight. That fact was crucial, just as it was with sport. Defeat the enemy, but keep within the rules. Knock out an opponent in the ring, but do not murder him. Have eleven men on either side, and never any more. Play up, play up, and play the game as it should be played. Of course machine guns had to be resented and despised. They had adjusted the equation in favour of death. They only served to kill.

Officers were traditionally given swords when receiving their commissions. In war these individuals, advancing with their men, could hold these weapons or carry only swagger sticks, the other emblems of their rank. 'Swagger: Walk like a superior among inferiors, show self-confidence or self-satisfaction by gait . . . Behave in domineering or defiant way,' as *The Oxford English Dictionary* so precisely sums up this attitude. The canes were also used for walking out, and considered no less suitable in action, where bravado, self-confidence, and superiority had to be displayed. Officers might carry revolvers, but such weapons were of no more use than canes until almost face to face with an enemy, and hand to hand, and looking him in the eye. They were certainly somewhat futile when 600 rounds per minute were arriving from each of the enemy's guns. The old rules of engagement were shifting, with glory no longer where it once had been. The majesty of war was vanishing within the mud, among the wire, and in the sheer quantity of death. To suffer 50,000 casualties on a single day, as on 1 July 1916, was a fact which should have been sufficient to entomb the past for good. No longer could anyone be unaware that former times had ended, along with all those men.

Ferdinand Foch, the French marshal and wiser than most, stated after the First World War that the Versailles peace treaty was no more than an interregnum. It seemed he had learned a thing or two because he had famously reported five years earlier: 'My centre is giving way, my right is retreating, situation excellent, I am attacking.' The remark was commended widely, even by the enemy. Douglas Haig, the British Commander-in-Chief, apparently emerged from the war rather less perceptive. Aeroplanes and tanks, he proclaimed, 'were only accessories to man and the horse'. In the future 'you will find as much use for the horse as you have ever done in the past'. 'Dead battles, like dead generals, hold the military mind in their dead grip,' wrote Barbara W. Tuchman in her brilliant book *August 1914*. Talleyrand, more a politician than a soldier, had said that war was too important to be left to the military. Others could argue that it was also too important to be left to politicians. World War One had ended with uncertainty everywhere, save in the knowledge that war had changed. The machine gun had had much to do with this alteration. It had killed, and that was that.

Glory of the old kind was difficult to find in the carnage of Flanders. Or beneath an artillery barrage. Or when infused by poison gas. Similarly, there was little opportunity for valour when sitting in a trench. Life below ground level became more a matter of survival, with the enemies being cold and rain, and filth and misery, as much as shells, grenades, and bullets. The machine gun had tipped the balance in favour of defence, yet to remain on the defensive gave scant occasion for heroics: there was little élan in catching lice or hoping for a blighty wound which would ensure repatriation. Keeping one's head down, and shivering on duck-boards in the muck, did not enlarge treasured regimental memories of former bravery. Attack was the only reasonable thing to do if fame and reputation were to be enhanced. Leap from that underground security. Stand up in no man's land. Face the rifles and the guns. Clamber through or over the wire. Encounter the human enemy. Use grenades. And gain a hundred yards or more, even if losing a hundred men, or very many more. Old thoughts of glory were not dying without a fight.

In one sense the generals, and the staff who sent the orders to attack or counter-attack, were wishing to reinstate the individual in a world of increasing industrialisation. The historian A. Vagts has called them romantics in an industrial age. Half a century earlier, G.K. Chesterton had summed up the workers' general situation: 'They go to hell like lambs, they do, because the hooter hoots.' Charlie Chaplin, in *Modern Times*, would lampoon the depersonalisation of people, with their single role to serve as cogs within faceless industry. The army, conversely and even perversely, was therefore doing its best to reverse this situation. Medals were presented for individual acts of valour, for the lone rifleman who silenced a machine-gun nest, for the man who saved a comrade, for anyone who stood out bravely from a general anonymity. Not many names were honoured for killing more of the enemy than anyone else had done. The war was one of attrition, and yet attrition itself was not rewarded. Personal heroism was what mattered, serving as a noble counterweight to the impersonal outrage of artillery and machinery.

Much the same contradictory distinctions would be made in 1940 during the Battle of Britain, when fighter aircraft restored the sense of individual combat. These machines were brutally mechanical, but single pilots were in charge of them. The Royal Air Force fighter pilot Richard Hillary acknowledges this fact acutely in *The Last Enemy*:

> In a fighter plane, I believe, we have found a way to return to war as it ought to be, war which is individual combat between two people, in which one either kills or is killed. It's exciting, it's individual, and it's disinterested. I shan't be sitting behind a long-range gun working out how to kill people sixty miles away. I shan't get maimed: either I shall get killed or I shall get a few pleasant putty medals and enjoy being stared at in a night club.

John Ellis, in *The Social History of the Machine Gun*, makes valid comments about tradition and correct styles of combat when discussing the U.S. Civil War. The United States then possessed such a small standing army that few people had 'any rigid conceptions of what war *ought* to be like'. Everyone, from the generals to the lesser ranks, was therefore ready and willing to adapt on behalf of the war effort. So much was new in that conflict — the steam-driven ironclads, rifles with magazines, land mines, and even a form of submarine, with all of these actively promoted by an open-minded attitude to war. This, Ellis reminds his readers, 'did not exist to anything like the same extent' in Europe. Indeed, it hardly existed at all.

Every European nation possessed a large officer corps, frequently with sons, fathers, and grandfathers adhering to the same principles in identical regiments. This corps was dominated by the aristocracy and gentry. To be an officer was to pursue an honourable career. The role was steeped in history, noble in its endeavour, and just right for a gentleman. Besides, what else was there for such a man to do? His older brother would inherit the property, plus the title (if there was one) and most of the money (if there was any). Another brother might go into the Church, but the army was always there for those in need of it. Industry and commerce were not items on a gentleman's agenda, and this kind of military tradition did not expire with the arrival of the twentieth century. Archibald Wavell, the famous field marshal of World War Two, wrote that in his youth he had felt no inclination to be a soldier. But he did become one, taking the line of least resistance, because all his male relations were already serving.

Until 1871, commissions in the British Army could be purchased. With money having such power over mere talent and ability, it becomes easier to understand why *Punch*, at the time of Crimea, chose to describe the British contingents as an army of lions led by donkeys. William Russell, the journalist who criticised virtually every aspect of that campaign, was not averse to pouring scorn on officers. Their brains, in his opinion, did not match their breeding. One Coldstream captain, seeing a bunch of men ahead, went to speak with them. 'They're Russians,' cautioned his men. 'Nonsense,' said their lordship captain, who was promptly captured. The government of the day favoured purchased commissions because the procedure was economical. An officer's salary was little more than an honorarium, therefore it was plainly satisfactory to acquire men of independent means. The Duke of Wellington had favoured purchase because it brought into the service 'men of fortune and character, men who have some connection with the interests and fortunes of the country'. Purchase, and then promotion by further purchase, coupled in his instance with ability, certainly benefited that particular man of fortune and character. Wellington became a lieutenant-colonel by the age of twenty-five.

Reading of the British Army's history, as, for example, in *Redcoat* by Richard Holmes, does make one understand why the organisation was slow to embrace new weapons such as the machine gun. Indeed it makes one curious how Britain ever won a war. The army, which fought with such distinction and success so frequently, was riddled with inconsistency, with ineptitude and folly. Generals, for example, received no pay whatsoever unless they had some formal posting, such as governing a fortress. Officers could lose their inherited fortunes by raising regiments. Others could gain fortunes by embedding themselves in fraud. Commissioning from the ranks could occur, with conspicuous bravery being the most fruitful stepping stone, but the practice was not everywhere applauded. Officers could be exceedingly unpleasant to commissioned rankers of 'obscure origin', and those still in the ranks could resent one of their number being upgraded, possibly because he was less likely to be deceived by malingering. And no one could deny that drink was a major problem in the army. Drunkenness could occur even during a battle, or particularly during a battle if wine cellars were encountered. In fact, drunkenness was achieved whenever there was opportunity. In 1912–13, 9,230 were fined for it, some 5 per cent of the regular army; but that was a steep decline from the 13.7 per cent of the army court-martialled for drunkenness in 1868.

In short, Britain's military had its rules, its particular customs, and idiosyncrasies — like any other long-standing organisation. Its inheritance was part of its excellence. The camaraderie it inspired was a prime ingredient. Men did wish to serve, not so much on behalf of their king and country, but for the portion of the army in which they were engaged. Massive loyalty was involved, forged partly by history, partly by the actual situation, and partly by a unique amalgam which is difficult to define.

There is a piece in all of us which favours earlier days, or at least some aspects of those times. Militarily it was wrong to disregard the machine gun as a useful weapon of war, but we can welcome the notion of individuals being superior to machines. The lone hero pitting himself against an evil horde is attractive. The solo warrior, in films, in books, is admirable, and likely to remain so. Each such paragon facing fearful odds may be inwardly concerned about the situation, but should never be subdued by it. He knows he is outnumbered, or short of firepower, or badly wounded, but he can demonstrate superiority by being disdainful of the facts. It is more courageous to attack a machine gun than to use one. The better man may then die, but he has lain down his life for his friends, just as his friends laid down theirs for him. It is all very honourable, and correct, and admirable, but it can be frighteningly wrong-headed.

Why, one wonders, did no one stumbling over no man's land in World War One carry defensive armour, as in former days when shields were always carried? Why not even dustbin lids to deflect the bullets, as so many prayerbooks, pocket diaries and St Christopher medallions seem to have done, most fortuitously, when bullets came their way. The Japanese held sandbags when attacking Russian rapid fire in 1904, and then hid behind them when the fire became severe. What a good idea, save that it countered the regimental spirit, the do-or-die bravado, the proof of excellence. Soldiers walking from the trenches were not silly, or mentally deficient, when so casual about life. Their intelligence was equal to that of other generations, but their time and code were different. It was correct to do what they did. It was good to be scornful, to carry a swagger stick, and to boot a football between the trenches. Such men perished in their tens of thousands as World War One progressed, but honour lived amidst the mud. It was madness to stumble towards machine guns, but the men who did so, and so vulnerably in Flanders, were not mad. They happened to be living at another time — until they died.

Julian Grenfell, soldier and poet, expressed his personal feelings within 'Into Battle', a poem published in *The Times* on 28 May 1915.

*And Life is Colour and Warmth and Light*
*And a striving evermore for these;*
*And he is dead who will not fight;*
*And who dies fighting has increase.*

Aged twenty-seven, he was killed in action shortly afterwards. He had also written with a similar presentiment:

*If this be the last song you shall sing,*
*Sing well, for you may not sing another.*

The trooping of the colour in front of the monarch is a fine ceremony. Men march in astonishing unison. The straight lines they form appear controlled by a lengthy ruler. When these lines are turned, they wheel as if they are spokes, each man knowing precisely what to do, and when and how to do it. The pageantry is splendid, and can stir emotions in almost all of us. Parade ground drill has regularly formed a crucial part of military training. Soldiers must learn to obey without question, and time spent quick marching, turning and halting is no less important than lecture hours on weapons. Men used to enter battle as if still on parade, column by column, and rank by rank, but those times had to change. *'C'est magnifique, mais ce n'est pas la guerre,*' said the French general so pointedly on watching the Light Brigade's suicidal charge at Balaclava. He could have said so even louder had he watched infantrymen rising from the trenches sixty years later, before they walked (or ran or staggered, or slipped and slid) at well-placed guns waiting to open fire.

Colonel Richard Meinertzhagen confided something of the sort to his diary when training in England in 1899 (and was quoted by John Ellis).

> Today we were taught how to assault an enemy position. The battalion moved forward in tight little bunches of about twenty men each, marvellous targets for modern riflemen and machine gunners, but the drill was splendid, shoulder to shoulder and perfect line. We should have been annihilated long before we reached the assaulting line.

Annihilations would be the order of the day a few years later, particularly when attacks were such an obligation and were the proper thing to do. Joseph Joffre, about to become French Chief of Staff, wrote in 1913 that the French Army no longer knows any other law than the offensive . . . All attacks are to be pushed to the extreme with the firm resolution to charge the enemy with the bayonet, in order to destroy him . . . Any other conception ought to be rejected as contrary to the very nature of war.

Even the Germans, much more in favour of machine guns than their opponents, held similar views about offensive operations. Their Infantry Regulations, published in 1899 and little revised until war began, make similar reading to Joffre's belligerent promulgation.

When the decision to assault originates from the commanders in the rear, notice thereof is given by sounding the signal to 'fix bayonets' . . . As soon as the leading line is to form for the assault, all the trumpeters sound the signal 'Forward, double time', all the drummers beat their drums, and all parts of the force throw themselves with the greatest determination upon the enemy.

British standing orders at that time were exceedingly similar. The Field Service Regulations (of 1909) stipulated that:

Decisive success in battle can be gained only by a vigorous offensive. Every commander who offers battle, therefore, must be prepared to assume the offensive sooner or later.

Retreat, of course, is less capable of winning battles but, if attrition is to be involved, victory can be achieved by a steady defence against enemy attacks, and then a final advance.

Hardly anyone in World War One was killed or even wounded by the bayonet, the direct descendant of the lance, but enormous numbers were killed after fixing bayonets and exhibiting the firm resolution which, allegedly, formed the very nature of war. It is easy to be at a loss about that nature, with war being a legalised killing by both sides without obvious principles or definition. Rules do not necessarily have a place in such brutality. Besides, what should be the correct nature of this particular form of murder? Is it somehow better and more correct to be cut up by a sabre than peppered by a gun? And why should certain kinds of bullet be preferred — for example, those which are not purposely deformed to increase the injury they cause?

The cavalry loved its horses and, in consequence, hated the passing of tradition more than most. The 300 Scots Greys at Waterloo — 'Go at them the Greys! Scotland for ever!' — had performed so valiantly, and so gloriously, that their charge was known to everyone. Surely such exemplary excellence could not be discontinued merely because another hundred years had passed and some different weapons had been devised? Let such a brutal change not happen, whatever has occurred. In the 1907 Cavalry Training Manual there is plainly no acceptance that times have altered, or that new forms of warfare have arrived. Indeed the lance was officially reinstated as a cavalry weapon in 1909.

It must be accepted as a principle that the rifle, effective as it is, cannot replace the effect produced by the speed of the horse, the magnetism of the charge, and the terror of cold steel.

Douglas Haig, quoted by B.H. Liddell-Hart in *The Tanks*, was also happy to promote 'the effect produced by sword and lance in modern war'. (Both he and John French were cavalrymen, a point not irrelevant when assessing their policies.) It was not so much the weaponry carried by the cavalry when it struck at the enemy, as Haig reported, but

> the moral factor of an apparently irresistible force, coming on at highest speed in spite of rifle fire, which affects the nerves and aim of the . . . [opposing] rifleman.

Unfortunately, a good machine gunner, provided he keeps his finger on the trigger, can cut down any number of horses and their valiant riders, even if aiming only moderately well. He can find them quite resistible. Besides, if such a force is thundering his way, he has every incentive to keep on launching bullets in its direction. The alternative of doing nothing, and then being trodden underfoot, has infinitely less appeal. As for the cavalry, they stuck to their horses whatever was happening. The trouble with mounted infantry, in a cavalryman's opinion, is that they liked getting off their horses and lying down to shoot when the going got difficult. That completely demolished the irresistible force coming on at the highest speed. Instead, it had come to an ignominious halt.

History ought to teach, and can do so, but its various lessons can be selectively chosen. There was considerable evidence for all to see (and read) that the machine gun's arrival had heralded a new form of warfare. It had suggested that defence was now the better option. However inglorious this policy, and lacking in élan, it had to be the proper way. For those individuals who loathed and resented the machine guns' arrival, there was some contrary evidence about their capabilities. This was very convenient, and spanned much time. Gatling's weapon, for example, could have been used in the U.S. Civil War, but was not actually employed. Therefore the Americans must have found deficiencies, either in the weapon or its use. During the Franco-Prussian war of 1870–1, the French mitrailleuses failed to perform satisfactorily, and were rebuked as weapons even by the French. Guns made by Gatling, Gardner, and Maxim had all worked efficiently against tribal armies, but those various massacres did not constitute a proper test. As for the British war against the Boers, neither side had been vulnerable to the machine gun. The South African landscape, with its rocks and cover, its kopjes and tussocks, had favoured the rifle above all else. When the Russians fought the Japanese in Manchuria between 1904 and

1905, only the Russians had started with machine guns, and yet they lost the war. Therefore, for those who wished to interpret the facts negatively during this half century of warfare, the new rapid-firing weapons had proved themselves inadequate in a great assortment of situations. The disadvantages of machine guns were clearly all too plain to see.

Every technical advance encounters resistance. Sailors loathed the arrival of steam. Every craftsman resented automation, and the cavalryman was unhappy to lose his horse. For well-drilled riflemen, skilled in firing with accuracy and speed, the switch to a machine gun must have been equally disarming. What had been the point of all that training, the gain in expertise, and the pride in being best? Much less expertise was required with a machine gun to fire off many times more bullets, and much less skill to launch more ammunition than a trained platoon of riflemen could ever do. (Once, when sitting with some fighter pilots during the demonstration of a heat-seeking missile, I watched one official light a sheet of newspaper in an open space before he vanished rapidly. An aircraft flying overhead then aimed its missile deliberately off course. The clever device promptly veered towards the burning paper and hit it explosively. 'Kind of takes the fun out of it,' said the pilot next to me. He had a point. What about skilled manoeuvring, and cunning, and years of training, when a missile can counter every move? Where is the fun in that?)

By the autumn of 1916 it was realised, regretfully by die-hards, that machine guns were a necessary instrument of war. Britain's Machine Gun Corps, formed one year earlier, was being generally accepted on the battle-front. But the Somme onslaught had begun, and had then continued, as if the machine-gun lesson had not been learned, and it was taking time for the new ideas to gain a hold. George Bernard Shaw later wrote that 'all great truths begin as blasphemies', and it had been a sin of sorts to accept the inhuman, mechanical style of death meted out by automatic weaponry. It was also, of course, a rather greater sin for nearly three-quarters of a million Allied troops, French and British combined, to become casualties before the Somme campaign finally ground itself to a halt. And when it did so, it was because the weather had become too foul for further fighting. The grand advance achieved for so much sacrifice had been half a dozen miles. This worked out at half an inch of ground gained per casualty, and did nothing to conclude the war (save in teaching what should not be done). Douglas Haig had hoped to reach Bapaume on the very first day. This objective had not been reached even by the last.

The stalemate of the trenches inevitably bred frustration. Put your head too high, and someone shot at it. Do nothing, and the enemy's artillery steadily took its toll. There could also be death even without assistance from the enemy: the miserable conditions fostered disease. Therefore attack, even if machine guns then start stammering, and killing, and cutting swathes, but not of everyone. A lucky few would survive. The Boer War had taught the value of trenches, as at Spion Kop, and of the spade as crucial companion. The Great War was teaching the horrors of the trench, and of life beneath the surface of the land. There had to be some escape from it without the certainty of death. Haig had hoped his cavalry would be first to reach Bapaume, but his horses had failed even more miserably than the men themselves.

Besides, the trench was such a pathetic barrier. The most powerful and industrialised countries in Europe were stuck within an inglorious deadlock that was totally insubstantial. They were not inside a fortress as in medieval times, with walls ten feet thick and often built on rock. They were not even in concrete blockhouses, which Belgium had constructed before the war and the Germans then destroyed within days of their invasion. Along the front line there were concrete emplacements, largely German-made, but for the main part the front line was no more than a straggling zig-zag of open dikes, of pathetic furrows in the land. It was a system of tunnels open to the air, with a maximum depth of five miles from front to rear (notably with the Germans), but it was still something the Romans could have dug, had they so wished, and had they seen the point.

Was this the best that modern nations could contrive? The industrial powers created colossal liners, aircraft, dreadnoughts, multi-storied office blocks, power stations, and many thousands of different objects every day, yet their undoubted energies for war had been channelled into miserable ditches that moles would scorn, there being (in general) no roof to them. More than a million men on either side were inside these troughs at any one time, occasionally making forays at each other, but largely impotent to change the situation. Why could not some pathway be laid down, enabling men to stream across it? Why could not some invasion elsewhere find itself in open country, in undefended open country which made real war feasible? Might parachutes get men behind the lines? Was nothing possible to break or circumvent those miserable, sodden, lethal and dishonourable open tunnels in the ground?

Then came the tank. 'Big Willie', weighing twenty-eight tons, started its trials in January 1916. Speed was modest — a slow walking pace — but it could cross trenches eight feet wide. There were high hopes that this ambling device, crunching wire, disregarding enemy positions, casual about machine-gun fire, and spurting bullets of its own, would solve the standstill. It certainly amazed those on either side, although its arrival should not have been quite so unexpected. Tracked vehicles had been moving artillery since 1910, and the man generally credited with putting one and one together — tracked propulsion and armour plating — had been a witness of the Russo-Japanese war. Ernest Swinton had observed the terrible effects of machine-gun fire. Unlike many others, he not only learned a lesson but had then acted on it. He was certainly first to call them tanks — there had to be a name for the huge containers being transported to the front — and he was probably the first to be disappointed when D-Day for these things arrived.

Technical advances often start as blunders. The early machine guns did jam — that word was more intimately linked with them than any other. It was so easy finding fault with those machines; they found their faults themselves. The first steam boilers had a tendency to blow, to explode, and kill their devotees. The Wrights' first flight covered 120 feet, lasted twelve seconds, and their craft was wrecked later in the month. Perfection never occurs at the outset, but its possibility is perceived — by some. Germany took particular note of the tank, and its Panzers were to rip through France in 1940. Germany had also taken earlier note of Maxim's gun, using it to carve up British infantry on the Western Front. Its steadfast stammering would also slaughter much tradition and convention, as well as the longing for a proper kind of war. The machine gun had come into its own when the European lights went out. Its day had dawned most dreadfully.

# Chapter 12

# Dash, Bravado, and Death

Robert Graves, poet and writer of historical novels, went straight from school to the First World War. Having served as a captain in the Royal Welch Fusiliers, he later wrote *Goodbye to All That*, a revealing book at innumerable levels, providing insights into war beyond the official histories. Ration biscuits, he wrote, were often used as fuel for boiling dixies, since kindling was scarce and the food combustible. Machine-gun crews were similarly innovative. They fired off their guns, with 'belt after belt of ammunition', thus bringing their cooling water to the boil for making tea. British and German machine gunners, after removing selected cartridges from the belts, 'exchanged courtesies' by rapping out the rhythm of the familiar prostitutes' song, 'MEET me DOWN in PICC-a-DILLy', to which the Germans would reply 'YES, with-OUT my DRAWERS ON'.

Machine-gun power is mentioned in every account of trench life — our men 'were stopped by machine-gun fire before they had got through our own entanglements' — but Graves held no particular loathing for them. Rain, mud, cold, gas, lice, corpses, shells, official stupidity, and terrible conditions were everyday fare, these more or less to be expected, but he found rifle fire particularly irksome, it being 'more trying' even than artillery fire. Bullets from the enemy's machine guns were much like all explosives, launched with little discrimination,

. . . but a rifle bullet, even when fired blindly, always seemed purposely aimed. And whereas we could usually hear a shell approaching, and take some sort of cover, the rifle bullet gave no warning. So, though we learned not to duck a rifle bullet because, once heard, it must have missed, it gave us a worse feeling of danger.

For the main part, trench life was a matter of surviving rather than directly engaging the enemy. That kind of contact happened in some sectors only on a very few days a year, but was equivalent — in terms of death and injury — to several months in the trenches. The actual length of the trenches was impossible to calculate because they not only zig-zagged — to prevent blast travelling far — but there were all the other communication and support trenches leading to the front. The front line itself varied in length, as it meandered from the Channel towards Switzerland, but its maximum was about 460 miles, whereas all the trenches must have totalled many thousands of miles.

The quality of each trench varied, of course, with the type of terrain through which it had been dug. Up by the Somme river, the land was largely chalk, making trench lines extremely visible from the air and permitting the trenches themselves to be well drained. All easy digging meant the subsequent trenchworks probably had to be effectively shored to prevent collapse. As for the region near Ypres, that had a high water-table, causing digging to be a very muddy business (even before shelling had got to work on the landscape). Duckboards were very necessary, and could be conveniently up-ended to serve as ladders when attacks were being prepared. In all kinds of trench it was important for sand-bags to serve as their parapet, and six million such sacks were sent, on average, to the front line every month. Sometimes the water-table was so high that the standard trench depth proved impossible to create. Parapets or balustrades then had to be built up so that men could stand rather than crawl behind their protection. There was no law concerning the proximity of trenches to each other, those of friend and foe. The environment was influential; so too were local commanders and chance. On occasion it was possible to hear the enemy, and certainly to exchange invective, whether lighthearted or more outspoken. At other times, and in other places, the enemy's front line could be little more than a distant smudge.

Night-time tended to be the busiest portion of each trench day, with patrols regularly despatched to cut wire in preparation for an attack, to discover information about the enemy (perhaps by capturing a soldier), and to reinforce one's own barbed-wire or — a high priority — to rescue men wounded in some earlier foray. Hand-to-hand fighting was most likely when opposing patrols encountered each other, either deliberately or by chance.

Hammering in stakes to hold the wire would probably earn machine-gun fire as immediate retribution, and so-called 'silent picquets' were preferred as they could be screwed inaudibly into soil. Efforts were made to provide everyone with at least one hot meal for each day in the trenches, but the food was mainly tinned and certainly monotonous. The smoke from cooking fires would often alert the enemy and lead to retaliation of some sort. No beer was ever allowed at the front line, but rum was often allocated to boost both courage and morale. Being relieved from front-line duty, and returned to the vicinity of some *estaminet* suitably distant from the danger zone, was obviously to be preferred. Those happily retreating might pass another group travelling forwards as their replacements, and could then sing 'The bells of hell go ting-a-ling-a-ling for you and not for me . . .' if feeling particularly merry and unsympathetic. In the rearward areas the local French were ready to relieve the men of their pay, this being (for a private) seven shillings a week (or £18 today) in local currency.

Post-war memories of those who served with machine guns oscillate between the awfulness of their experience and the levity which helped to make it bearable. Perhaps that is an accurate reflection of front-line life. It is the horror which makes the light-hearted comments so poignant and astonishing.

'We followed as mildly as sheep, but
  without the bleat.'
'That foot you got shot, was that the
  one with the chilblains?'
'We dug as if our lives depended on it
  — which they did.'
'I saw a comfortable shelf in the
  darkness, and rested on it.
  When dawn came it proved to be the
  knee-joint of a German.'

It must have been difficult adhering to the civilities of peacetime life when warfare was proceeding, such as a tricky incident during Christmas 1915.

We [from the M.G. section of the 11th Inneskillings, 36th Ulster Division] were very tired — not too tired to notice seven ducks — we silenced the ducks but much noise came from their owner — 'I'm going to see your general,' he said — We saw he had an empty pipe — gave him some platoon

339

issue tobacco — nobody smoked it as made from rubber cuttings and weeds — duck owner gleefully accepted the gift — smelt like a blacksmith shoeing a horse — so gave him forty four-ounce tins — he said general could go to warmer climes — duck owner returned with ten stone of potatoes, several turnips, crate of honey, barrel of cider — we invited Frenchman and wife to dinner — they accepted but he wouldn't stop smoking that tobacco — presented Madam with few tins of bully beef and Tickler's jam — farmer and wife escorted us 'up there' for four kilometres.

In short, happiness for all concerned, save for seven ducks, with the entente fortified, and Christmas duly celebrated.

Sickness, and a longing for repatriation, also went hand in hand, as with mud and rain, and life and death, during the two weeks in the trenches and the one week behind the lines. A famous medical cure-all was the No. 9 pill. According to one ex-gunner it was good 'for trench feet, acheing tooth, ingrowing toe-nails, lowering the temperature, restoring lost appetite, regulating the pulse, mending the boil, curing scabies'. Medical officers found the pill most satisfactory when confronted at seven a.m. with thirty to forty men each wanting 'a ticket to blighty'. It was 'either a No. 9 or a come back in the morning if you don't feel any better'. The task was easier, said this former gunner, for a camel to get through the eye of a needle than for a bold hero to do so.

Cunning was always feasible. Two men, wrote an M.G. diarist, were once carrying a 'gassed artful dodger' on their stretcher. Shelling then started; so they stopped, put the stretcher down, and ran for cover. When they returned the man had gone. Apparently, as they later learned, he had picked up the stretcher, proved himself to be running — rather than walking — wounded, found a field hospital, lay down on his stretcher once again, and 'was soon on his way to Blighty'. 'It's only fair to say,' wrote the compiler of these notes, 'that the sick hero was not a machine gunner.'

Seemingly everything was described in such memoirs, the 'fickle' rain, the mud that was such an 'old acquaintance' of the military, but curiously, there was never a forthright description of machine-gun fire, whether it was coming or going. What noise did it make when it hit a comrade? Did he always receive several bullets from the fusillade? Did a gunner aim deliberately at certain human concentrations, or tend to spray more casually much like watering the garden when thirst is everywhere? The gun's sound is said to be rat-a-tat, or a drumming, or a clatter, but is never given more precision. There was never — for all the seeking — any clear indication of the different noises from the different guns. The sounds were surely memorable, but apparently impossible to describe.

The whereabouts of enemy machine guns were always well known. Everything about the front line was unpleasant, the shelling, the accommodation, the corpses, the foul conditions, and the omnipresent likelihood of death; but when the time came for some major assault against the enemy, its opposing machine-gun nests were most particularly loathed. The 'trying' snipers were then of lesser consequence, and the lethal chatter from machine guns needed to be tackled first, and then silenced, if any progress was to be achieved. A total of 578 Victoria Crosses was awarded in World War One, with two being a bar to an earlier V.C. About a quarter of that large number were for courage in attacking the rapid-firing weapons. An even greater number of these medals 'For Valour' were for rescuing wounded comrades, this usually involving a cold-blooded kind of bravery. Attacks on machine guns were more impulsive, being mounted with a headlong recklessness.

Lieutenant-Colonel Harry Greenwood's (King's Own Yorkshire Light Infantry) citation is typical of such bravado.

The advance of his battalion was checked, and a German machine-gun post was causing many casualties. Lieutenant-Colonel Greenwood unhesitatingly and single-handed rushed the post and killed the crew, and so like magic cleared away the menace to his troops. After that brilliant achievement he again rushed a machine-gun post . . . and, with the help of two battalion runners, killed the occupants.

Private R. Mactier's story is similar, and displays the same extreme audacity:

[He], single-handed and in daylight, jumped out of a trench, rushed past the block and fearlessly closed with and killed the machine-gun garrison of eight men. This he accomplished with his revolver and bombs, finishing this particular task by throwing the machine gun over the parapet. Mactier now rushed forward about twenty yards and jumped into another strong point which was held by a garrison of half a dozen men. Probably these knew of the fate of their countrymen, at any rate they promptly surrendered. Private Mactier continued through the trench to the next block and disposed of a hostile machine-gun which had been enfilading our flank advancing troops; he then, unfortunately, was killed by another machine-gun at close range.

It is easy, even at a distance, to understand the antagonism towards the enemy machine guns which mowed down one's comrades so relentlessly. Their 600 lethal rounds a minute had to be halted, somehow. The human purveyors of so much death, squatting smugly behind their weapons, became a focus for all the pent-up anger caused by life within a trench.

There was heavy machine-gun fire, but disregarding this [Sergeant A.D. Lowerson] moved about fearlessly, directing his men and encouraging them to still greater effort that at last led them on to the objective. Having reached this Lowerson saw that the left attacking party was held up by an enemy strong post which was manned with a dozen machine guns. Under the heaviest sniping and machine-gun fire he rallied seven men, and with this mere handful as a storming party he rushed the post, having directed his band to attack the flanks, and so effectively bombed and fought that the whole of the twelve guns were captured, with thirty prisoners. The sergeant had been severely wounded in the right thigh, but he refused to leave the front line until the prisoners had been disposed of and the post thoroughly organised and consolidated.

There is a similarity to such citations, with extreme dash, grim resolve, and bravado of the highest order being repeated, again and again. The only difference resided in the final line. Would the soldier in question, displaying so much courage, actually survive or succumb to hopeless odds?

Corporal Gordon [41st Battalion A.I.F.] attacked a German machine gun which was enfilading the company on his right. So swift and skilful was this individual onslaught that the corporal killed the man on the gun and captured the post, which contained an officer and ten men; then he cleared up a trench, seizing two machine guns and taking twenty-nine more prisoners. Amazing as these deeds were, they were not the total of Gordon's achievements, for in clearing up further trenches he took twenty-two prisoners, including an officer, and three machine guns. Practically unaided, he captured, in the course of these operations, two officers and sixty-one other ranks, and throughout he showed a wonderful example of fearless initiative.

In short, Gordon did survive, even if readers of his exploit cannot comprehend how this was possible. Or how many others lived who so vigorously attacked the nests, as these emplacements were always called, of such well-defended rapid-firing guns. Over and over again the loathing engendered by automatic fire is repeated. Even in the *Dictionary of National Biography* it is frequently cited. Frederick Septimus Kelly, Eton, Balliol, distinguished composer, and skilled oarsman served with the poet Rupert Brooke, and survived Gallipoli, only to be killed in France 'when rushing a German machine gun that was holding up the attack'. Among his final compositions was an 'Elegy for String Orchestra' in memory of Brooke, whose burial he had attended.

Detestation of rapid-firing weapons was, of course, equally strong among the enemy. German soldiers were no less resentful of machine guns aimed at them, and regularly requested their artillery to silence all such British weapons. The British soldiery at the front could therefore be dismayed when a machine gun was deployed in their locality, ostensibly to assist their cause. 'Get that bloody thing away from here,' formed the gist of their remarks; 'You'll get us all blown to hell.'

The war was followed by the publication of countless memoirs, but these are all short on detail concerning what it felt like to be either at the receiving end of machine-gun fire or directing it at the enemy. C.E. Crutchley's *Machine Gunner 1914–18* is typical of many, with rapid-firing weapons being just another ingredient of hellishness in general, and with the prevailing sounds of warfare being the scream of the shells, the dull boom of the burst, the chatter of the machine guns, and the spat-spat of heavy rain drops lashing the surface of the quagmire.

Crutchley becomes more eloquent in his recollections, and rather more revealing, about haircutting, shaving, frying bacon, new socks, tins of condensed milk, pork, and beans, Woodbines at a penny for five, brass hats, fatigues, blighty wounds, Jack Johnsons (5.9 shells), 'chatty' (louse-ridden) clothing, 'awful' Tickler's jam, and 'magnificent Machonachie', a tinned brand of meat and veg. 'To get a decent wash' you went to a water-filled shell-hole, and took care 'not to scoop too deep'. One particular trench, 'cut through a cemetery', had 'bits of bodies' all along it. Death is mentioned in his account only too frequently, but neither the procedure of inflicting it nor watching it cut swathes through scores of comrades on either side. Occasionally Crutchley received praise from authority for his 'gallant work', which meant killing the enemy.

No one knows how many of that world war's formidable total of casualties were the direct result of machine-gun fire.

Guesses have been made, such as 80 per cent of those who died on the Somme's first day, but that particular event was exceptional, with so many tens of thousands of individuals exposing themselves so brazenly to enemy fire. Whether, in the normal circumstances of trench existence, men were killed by shrapnel, bomb-blast, rifle bullets, machine-gun fire, grenades, or some other weapon of war, was not of major concern. In any case, so very many thousands were simply posted as missing, with no one knowing how they had met their ends, even at the time. Worse still, in all that monstrous killing, so many other thousands of servicemen became only bits of corpses, so that Kipling's tombstone phrase of 'Known Unto God' became widely used for burials. Suffice to say that rapid-firing guns were extensively used as killing machines, and they did kill with extreme efficiency. David Lloyd, Britain's prime minister for the War's second half, was prone to making extreme statements about the proportions killed by machine-gun fire — he even went as high as 90 per cent in one debate in the House of Commons; the probable figure was somewhat less than his more usual estimate of 80 per cent, but the prime-minister-to-be was making the point that machine guns were highly effective killing machines.

The manner in which machine guns were increasingly welcomed by the army is a form of death statistic in itself. Shortly after the outbreak of World War One, the British possessed between 200 and 300 machine guns, with the expeditionary force to France taking 108 guns to serve its six divisions (totalling 70,000 men). Britain's manufacturing output of these weapons was extremely modest: only 109 of the most modern Maxims, known as the Vickers C, had been delivered before the war broke out. Germany, on the other hand, started the war with some 5,000 machine guns, all of a much-improved Maxim type, and further tens of thousands were being manufactured. France's total, although only half of the German quantity, was greatly better than Britain's, being 2,500 or so. Russia also had large numbers, many of which were soon captured by the Germans and transported to the Western Front. The strangeness of these numbers lies not with Germany, France, and Russia possessing such large quantities, but in the diminutive British total. Not only had Maxim invented his gun in Britain, but its army had made greater use of the weapon, notably in Africa and Asia, than any other nation.

Not until 1918 did production levels in Britain reach quantities thought appropriate for the fight in France: as many guns were made in the final year of the war as during the four previous years. (Maxim weapons are not mentioned in the table below because, following the development of the Vickers gun in 1912, the old guns had been sufficiently altered to earn the new name of Vickers.)

**British machine-gun manufacture 1914–18**

|  | Vickers | Lewis | Hotchkiss | **Total** |
|---|---|---|---|---|
| **1914** | 266 | 8 |  | 274 |
| **1915** | 2,405 | 3,650 | 9 | 6,064 |
| **1916** | 7,429 | 21,615 | 4,156 | 33,200 |
| **1917** | 21,782 | 45,528 | 12,128 | 79,438 |
| **1918** | 39,473 | 62,303 | 19,088 | 120,864 |

Rifle production was quite another matter. Experience in the Boer War had boosted their popularity, and the manufacture of British rifles had been running at 8,000 a month until July 1914. During the final five months of that critical year, 120,093 were produced, and by 1918 the annual figure had risen to 1,062,052. Therefore yearly rifle production rose sixfold between 1914 and 1918, whereas machine-gun production during the same period increased 441-fold. In theory, two machine guns were allocated to every 1,000 men in the pre-war army, or fewer than two weapons for each battalion, this paltry arrangement reflecting the lack of enthusiasm for them. As there were 26,774 officers and 777,425 other ranks in the British Army on 1 August 1914, there should have been some 1,600 machine guns at least, but there was nothing like that number. Neither officers nor other ranks were much in favour of them, as Arthur Russell wrote in *The Machine Gunner*:

> Most of the Regular Army infantrymen had little good to say about the machine gun, although by October 1915 this mechanical device for firing 500 bullets per minute was being debated by the brass hats and top-level Ordnance officials.

The Germans, in contrast, had entered the war with machine guns as a special arm. They certainly possessed many more at the outset, although estimates vary widely. By the end of 1915, they had 8,000; by the all-important (Somme) month of July 1916 the number was nearer 11,000, and by the war's end three times as many. Right from the war's start, as for several years beforehand, Germany had been more percipient about the potential of such rapid fire. British officials increasingly thought the German concept a good idea, but the notion advanced in somewhat laggardly fashion. Only late in 1915, with the war more than one year old, did a Royal Warrant establish the British Machine Gun Corps, with Kitchener agreeing to sign the formal proclamation.

George, R I
Whereas we have approved of the formation of a Machine Gun Corps, our Will and Pleasure is that the Machine Gun Corps shall be deemed to be a Corps for the purpose of the Army Act.
Given at Our Court of St James's this 14th day of October, 1915, in the Sixth Year of Our Reign.
By His Majesty's Command
Kitchener

Despite that royal approval on top of Kitchener's signature (and the king himself becoming Colonel-in-Chief of the Machine Gun Corps), the corps only contained 153 officers and 3,383 other ranks the following February. (The Cyclists Corps, by contrast, possessed over 13,000 men in 1914 and more than 30,000 at the end of 1915.) By March 1916 the poor supply of machine gunners was being debated in the House of Commons, with unhappiness being expressed that the new corps was so small and its members were so wrongly recruited. Men, sometimes labelled misfits, had allegedly been sent to the training centre near Grantham 'without the full capacity required'. It was further argued that the dismal rate of pay for the job in hand, requiring more skill than was necessary for ordinary infantrymen, should be 'rendered a little more attractive'. Mr Millar, M.P., addressing the House when the war was almost at its halfway stage, said:

I believe that if we had in the field today, following the example of our enemy, a much larger proportion of machine guns, it would tend to shorten the War as these guns can be used not only for defence but for attack . . . I trust (the right hon. gentleman representing the War Office) may be able to give some assurance, at any rate with regard to the machine gun service, that everything is being done to encourage the development of this splendid arm of the service.

The British saw the light eventually. They realised that several hundred rounds per minute from a single weapon did have advantages, this terrible power outclassing even brilliant riflemen. Machine guns ought to have been issued in huge numbers, as they were by the Germans, but they were not. Therefore, until that happened, the British rifleman had to make up, as far as was possible, for this deficiency. To a large extent he did so, as Major-General Sir Reginald Pinney has written in an official history:

In defensive actions, during the first six months of the war, the marvellous fire power of the highly trained regular infantry beat the enemy to such an extent that the German Higher Command excused their defeat by saying 'the British machine guns rendered any advance impossible'.

This was undoubtedly laudable, and the so-called Contemptibles did do brilliantly, but they should not have been put to such a test. Although the German Army is thought to have been the best equipped and trained in August 1914, the British Army possessed the advantage of being a volunteer force. Men joined in Britain for a seven-year period, whereas troops of European armies were mainly conscripted, with 50 per cent of German youth called up for two years, and 80 per cent of French youth for three years. Plainly there was merit in a longer, and less obligatory, period of military service without enforcement.

Edward Spiers, in his writings about the war, has stated that good riflemen in 1914 could fire fifteen accurate rounds per minute at a range of 300 yards. This was impressive but, as another historian phrased it, the writing (about machine-gun power) had been 'on the wall' for quite a time, even if only a few had bothered to observe this warning. In the *History and Memoir of the 33rd Battalion Machine Gun Corps* there is a blunt assessment:

Although every reading soldier knew that one of the great lessons of the Russo-Japanese war had been the extraordinary effect of machine guns, a sufficient number had been denied to the Army, and it was left to do the best it could . . . with rapid fire from rifles.

Every kind of soldier, reading, non-reading, general, private, and even arm-chair warrior, knew by 1916 that machine guns were not just an asset but indispens-able. Rapid fire, by whatever means, was all important, but the new and volunteer recruits, 'Kitchener's Army', were not as capable of accurate rapid fire as the pre-war army had been. Moreover, so many of those who had been well trained when the war began had already vanished from the scene. They had lain down their lives, as memorial services up and down the land were proclaiming so repeatedly, for their King and Country.

Kitchener's demand had been for men rather than machines to help them fight. Right from the start, Kitchener considered it necessary to raise a million men, even if some members of the Cabinet thought the war would be concluded before such a quantity of recruits could possibly be trained, but Kitchener got his way. The British Expeditionary Force had been in France for only four weeks when that fa-mous recruiting poster — Your Country Needs Y O U — was first drawn. The editor of *London Opinion* had suggested to the artist Alfred Leete that 'something topical' should illustrate its front page for that week's issue on 5 September. By then 100,000 men had already volunteered, and recruitment was all the rage. Leete's drawing was a huge success, with reproductions being frequently requested. The War Office was soon asking for permission to use it (and thereby helped to make it one of the most famous posters of all time, if not the most famous). It undoubtedly helped to raise the million men Kitchener so desired. In fact, a million men joined up in 1914, with a maximum of 30,000 recruited in one day. Another 1.5 million enlisted in 1915, but there was still a demand for men. The height stipulation was dropped from 5 ft 8 in at the war's start to 5 ft 2 in. Insistence upon a minimum age of nineteen became more lax, particularly when many youngsters were lying about their age. Despite the considerable numbers of volunteers, the demand continued and conscription (already employed by Germany and France) was initiated in January 1916. For that reason, as it took time to train the conscripts, the great losses around the Somme six months later were almost entirely of volunteers. By the war's end some six million had been recruited, half that number entirely willingly.

Kitchener's poster, plus all those others of women urging their men to go, or of children asking daddies what they did in the war, did little or nothing to improve the supply of weapons with which the brand-new soldiers had to fight, such as machine guns. That had not been Kitchener's proclaimed concern, despite his experience at Omdurman when the machine gun had won the day and covered him in glory. 'Give us the tools, and we will finish the job,' said Winston Churchill twenty-six years later in the Second World War, thereby striking quite a different, and more pragmatic, sense of priorities.

The field-marshal's renown as soldier was outstanding, and this was fundamental to his appeal. Kitchener, so immaculate in uniform, stood head and shoulders above everyone else. His principal rival in the nation's affection, Lord Roberts of Kandahar, was then eighty-two, and would die in November of the war's first year, after catching a chill while visiting the troops in France. It was certainly Kitchener's name, and his particular form of fervour, that concluded a personal message to every soldier then going overseas to fight.

You are ordered abroad as a soldier of the King to help our French comrades against the invasion of a common enemy, you have to perform a task which will need your courage, your energy, your patience. Remember that the honour of the British Army depends upon your individual conduct . . .

In this new experience you may find temptations both in wine and women. You must entirely resist both temptations, and while treating all women with perfect courtesy, you should avoid any intimacy.

Do your duty bravely.

Fear God. Honour the King.

At least song was permitted, if not drink and women. Kitchener's new recruits marched off to war, and to help them, and their 'boots, boots, boots, movin' up and down again' (as Kipling had spelt it out), they used a mixed repertoire of music hall favourites, of popular hymns (with even more popular new wordings), and of new creations, such as 'It's a long way to Tipperary', which had been composed by Jack Judge and Harry Williams in 1912.

Although Kitchener, Britain's revered and most decorated soldier (seven orders of knighthood, and the Order of Merit), complained that his country had gone to war against the world's mightiest army without either the men or munitions to fight it, he stressed more vigorously the need for human reinforcement rather than equipment. In time his forthright and independent manner, coupled with the wretched progress of the war, began to earn him criticism. He had been placed upon a pedestal, perhaps too high a pedestal, and soon became the butt of every dissident.

By 1916 politicians were becoming increasingly vociferous — about the war's conduct, about the generals in charge, and certainly about Lord Kitchener, Secretary of State for War. The initial confidence, so boldly expressed in 1914 by recruits hurrying to join up, to see 'some of the fun', to get involved before it all ended (allegedly by Christmas), had by now utterly waned. Everyone knew the war had become a slaughter. No one knew how it might end, save that it might do so sometime. Many a soldier merely wished for it to be concluded, without caring much who would prove victorious. 'What concerned most of us was not who won the war, as to when it would be won,' as one anonymous machine-gunner phrased it in a small volume of collected memories. Men sang 'When this bleeding war is over' and did not emphasise the need for victory. Indeed, try thinking of a song with that word in it, or conquest, or triumph, or any form of success. For the time being, and for those involved, the war remained just a monster, consuming countless lives.

# Chapter 13

# Known Unto God

As soon as a Ministry of Munitions had been formed, David Lloyd George, then fifty-two, ceased being Chancellor of the Exchequer and became its first Minister. Inevitably, he now more closely encountered the Secretary for War, the 'greatest soldier' and 'leading expert' of the day (as Lloyd George described Kitchener in his memoirs). Equally inevitably, he wished to learn the details of weapon requirements from the distinguished fighter, and sent two men to seek some answers, such as the numbers of rifles and machine guns required for the next nine months. 'Do you think I am God Almighty that I can tell you what is wanted nine months hence?' exploded the field-marshal. After being pressed, he added that he wanted 'as much of both' as could be produced, with the military requirements being 'two machine guns per battalion as a minimum, four as a maximum'.

In theory the Secretary for War was only 'expected to fulfil the requirements of the War Office', as Lloyd George wrote, but the Minister was indignant at Kitchener's reply. According to a subordinate, he made his own judgement after Kitchener's outburst, 'Take Kitchener's maximum; square it, multiply that result by two; and when you are in sight of that, double it again for good luck.' For all those who had visited the troops, and had heard their comments about machine-gun fire, this outspoken calculation of sixty-four weapons per battalion, as against Kitchener's two, was certainly a better estimate of requirements, but the guns still had to be produced. On 19 July 1915 Vickers received an order for 12,000 of its (formerly Maxim) guns. It also received financial assistance to extend its factories, and was eventually manufacturing 5,000 machine guns every month. Reality had begun to assert itself after eleven months of war.

Unfortunately the 'wastage', as it was termed, of men at the front made the expansion of production extremely difficult. The very men who should have been able to make the guns had either been slaughtered or were in France awaiting their turn. Skilled operators had answered Kitchener's call just as readily as the unskilled. There were 'reserved occupations', such as farmers, but the headlong rush to the recruiting offices had led to countless individuals putting on uniform who should, had recruitment been more intelligently undertaken, have stayed at home to make the guns the soldiers needed. Despite the sudden appreciation that armaments, like machine guns, were no less necessary than men, and despite the urgent governmental demand for 12,000 guns, Vickers found it difficult to fulfil the order. Some officers, unhappy at the shortage for their own battalions, actually purchased the guns themselves rather than wait for delivery through official channels.

Production figures from Vickers' Erith and Crayford factories (which had been Maxim-Nordenfelts') tell their own tale of a nation getting to grips with actual requirements. It did take time to stoke up steam.

### Annual Vickers production
### of machine guns

| | |
|---|---|
| **1911** | 26 |
| **1913** | 45 |
| **1914** | 377 |
| **1915** | 2,433 |
| **1916** | 7,468 |
| **1917** | 21,751 |
| **1918** | 41,699 |

In 1914, a mere thirty-eight had been produced before the war began. In 1918, some 10,000 more guns were produced than in all of the earlier wartime years. Not only was the army wanting increasing numbers of the weapons, with eighty per battalion sometimes achieved (as against the two with which the war started), but the Royal Flying Corps was also demanding them for its thousands of bombers and fighters. Vickers had to boost its workforce in similar style: the total number of employees became 107,000 at the peak period, with 32,500 being women and girls. (With thanks to *The Grand Old Lady of No Man's Land* by Dolf L. Goldsmith for these figures.)

Lloyd George made certain that machine guns became a subject to be debated within the House of Commons. In part this was a political manoeuvre. The war was going badly, and the so-called Welsh Wizard was wishing to oust Herbert Asquith as coalition prime minister. The lack of proper weapons was a very useful stick with which to berate the man in charge, along with the nation's most renowned, and most exceptional, military man. Inside the sanctity of Parliament, that famous and revered Secretary for War was being labelled 'stupid' and 'wrong-headed'. 'The charge we make against him,' said Arthur Markham, M.P., 'is that he never ordered the material, and he never gave the orders which he could have given, until the Prime Minister came on the scene.'

The Minister of Munitions was also most clear and forthright in his denunciation of the war's management, and of machine-gun production in particular.

We were rather late in realising the great part which the machine gun plays in this War, and I think I am entitled to say that the first time the problem was impressed upon me, in the gravest possible language, the importance of supplying a large quantity of machine guns, we immediately placed large orders at home and abroad.

Arthur Markham (who died three months later) then made the same point with even greater emphasis.

Lord Kitchener had been time after time to France, and are we to have a civilian to go to France in order to find out that it is necessary to have more machine guns? We have the extraordinary position that the Prime Minister goes to France, and with his great foresight . . . he comes back and impresses on the Minister of Munitions the necessity of having more machine guns. What is the good of having a War Minister when the Prime Minister has to go out to ascertain that there is a shortage of machine guns?

The House gave Kitchener's reputation a very rough ride. One member called him 'incompetent, obstinate and wholly lacking in brains'. Another said 'his deficiences were so great and the inefficiencies so apparent' that he ought to be removed. Dismissal was then made harder by the prime minister, Herbert Asquith, who — to the accompaniment of cheers — said:

The army, the country, and the Empire are under a debt which cannot be measured in words for the services Lord Kitchener has rendered since the beginning of the war.

According to John Pollock, in his book *Kitchener*, Andrew Bonar Law (a later prime minister) then complimented Asquith on his words, before whispering:

'That was a great speech, but how after it shall we get rid of him?' To a large degree this debate was party politics, despite the fact that a coalition was in charge. Markham was a Liberal and a strong supporter of Lloyd George. A considerable movement was already in place for installing Lloyd George as prime minister (an event which took place during the following December).

Kitchener's drowning early in June 1916 when on his way to Russia was therefore not without certain advantages. Instead of the nation's most favoured soldier (and principal recruiter via his poster) having to be ignominiously sacked, he could die as a hero. The notion of a Russian visit — to boost morale there and discuss munitions — had been mooted by the Cabinet, but nothing had been decided until King George V received a telegram from his distant relation, the Czar of Russia, welcoming the idea. When a mine off the Orkneys sank H.M.S. *Hampshire*, killing almost all the 650 on board, there must have been relief, as well as lamentation, that the great man was no more.

The abrupt vanishing of Britain's most important soldier also caused suspicion in certain quarters that it was all a fiction, cleverly designed to mislead Britain's enemies. For those who knew he had been on board, the cruiser's sinking so close to shore and lifeboats being on board raised expectations that he might have survived; but only two floats (with twelve men on them) reached the land and not a single lifeboat. The problem of Kitchener's possible dismissal, and his lack of enthusiasm for machine guns, therefore departed with him. In a sense the submarine U75, proud to claim credit for laying the mine which caused the sinking, had done Britain a favour by laying its deadly ordnance in forty fathoms so near the British naval base at Scapa Flow. And so had the raging storm which made survival by anyone, let alone a sixty-six-year-old, extremely difficult. Many in Britain wept when they heard the news, but not everyone can have done so and Kitchener's departure led to some distinct gains. Almost at once, for example, David Lloyd George took over the reins of the Ministry of War. He could therefore demand the weapons which the troops required without experiencing blunt objection from the nation's favourite military man.

Twenty-six days after Kitchener's disappearance, the long-prepared Battle of the

Somme began on 1 July 1916, and as that man's enthusiastic volunteers quickly learned, those engaged in this massive attack would be mown down most horribly. German machine gunners, seemingly undamaged by the massive and earlier artillery bombardment, had emerged from the depths of their dugouts to fire their guns relentlessly. They did not have to aim. They merely kept their fingers on the triggers and speedily reloaded. Making everything worse, from the British point of view, was the fact that holes had been cut in the wire for easier access towards the German lines. Therefore, not only were many thousands of men suddenly exposed to the machine gunners, but they made an even better target as they concentrated themselves within the gaps in the wire.

The British had been told that their attack would be a pushover following the artillery barrage, and they were so confident that they merely walked across no man's land, giving the German gun-crews yet more time to effect their carnage. The horror of 19,240 British soldiers being killed on the Somme's first day, and of British casualties overall amounting to 57,470 during those initial twenty-four hours, helped to convince every remaining doubter that a new kind of killing from a new kind of killing machine had arrived. That casualty total is equivalent to the number of men passing a fixed point in eight hours if marching four abreast in an unbroken column, and it was the greatest one-day loss in the entire history of the British Army. Machine guns had been known to be inglorious and unpopular, but had proved the point that, if attrition of an enemy was required, they could do the job very satisfactorily.

In theory, the German front line should have been pulverised, almost to annihilation, by the week-long artillery bombardment which had preceded the battle. More than a million and a half shells, totalling over 20,000 tons of steel, were fired, mostly into a central area approximately fourteen miles wide and one mile deep. The British felt confident that their own grand attack would win, even though the German and French assaults at Verdun had each failed (and were still failing when the Somme assault began). With the British barrage not only were most of the heaviest shells to be straightforward, in that they would explode on impact, but there were to be others primed to detonate and disintegrate into shrapnel when a short distance above the ground.

Surely nothing and no one could possibly survive such a cannonade? Those several prior days of gunfire were horrendously deafening and disarming even for the British in their trenches. They had to be ten thousand times more damaging for the Germans who were sheltering in theirs.

Practice proved quite different from theory. Official British optimism concerning the barrage had been entirely faulty. The German trenches had been dug extremely deeply, and most of them — up to thirty feet below the surface — could withstand even direct hits. Hints of this considerable depth should have been taken, following aerial reconnaissance, from the great quantities of excavated chalk which parallelled the German front-line trench system.

A further problem with the British barrage resulted from a large number of the poorly manufactured shells failing to detonate. Frenzied demands from the artillery in France for additional ammunition had caused excessive haste back home. This fervent rush may have been, in part, to blame, or perhaps the brand new workforce had been at fault. Even Douglas Haig wrote in a subsequent despatch that 'enhancement of ammunition production by 1916' had been offset by 'poor quality fuzes which resulted in dudding rates of one third during the preparatory bombardment'. In any case, whether or not the ammunition did its job effectively, and exploded on cue, as many shells were launched during those six days at the end of June as had been consumed during the war's first twelve months. Soldier poets at the front not only harangued the loss of life, the waste, the horror, the pity of it all, but were forever aware of monstrous anger from the guns and the choirs of wailing shells. Silence was yet another major casualty of that war.

As for the million shrapnel shells despatched before 1 July 1916, their moments of detonation were often sufficiently inexact to prevent explosions at suitably lethal heights. Even when set correctly, their vehemence did not much affect an enemy that was sensibly sheltering so deeply underground. Worse still, the acres and acres of the German barbed-wire entanglements were not greatly damaged by the explosions and remained a formidable barrier. 'The wire has never been so well cut,' wrote Haig to his wife on the day before the battle, but he was letting his wishful and enthusiastic judgement get the better of him.

It is sometimes reported that the man in charge of the Somme offensive could not possibly have appreciated the power of the machine gun. Otherwise he would not have despatched so many men into the teeth of enemy fire. There were generals who still resented the weapon, but Haig was not among them. According to Brian Bond and Nigel Cave (in their *Haig: A Reappraisal 70 Years On*), 'the utility of the light machine gun was identified by Haig in mid-1915, and its battle-winning value . . . was emphasised by him at an Army Commanders' Conference in March 1916'. Haig himself wrote, as quoted by Duff Cooper in his very readable biography on the C.-in-C., that in early 1916 he had wished

> to bring home to units the need for thorough development of the use of the Lewis machine guns for an offensive. I think units have hardly begun to realise the great addition which they have recently received to their fire-power by the provision of Lewis machine guns and machine-gun batteries.

The lightweight and bipod-mounted

Lewis's were different from the water-cooled Maxim-type weapons so favoured by the Germans, but Haig was well aware of the boost to fire-power provided by any such gun. Nevertheless, the tens of thousands of British soldiery were to rise up on 1 July and meet everything that Germany could deliver in terms of rapid fire.

A final and particularly unfortunate error was the length of time which passed between the artillery gunfire's abrupt cessation and the attack's initiation. For days and nights those guns had been firing at an average of over two shells every second. Everyone knew an attack was imminent. To the Germans, the warning signs were all too clear. Indeed, they hoped the fight would begin sooner rather than later, as the bombardment was disrupting their food supplies. Although it was a British assault, the French, for reasons of diplomacy and international cooperation, had been allowed to choose the place, the date and the very hour of the attack. Haig had wanted the attack to be further north by the River Lys and had also wished for greater preparation time. But the French, hard-pressed at Verdun much further to the east, had urged a June beginning, and 1 July was the eventual compromise.

Hence the launching of those 1.6 million shells during June's last six days, and everything primed for the 'great push', as all called it, on the very first day of a brand new month.

Quite suddenly this artillery assault was halted. The consequent quiet must have been extraordinary, and even somewhat eerie, with birdsong then the loudest thing to be heard. Had there ever been such silence at the front line in the normal course of events? After dawn on that 1 July 1916, this peace lasted for a full ten minutes, giving the Germans ample opportunity to climb from their bunker depths, to settle behind their machine guns, and await the certain assault. One American critic (unnamed) of this fight said the Battle of the Somme 'was lost in the first three minutes'. He had a point. It took the Germans time to scramble from their depths, to line up their guns and ammunition, and to squat in readiness. The British, with their unfortunate delay, gave it to them.

The whole German army, and certainly those in the bombarded sector, knew the assault was coming no less assuredly than did the British who, with their full sixty-pound packs, were waiting to go over the parapet. It had never been a secret that a huge attack was imminent. Back in January 1916, at the Chantilly Conference, it had been decided that a major assault should be mounted, mainly by the French. But the ghastliness of Verdun had begun soon afterwards, and the French army's ability and willingness to play a similarly major role around the Somme had gradually been whittled down. The British were therefore compelled, partly to bolster the entente and help their battered allies, to accept and then experience a much bigger share of the action, notably over territory which had not been of their choosing. An early British plan had stipulated that the attack should begin when the night was ending, and when semidarkness would favour the attackers. Anyone who had witnessed the Battle of Omdurman eighteen years earlier (as quite a few of the officers had surely done) would have known of the Khalifa's decision to postpone his Mahdist advance until daylight had arrived, thus permitting the British gunners to see their running and galloping enemy all too clearly. But the French had insisted upon it being a daylight affair, and so it was. Worse still, on the Somme the British regiments would stroll almost casually in disciplined fashion rather than running impulsively at the guns, as the Dervishes had at Kitchener's Maxims, but their downfall would be much the same. Supersonic bullets, spewing forth in such abundance, were equally disdainful of both kinds of men.

Kitchener had reportedly been calm before the Battle of Omdurman, in great fettle and even cheery, and Haig was (apparently) similarly relaxed. Quite how generals manage to sleep, let alone be calm or cheery, when committing soldiers to unknown quantities of death can be a mystery, but Haig was able to write:

> With God's help, I feel hopeful. The men are in splendid spirits, several have said they have never before been so instructed and informed of the nature of the operations before them.

And yet 57,470 of those in such high spirits were to become casualties before that first day was concluded, with over 19,000 never seeing any other kind of day. To his wife Haig wrote on the eve of battle:

> I think it is Divine help which gives me tranquillity of mind, and enables me to carry on without feeling the strain of responsibility to be too excessive.

Of course the same god was being urged among Haig's opponents to give them a similar tranquillity of mind, and *Gott mit Uns* formed a similar inspiration. As for the men about to be enmeshed in the battle, they surely mouthed ten thousand different prayers, and possessed little by way of tranquillity, but wished that whatever was going to happen would happen soon. Waiting is never a happy circumstance.

After those ten silent minutes of expectation, the Germans could hear whistles being blown right along the British line. As a further signal of an attack's imminence, the tremendous Hawthorn mine and others were exploded beneath sections of the German trenches. Hawthorn killed twenty-eight of the enemy at 7.20 a.m. and, with daylight well advanced, 60,000 of the first British wave were then climbing from the relative safety of their trenches to experience whatever hellishness was about to come their way. Hardly any of them, perhaps one in several hundred, had been over the top before, and very few of them were regular soldiers. Instead they were clerks, delivery boys, stevedores, railway porters, postmen, factory workers, shop assistants, farm hands, road sweepers, builders, teachers, miners — a cross-section of the British population. They had not dreamed of wearing uniform until August 1914, but then did so in abundance (with more men joining the army every day than were normally recruited in a year). The earliest volunteers had, by mid-1916, been in khaki for almost two years, and huge numbers of them knew a very great deal about the stalemate of trench existence, accompanied by all its miseries.

The Battle of the Somme, as it would come to be known, was also the first great opportunity for Kitchener's army, as all the volunteers were called, to prove itself. Regular officers had often despaired, out loud, that such a disparate bunch of civilians could be honed into a proper fighting unit. The new men were keen, and determined to 'have a crack', but they were not regular material, accustomed to army ways and discipline. On the other hand they were, in general, fitter, taller, and healthier than the average peacetime recruit, so often obliged to join the army because of penury and unemployment. Gradually those in charge of the new arrivals improved their attitudes. Rivalries developed, with battalions and their commanders believing they were the best, and wishing to prove the point. What better way to win confirmation of all their excellence than by attacking the dastardly Hun? It had been difficult showing merit when living in the trenches, suffering mud and shot and shell, and being miserable in a thousand different ways. How much better to prove superiority, not only above other regiments but over the enemy, than by assault? The big trouble, of course, was that the waiting machine guns were not concerned with ability or excellence. They would fire their bullets quite impartially, with all those confronting them uniformly vulnerable, the clerks, the errand boys, the road sweepers, and the long, and the short, and the tall. Any form of superiority was totally irrelevant, whether officers or men, whether the best battalion in the regiment or quite the worst.

When the battle began 'nothing seemed to happen at first', as one man wrote,

> then, suddenly, we were in the midst of a storm of machine-gun bullets and I saw men beginning to twirl round and fall in all kinds of curious ways as they were hit — quite unlike the way actors do it in films.

Shells were also raining upon the advancing infantry, and more and more replacement men were being despatched in further waves. No one in authority seemed to know that a disaster had begun, and these additional reinforcements would only serve to make the day yet more disastrous. By noon, about 100,000 had been committed to the fight, and casualties were already horrendous. Junior officers suffered more than most, mainly because they walked at the head of their men. The British dead-to-wounded ratio was two to one, a proportion twice as high as for the Great War as a whole. As for those Germans squatting behind their rapid-firing weapons and their comrades on either side of them, some 8,000 were to die on that first day of July. This number was also considerable: the assault by the British was the most violent in that war's history. The defenders therefore also suffered, but attack — so widely proclaimed as the 'proper' kind of war — had firmly proved itself so much more lethal than defence when machine guns were in place.

The time soon came when burial parties set to work, collecting the identity disks (and rifles and equipment) from the dead, and then pitching the corpses into convenient craters. Joe Hoyles, of the Rifle Brigade, was one man detailed for this task (and quoted by Lyn Macdonald in her book *Somme*).

There was a terrific smell. It was so awful it nearly poisoned you. A smell of rotten flesh. The old German front line was covered with bodies — they were seven and eight deep and they had all gone black . . . I don't know how many we buried. I'll never forget that sight. Bodies all over the place. I'll never forget it. I was only eighteen, but I thought, 'There's something wrong here!'

Rupert Weeber, of the same battalion, was similarly engaged.

As far as you could see there were all these bodies lying out there — literally thousands of them, just where they'd been caught on the First of July. Some were without legs, some were legs without bodies, arms without bodies. A terrible sight. They'd been churned up by shells even after they were killed. We were just dumping them into the crater — just filling them over. It didn't seem possible. It didn't get inside me or scare me, but it just made me wonder that these could have been men. It made me wonder what it was all about. And far away in the distance we could see nothing but a line of bursting shells. It was continuous. You wouldn't have thought that anybody could have existed in it, it was so terrific. And yet we knew we were going up into it, with not an earthly chance.

Machine guns, in the main, had seen to it that attack over open ground had become so lethal. Back in Kent, Hiram Maxim, the man most responsible for this tactical alteration, and for the machine gun's introduction, was then thinking more of his bronchitis, and he would die when the Somme offensive was being finally concluded. Basil Liddell Hart, World War One soldier and war historian, wrote later of that aged individual:

His name is more deeply engraved on the real history of the World War than that of any other man. Emperors, statesmen and generals had the power to make war, but not to end it. Having created it, they found themselves helpless puppets in the grip of Hiram Maxim, who, by his machine gun, had paralysed the power of attack. All efforts to break the defensive grip of the machine gun were vain; they could only raise tombstones and triumphal arches.

Both before and after that terrible day in July 1916, very large numbers of men were learning of Hiram Maxim. It did not take them long to know of the Anglo-American inventor's dastardly creation. As one British ex-machine gunner summed up the situation in his memoirs:

From the outset of trench warfare in France and Flanders the Germans had relied on their heavy Maxim-type machine guns to support their attacks . . . [they were] operated as a special *corps d'élite* . . . So devastating was the effect of the fire from the enemy machine guns when an attempt was made to break through the German trenchworks that most of the men in the waves of attacking infantry were killed or wounded before they could cross no man's land, and the few who did reach the enemy's barbed-wire fences were usually blasted to death by the stick-bombs thrown at them by the Boche defenders.

As the song then phrased it, with the all-too-accurate and courageous jollity of those terrifying days:

If you want to find the old battalion,
I know where they are, I know where
    they are, I know where they are.
If you want the old battalion, I know
    where they are.
They're hanging on the old barbed wire,
I've seen 'em, I've *seen* 'em, hanging on
    the old barbed wire,
I've seen 'em, I've seen 'em, hanging on
    the old barbed wire.

There was also a popular rendering of the sentimental 'Though your heart may ache awhile, Never mind' which, in its final (much-amended) verse, referred to the lethal and barbed entanglements the soldiers had to face.

If you get stuck on the wire, Never mind!
If you get stuck on the wire, Never mind!
Though the light's as broad as day
When you die they stop your pay,
If you get stuck on the wire, Never mind!

Whether from wire or grenade, machine gun or artillery, the casualty lists were formidable. 'Come on, men,' an officer might say, only to realise he was on his own. The 1st Newfoundland Regiment suffered 684 casualties out of 752 within thirty minutes. Four members of the same Ayre family, a captain, two second lieutenants, and a lance-corporal, all of that single Canadian regiment, died that day. So did a fifth member serving with the 8th Norfolks. As for the 1st Newfoundlanders, the formation had virtually ceased to exist, but it was certainly not alone in its ill fortune.

> I could see men of the 1st Queens passing up the slope [wrote G.S. Hutchison in his memoirs] . . . they wavered and a few of the foremost attempted to cross some obstacles in the grass. They were awkwardly lifting their legs over a long wire entanglement. Some 200 men, their commander at their head, had been brought to a standstill at this point. A scythe seemed to cut their feet from under them, and the line crumpled and fell, stricken by machine-gun fire.

Hutchison's memories were often disturbingly vivid:

> On my right an officer commanding a

machine-gun section had perished and all his men, with the exception of one who came running towards me, the whole of the front of his face shot away.

'We've been lucky,' wrote one man from another unit two days later; 'we only lost 40 out of 150 . . . but struggling over dead bodies and pieces of dead Germans — it was horrible.' That was Private Ernest J. Coleman, who had enlisted aged sixteen (claiming to be nineteen). He had been sent to France in early 1916, and would die in 1917 with no known grave. Over and over again, others caught up in the battle told the same dreadful tale — 'There were six officers and 100 other ranks, but only one officer and thirty-seven men came back'; 'The company was no longer the unit it had been'; 'Our battalion's roll-call was the saddest thing I ever heard'. How anyone could sleep, having been in charge of such fighting, and having ordered so many men to their deaths, is assuredly confusing in modern times, but Richard Holmes has a kind of explanation in *The Western Front*. In this book he quotes Michael Howard's chilling assessment: 'The casualty lists that a later generation [would] find so horrifying were considered by contemporaries not an indication of military incompetence, but a measure of national resolve, of fitness to rank as a Great Power.' In which case Britain was indeed a great power, rich with national resolve.

The British, even when they did possess a substantial number of machine guns, still had much to learn about the right and wrong ways of using them. It was all very well 'to move forward in close support of the advancing waves of Infantry', as one machine-gun commander described it, but not if this led to 'hails of machine-gun bullets [killing] sections almost to a man', when all to be seen thereafter were 'tripods of the guns with their legs waving in the air, and ammunition boxes scattered among the dead'. The right way of using machine guns was entirely different. G.S. Hutchison, already mentioned, has been described as 'the man who led the most famous machine-gun barrage of the war'.

The order had been given before a particular attack that ten guns, well situated with a fine view of the German line 2,000 yards away, should maintain rapid fire continuously for twelve hours. This would 'cover the attack and consolidation'. 'It is to the credit of the gunners and of the

Vickers gun itself that this was done,' stated the official history of the M.G. Corps' 33rd battalion. A prize was even offered to the team who fired the most, and the winners loosed off 120,000 rounds during those twelve hours. In all a staggering 999,750 bullets were fired by the ten guns during that time, which does indeed speak well of the men and their machines. Even bringing up and transporting the necessary quantity of belted ammunition would have been a daunting business. As for that attack (of 24 August 1916), it was a 'brilliant success', with 'all objectives being taken'. German prisoners captured at the time said the barrage 'had been annihilating', with every attempt to retake lost ground 'being broken up'. Plainly the first problem for the British Army was to equip itself properly with machine guns. The second problem, just as great, was to learn how to use them. August 1916, the day of that success, was exactly two years since the war had begun.

Private Coleman, the sixteen-year-old who had claimed to be nineteen, possessed a wise head upon his shoulders — before it was blown away. He, an impassioned member of the Machine Gun Corps, knew when he joined that it had not yet found absolute favour among the hierarchy, or even the rank and file. In June 1916 he confided to his diary that 'The M.G. Corps has yet to prove itself; it now has a chance.' There was no such corps until, very late in the day as Parliament had abruptly appreciated, enthusiasm slowly grew for a greater adoption of the killing weapon. The new arrangement of a special corps, formulated in 1915 but not truly actioned until 1916, asserted that each M.G. company should have sixteen guns, and there would be three such companies to every division. This was nothing less than a revolution in thinking, in policy, in practice. The former, and hopelessly inadequate, system of two weapons for every 1,000 men (with one usually stored as a spare) was suddenly ancient history. Many tens of thousands of courageous individuals had given their lives to put it there.

Personal reminiscences of those who joined this brand new corps give a flavour of life within that organisation. Although Army Order No. 416 had initiated this separate arm, little was done immediately thereafter to transfer personnel its way, mainly because battalion commanders 'were reluctant to release any of their men', particularly the better ones. The new corps wanted a superior grade of individual as machine guns demanded greater technical expertise than mere rifles or grenades. Hardly anything happened concerning the new corps until February 1916, when the war was eighteen months old and had another thirty-three to go.

Machine guns had been in action, although inadequately, on the British side before that time, and their crews had not been envied for their vulnerability. The unhappy sobriquet they earned of 'Suicide Squads' then became attached to the Machine Gun Corps as a whole, and this title was more than justified. (Machine gunners were also known, rather more happily, as the Emma Gees, much as Ack Emma was a.m. and Ack Ack was anti-aircraft.) Not only did British forces often attempt to destroy the enemy's machine guns, thus earning so many V.C.s, but the Germans would rain particular destruction upon the emplacements of the British M.G. Corps. Its members were often 'picked off like rabbits', according to one ex-gunner in his reminiscences, with words like 'decimated', 'great havoc', and 'shot to pieces' frequently peppering his pages. Of the 130,500 officers and men who served with the M.G. Corps, a total of 62,049 became casualties during the two and a half years of its wartime existence, and 12,498 of these were killed in action. One recruit volunteered for the corps 'despite — or perhaps because of — the rumour then circulating that the average expectations of life of a Maxim gunner in action was twenty minutes'. (His later diary included the engaging couplet: 'Our hearts were filled with weary thoughts: our boots were filled with feet.')

Machine-gun training began at Harrowby Camp, near Grantham, and later at Clipstone, near Mansfield. The recruited infantrymen had already been taught about the rifle and bayonet before encountering the machine gun. 'It can't hurt you,' jested the instructors — no doubt to every intake as its individuals cautiously inspected this novel weapon; 'the bullets come out the other end.' One such recruit made a note of the instructions he received, and of the routines to be enforced:

Each gun was fed by a second man on the right . . . he pushed the tag of the belt through the feed block when No. 1, the man who fired the gun, pulled the belt-tag . . . The belts held 250 cartridges. To fire, No.1 had to lift the safety catch and press the thumb piece . . . This sent the first bullet away, which automatically set off the remainder . . . [Firing] would continue until the gunner released pressure from the thumb-piece or all the rounds were expended . . . Usually there were six men to a team who took it in turns to fire when in action. [This was to prepare all of them for that task in case of casualties.] The time for getting in action at drill was about three to four seconds . . . Everything was done at the double . . . You had to be very alert in the Machine Gun Corps.

The gun's surrounding container of cooling water became extremely hot if the weapon was fired continuously; 600 rounds were sufficient to bring it to the boil. If urine was ever used in lieu of water (with good water often scarce at the front line) the 'stench was most unpleasant', with evaporation — of either liquid — causing the loss of 1.5 pints for every 1,000 rounds. To assist in water conservation, a condenser bag could be attached to the gun by a tube, thus turning steam into water once again. During cold weather, a not unfamiliar feature of the Western Front, each gun's vital water jacket froze if glycerine had not been added or if the gun had not been fired from time to time, with firing being the simpler expedient. Who cared about the waste, Robert Graves asked, before suggesting — only too correctly — that his country's post-war tax-payers would have to foot the bill. Being economical — with anything — was not a feature of life in the front line. The present was sufficiently worrying to care about the future. Besides, who would meet that future?

'Stoppages and their causes' formed a crucial part of training, since tight pockets in the belts — these resisting or preventing cartridge extraction — were a major problem. Another was uneven manufacture of cartridges, notably at their bottom end. The army supplied appropriate tools to remedy all faults, and these were carried in a spare kit-bag which therefore added to the burden. As each of the commonest type of machine gun weighed thirty-eight pounds (when topped with water), its tripod forty-eight pounds, and every box of its belted ammunition twenty-one pounds, these considerable loads, usually to be carried over difficult — or near impossible —

terrain, help to explain why six men formed a gun team, even if only one of them was necessary to pull the trigger.

Germany's army, so much more adept from the start with this deadly weapon, not only used it over open sights to mow down attacking infantry, but also regularly raked the tops of British parapets, particularly at night. 'The life of the British Tommy (when) on duty on the fire step in the front line,' as one man recorded, 'was then in deadly peril.' So were other individuals a thousand or so yards behind that forward trench, notably during darkness. The Germans habitually preset their guns to hurtle bullets at the distant but much-used supply routes leading to the front.

Following their enemy's example, the British recruits at Grantham had to learn range-finding, generally with a Barr & Stroud instrument. Vickers guns could be effective at distances greater than 1,000 yards (or three times as far by the war's end), thus firing their projectiles over the heads of British infantry, much as the artillery always did when launching its rather heavier shells at the enemy. An officer was expected to select the machine gun's range (using the gun's clinometer) after some suitable German weakness had been detected. The gun crew-man appointed as the section's range-taker also received a major blessing — no longer did he have to carry rifle and bayonet as, in general, did the remainder of his crew. Instead, he was issued with a Smith & Wesson .45 revolver, a most prized alternative.

Training was all-embracing. Commands were barked out: 'Mount Gun', 'Fire', 'Fall Out One', 'Dismount Gun'. The trainee crews had to run twenty-five, fifty, and 100 yards carrying the eighty-six pounds of gun plus, perhaps, eighty-four pounds of ammunition. 'Hand bombs' were then thrown at them, and illuminating Very lights were also fired at night to make everything realistic — save that no Germans were firing back and wounding or killing these recruits with as much compunction as the Grantham crews were learning to annihilate their enemy. Gas-masks were also tested, and these were known as P.H. helmets. They had eye-pieces, with ointment to keep them clearer, as well as nose-clips to enforce mouth-breathing. Inevitably there was also 'weapon cleaning', with hot water, a rod, and the white-pink flannelette known (from its dimensions) as four-by-two. 'What you have to pull through your barrels is your pull-through,' intoned the instructors, with the same old heavy levity they regularly enjoyed. Then, as a final exercise, all guns and equipment had to be loaded on to trains, along with mules and horses. The major port of embarkation was Folkestone, with Boulogne the most common arrival point. Finally, in columns of four, the fresh contingents set off, usually for Camiers, the normal halting place for gunners, before they moved up to the front.

From that time on fortune played the major role concerning possible survival. Some 47.5 per cent of the M.G. Corps would become casualties, with 9.5 per cent being killed. One officer was killed to every fourteen other ranks, a high proportion. Seven members of the Corps received V.C.s — four officers and three other ranks — with two of them being granted posthumously. The first two V.C.s of the war were awarded to machine gunners, their valour exhibited during the Mons retreat, and long before the M.G. Corps was formed. This unit would grow in strength as the war progressed, with 54,000 of its gunners attached to the infantry by the end of 1916, 84,000 by the end of 1917, and 120,000 at the war's end. During the same period, the British Expeditionary Force as a whole also rose in its numbers (despite the massive losses), but nothing like so dramatically as the Machine Gun Corps. There were 2,054,000 soldiers within the B.E.F. in November 1916, 2,486,000 in April 1917, 3,180,000 in September 1917, 3,315,000 in December 1917, 3,251,000 in June 1918, and 3,265,000 in September 1918. The army itself therefore increased by one-third during that period of 1916–18, whereas its machine gunners more than doubled. The entire war had to pass before everyone became convinced that machine guns were an essential ingredient of such a conflict of attrition. Yet by its end, the weapon's status in the B.E.F. had merely reached the level of interest in machine-gun capability that Germany had acquired before the war began.

The machine gunners, once they had become a cohesive unit, even acquired some poetry of their own. Most wartime poetry concentrated, only too understandably, on the pity of war, of those who die as cattle, of a drawing down of blinds. John Hobson chose a different tack, once the machine gun had arrived, and he lay with one in the grass. A lieutenant in the M.G. Corps, he would die at Passchendaele in 1917.

*Come ye who may,*
*Foeman in air, or Earth!*
*For my machine-gun*
*Sings for you alone,*
*And in his lay*
*To silvery death gives birth.*
*Now lifts now lowers he*
*His deady tone.*
*Here do I lie,*
*Hidden by grass and flowers,*
*With my machine-gun,*
*Ghost of modern war.*
*The sun floats high,*
*The moon through deep blue hours,*
*I watch with my machine-gun*
*At Death's grim door.*

He was then aged twenty-three.

# Chapter 14

# The Omnipresent Chatter

The Duke of Wellington famously said that 'you can no more describe a battle than a ball'. So much is going on at so many levels (in both of them) that the events are too multitudinous for subsequent analysis. Certainly, Haig's bland despatches during the Somme are devoid of detail but rich in confident assertion.

[There is] sufficient evidence to place it beyond doubt that the enemy's losses in men and material have been considerably higher than those of the Allies, while morally the balance on our side is still greater . . . While some have been more fortunate than others in opportunities for distinction, all have done their duty nobly.

Perhaps those are the kind of bland assurances that commanders have to write. Gain the moral high ground. Do your duty. Grasp opportunities for distinction. As for the individual units engaged in the battle, they painted a less glorious picture, but could only indicate what they themselves experienced in their section of the front. Yet these accounts give a flavour of the fighting which was no doubt duplicated, again and again, in other areas. The summary reported by the '33rd Battalion Machine-Gun Corps in the Third Stage of the Somme Offensive' is perhaps typical, or perhaps not, but is certainly enlightening. Even if given in piecemeal fashion, it helps to illustrate the whole. It describes the active role the battalion played in the third portion of the Somme offensive, this beginning on 14 September 1916. The corps had been 'badly cut up' on 1 July, and the whole Division had been withdrawn 'for re-grouping and reinforcements'. Then came that third assault.

The weather had entirely broken. The roads were a morass of treacly mud . . . Cover of every description had been swept aside . . . every yard of ground was pitted by shell holes . . . Desolation was everywhere . . . It was obvious that the intention was to outflank Bapaume . . . It was equally obvious that an attack at this time of the year across a quagmire would be an almost impossible task . . . It was almost impossible for an armed man to move himself, let alone carry a wounded comrade.

The horror of the day spent in shallow, waterlogged trenches under unceasing fire was even surpassed at night when the full fury of the German guns was let loose . . . Men disappeared into the night; no one knows to this date their fate, whether destroyed by shell fire, or swallowed up in the yawning shell holes, stifled with mud and water, gripped and paralysed with cold and wounds. The scream of the shells, the dull boom of the burst, the chatter of machine guns and the 'spat, spat' of heavy rain drops lashing the surface of the quagmire was incessant . . .

The sole duck-board was torn up or sunken beneath the oozing surface of the ground. Boots were torn from the feet of men held fast in the octopus grip of the mud . . . Men were seen working without any clothing except shirts and jackets. Exhaustion became a plague. Horses and mules remained to die, stuck fast in their tracks. Wagons were abandoned and became the sport of shells . . . The little wooden crosses daily increased . . . Every man was buried where he fell, it being impossible to bear him away.

Multiply that kind of chaos a thousand-fold or more, and Wellington's comment becomes yet more comprehensible. What on earth was happening? What on earth did happen? The neat memorial rows of the later cemeteries clearly indicate the numbers of men killed, but not the shambles of the actual battle in which they perished. Neither do they tell of individual acts, such as that of a machine gunner serving with 151 Company.

During the Somme battle of September 1916 the Infantry of 151 Brigade was held up by a German strongpoint. Lance Corporal Bill Leftley . . . crawled across no man's land in broad daylight and reached the enemy trench. He discovered that the first traverses were empty, and assumed the Germans had retreated. Leftley then stood up, slowly walked down the trench, and suddenly surprised twenty Germans who, not realising the fact that there was just one British soldier to deal with, immediately put up their hands in token of surrender.

Leftley beckoned the party to come with him in single file, and was scared stiff in case the first German should rumble the actual situation and shout a warning to his mates. Leftley brought the twenty Germans back to his machine-gun position, and handed over the prisoners to an Infantry officer. The attack then progressed according to plan. Leftley was recommended for the V.C., but the Infantry officer had also been recommended for the same capture . . . Eventually an enquiry was established . . . The outcome was that Bill Leftley was awarded the Medal Militaire (French decoration). The officer got the M.C.

Haig's despatches were inevitably different, and more general, but do provide additional insight.

Many of the troops, especially among the drafts sent to replace wastage, counted their service by months, and gained in the Somme battle their first experience of war.

In other words, into that quagmire of mud where men and horses drowned, and into that chaos of shell holes with the little crosses in between, Britain's volunteer soldiers, who were hurried forward to overcome the wastage, soon learned about this particular form of life and death. No wonder, when the quieter times arrived, they might sing: 'When this bleeding war is over, oh how happy I shall be; I shall put my civvy clothes on, no more soldiering for me.' Kitchener's army had rushed to join by the thousand. They had been shouted at by sergeants at Aldershot and on Salisbury Plain. Drill and the rifle had been their daily fare. Then off to France, and marched up to the front line. Long days of waiting in and out of trenches, and eventually the push. Rain, mud, horror, wire, the whine from shells, the boom when they landed, the omnipresent chatter from machine guns, the sudden death of chums, and all those little crosses standing where there had been men. Let's get our civvy clothes back on, and have no more of this soldiering.

Haig had asked for more time before the Somme attack to train the brand-new army, but the French kept on pressing for an earlier assault. It was not an easy time for anyone. The Russians were saying the French were not doing enough. The French were saying much the same about the British, and the British were never much in favour of the French. The French commander-in-chief, for his part, could be particularly vitriolic and outspoken. *'C'est trop tard; c'est la mort,'* said Marshal Joffre on one occasion when dismayed by apparent British unconcern for France's mounting problems as its army shrank by the day. Haig greatly — and understandably — preferred dealing with the seventy-five-year-old Georges Clemenceau, about to become his country's prime minister and usually less fiery. Haig could also be antagonised by his own nation across the Channel. When he travelled to England in April 1916, wishing for speedy agreement of his big push plans, he discovered that everyone was missing, and all troop movement had been curtailed. The Easter holidays were in full swing.

After the Somme battle, Haig did not make an apology for misjudging German fire-power, so exaggerated by machine guns — perhaps commanders-in-chief are consistently weak in this respect — but he continued to applaud rapid-firing weapons as useful adjuncts to military activity. As some 60 per cent of the British casualties by the Somme were subsequently assessed to have been caused by them, he could hardly do otherwise, but he was effusive in his praise.

Machine guns play a great part — almost a decisive part — in modern war, and our Machine Gun Corps has attained considerable proficiency in their use, handling them with great boldness and skill. The highest value of these weapons is displayed on the defensive rather than in the offensive . . . The Machine Gun Corps will increase in importance.

The guns had undoubtedly been critical, if not decisive, but it had been the Germans who had been on the defensive, and were therefore exploiting that advantage. Their machine-gun corps had been training for such an assault over very many years, and then reaped the reward of all that preparation.

Before and during the Somme, which proved to be the longest such fight in Britain's (and the world's) history, Haig was having to meet important individuals. King George V arrived, and then wrote a letter of thanks: 'I have enjoyed my visit to your splendid army . . .'. Lord Northcliffe, proprietor of *The Times*, arrived, expecting and receiving total cooperation from Britain's commander-in-chief, with many lengthy conversations between the two of them. David Lloyd George made several visits, and even in September 1916 despatched fervent congratulations concerning Haig's activities. (Much later he would write of 'the horrible and futile carnage of the Somme'.)

Haig's despatches and diaries are full of meetings, of important lunches here and there, of chateaux and scenery, but hardly a word about casualties, save to say they were worse on the German side and 'a price to be paid' by the British. (Although the Somme was largely a British assault, the Germans' enthusiasm for regaining lost ground boosted their own casualty lists. In one sector the Germans made eleven counter-attacks in a single day.) At all events, precisely 136 days after it had begun with such high hopes, with Kitchener's army no longer afraid they might 'miss out on the fun' (as so many had feared), the last big attack by the Somme was launched. On 13 November forty-three battalions were ordered to advance, and a final slaughtering soon occurred. Shortly afterwards the weather worsened considerably, causing the whole dismal business to grind to a halt. It so happened, back in Kent, that Hiram Maxim's life was also grinding to its end. He died on 24 November 1916, the principal perpetrator of a new form of killing machine that had reached the high point of its capability 160 miles from his bedside. 'Invent something that will help these Europeans kill each other,' the friend had said, and he had done so with skill and enterprise.

No one sounded a retreat when the Somme battle was concluded. Each side kept quiet and licked its wounds, with hundreds of thousands of the fallen keeping quieter still. Allied casualties, of dead, wounded, and missing had been 700,000 (or so), and the vagueness is one further indictment of that battle. Fancy not knowing how many men had succumbed! It is thought that 'about' two-thirds of the whole were British. The German total is believed to have been about 100,000 fewer, with a similar uncertainty on their side.

Back in Britain, when the news was fully absorbed about the monumental losses set against the pitiful gains, and with objectives up and down the line still not achieved, the mood changed dramatically. 'No more Sommes,' became a rallying cry; no more such waste of men (a prayer which was also muttered over in Germany). Until that time there had been a British expectation that the new army would do wonders once fully trained and at the front, that the munitions pouring from the factories would deal a deadly blow, and that Germany's reckless venturing into foreign territory would be triumphantly repelled. After the battle, with the front line more or less where it had been for the past two years, there was disillusionment. The glory had quite gone. The hope had been vanquished in that welter of doomed youth. Therefore when and how would this dreadful war be curtailed?

Had the Somme not been fought, said military analysts, it would have meant the abandonment of Verdun by the French and the breakdown of cooperation with them. The entente therefore still existed after the battle, just as the front line still existed more or less as it had been before the fight began. So what had changed? There had been no breakthrough, and the war's end seemed further away than ever.

On the other hand, it was also plain that everything had changed. 'The illusions of one century had given way to the realism of another,' as Winter and Baggett phrased it (in *The Great War*). 'More than chivalry was lost' on those battlefields. The Somme had broken the mainspring of their old regular army, said the Germans. Despair had crept into the rank and file. The same was true of the inhabitants of the British Empire. Three Australian divisions, recently arrived, lost over 20,000 men. 'If Australians wish to trace their modern suspicion and resentment of the British to a date and a place,' wrote Peter Charlton, Australian historian, 'then July–August 1916 and the ruined village of Pozières are useful points of departure.'

The 'powers that be' were becoming restive, said Britain's commander of the Fourth Army to Haig. Indeed they were, and Britain herself, along with her fighting men, had been transformed. The Somme, it was reported, had been a cultural shock, with supremacy no longer inevitable. Even the songs were altering, with a lingering sadness replacing the former merriment. The haunting 'Roses of Picardy' was written in 1916, and so too 'Take me back to dear old Blighty'. 'Send out me brother, me sister and me mother, but for Gawd's sake don't send me' arrived in 1917 from music halls (where the words had a different meaning). 'Good-bye-ee' also arrived that year, and all four of these songs were quite contradictory in their mood to those of 1914, when volunteering had been the rage. A hospital nurse touchingly describes hearing 'There's a long, long trail a-winding' while watching a stream of ambulances moving in one direction while a train travelled the other way, laden with horses, guns, and men. Such sentiment was increasingly commonplace. 'People, both here and in other countries, are crying out for the war to end,' wrote a German student on 14 July in that dreadful year, 'and yet it does not end. Who is responsible?' He was killed thirteen days later.

For those who knew about it, there was one bright hope as the Somme proceeded that a way had been found to break the deadlock. 'I saw a huge toad-like monster,' said C.E. Crutchley, observing a tank for the first time, 'and at the rear were two rather large wheels.' The slow progress of such behemoths has already been described. There should have been a thousand of them at the Somme, a functioning thousand, and they might well have punched a hole in the enemy's defences. And they should somehow have been able to dodge the enemy's artillery which had such sport with these lumbering 'land battleships' or 'land cruisers', as some were calling them. There were not one thousand because new instruments of war cannot readily be accepted by authority until they have been tested in a battle. Therefore only sixty of the 150 already manufactured were sent to France, only forty-nine were available on 15 September to see action, no more than eighteen managed to reach no man's land, and only nine of those survived. This test of their ability, in which they wasted the element of surprise, was not really sensible or fair, much like despatching only forty-nine soldiers on some major enterprise. 'We are puzzling how best to use them,' said a general before the attack, 'but they are not going to take the British army straight to Berlin as some people imagine.'

Haig had only heard of tanks in December 1915, and had used their existence as one further reason for delaying the great push. He wanted to get hold of more of them. In his despatch following their limited use he was in favour, but somewhat lukewarm.

These cars proved of great value on various occasions, and the personnel in charge of them performed many deeds of remarkable valour.

Richard Holmes, in *The Western Front*, is rather more specific and certainly less flattering.

The tanks could help break into the German position but, short-ranged, slow, prone to breakdown and ditching, bone-cracking and nauseating for their crews, they could not yet assist with the breakout.

Even had they broken through, and found themselves in open country behind the front line, it is possible to wonder whether advantage could have been taken of such an achievement. In theory it was everyone's dream to disrupt the status quo. In practice nothing was in readiness for such advance; there were no further and supplementary lines of tanks, no transport across the mud. The stalemate had become too stale, the trenches too entrenched. Nevertheless tank potential had been observed, and their day would come, with May 1940 in particular showing what tanks could do when properly developed. And properly armed. And unlikely to break down.

The infamous Battle of the Somme is often mentioned as if it alone encapsulated the Great War. It had been so horrendous, and such a carnage, that other battles in other years can pale if set beside it, but these other engagements were by no means trivial. After all, most of those who died during those four long years did not perish during the Somme's long months. Artillery, rifles and machine guns were taking their toll on almost every day, and there were killings galore long before and long after that big push by the gentle River Somme. For example, there had been the Battle of Loos which began on 25 September 1915. With an apologetic tone John French, the first commander of the British Expeditionary Force, reported back to Kitchener when the fight was done.

I deeply regret the heavy casualties which were incurred in this battle, but in view of the great strength of the position, the stubborn defence of the enemy, and the powerful artillery by which he was supported, I do not think they were excessive.

[In this report he gives no details of British casualties, apart from naming some of the generals killed.]

He also could have mentioned the enemy's machine guns. At one place the Germans were astonished to see ten columns of extended lines of infantry 'coming on', as Richard Holmes phrases it, 'as if on parade'.

A target was offered to us (as German reports were later to describe the day) such as had never been seen before, nor even thought possible . . . Never had machine-guns had such straightforward work to do, nor done it so effectively . . . With barrels burning hot and swimming in oil, they traversed to and fro along the enemy's ranks unceasingly: one machine gun alone fired 12,500 rounds that afternoon.

Very soon, with some of the British even managing to reach German wire, the survivors 'began to retire', as the Germans phrased it. In the battle as a whole 43,000 British soldiers were no longer able to do so.

Loos should have served as terrible

warning. Men travelling over open ground will be cut down in their thousands if opposed by machine guns. The Russians and Japanese had proved this point in far-off Manchuria. They had done it with the older weapons available to them. Now machine-gun power had been demonstrated all over again, rather nearer home and with a more competent army (if not the very best) in charge of them. Therefore never, never again send troops, marching, walking, or running, against concentrated rifle and machine-gun fire. Do not even contemplate it. And yet, a mere nine months after Loos, an even greater assembly of men was similarly despatched against similarly withering fire. The Somme was not a mere replication of Loos. It was greatly worse.

The British used gas at Loos, hoping it would punch a hole in the German defences. By now both sides had gas masks, with German machine gunners having the best variety, but it was hoped the British gas would linger around the German lines sufficiently long for the masks to be ineffective. Light wind was required, as it would permit such lingering, but light winds are notoriously fickle. The Germans did suffer in that engagement, but so did 2,632 British soldiers, all victims of British gas (although only seven died). Even if lessons were seemingly unlearned about machine-gun fire, the truth about gas, as an accessory of war, was gaining ground.

The Battle of Loos certainly helped to cause the switch of commanders-in-chief, with French being forced to make way for Haig, and with Haig himself being vigorously outspoken concerning French's deficiencies. A lack of reserves, ready to exploit the British successes which did occur, became — quite rightly — a contentious issue. France's commander, Joffre, ever willing to paint a picture stridently, said of French's dismissal: 'If they do things like that, how can we hope to win the war?' He could perhaps also have said that, if they do things like exposing men to machine-gun fire, they could never win anything.

Books of reminiscences from men of the Machine Gun Corps are reminders that many more battles were fought than the major engagements. The sentences and phrases tell incompletely of each foray, but when accumulated give an idea of attrition between the more famous contests.

Sergeants McLellan and McCullum were reported missing, and no trace of them was ever found . . . The gunners had their first experience of carrying intolerably heavy loads across country which, in peacetime, they would have called impossible . . . the machine gunners were left stranded, and suffered many casualties . . . Both legs smashed, the guns of his section destroyed, he ordered the few surviving gunners to get back and leave him . . . To our amazement the other five Germans trooped up from the dug-out with arms raised . . . Sergeant Beard with two guns did great havoc among masses of enemy troops before they deployed; he was wounded during the subsequent Boche attack . . .

As daylight came it was seen that the German machine gun nests had not been captured . . . By mid-morning the situation of the Queens was desperate; they had run out of ammunition . . . The 16th K.R.R.C. attempted to supply them and, despite heavy losses, carried bombs and ammunition to them . . . As the men came back, the well posted enemy machine guns picked them off like rabbits, and scarcely a man returned unwounded . . .

One machine gunner, serving near the Messines Ridge in 1917, encountered the men who had been tunnelling nearby.

I well remember seeing the sappers, looking very begrimed, and me feeling sorry they had to work in such appalling conditions . . . As zero hour approached [for detonating the explosives] my heart beats thumped . . . Then in a flash it all happened . . . The earth shook and all hell was let loose, as nineteen mines were exploded . . . No words can adequately describe the horrors of that cataclysm. Vast masses of earth and mangled bodies were hurled skywards, and surviving masses of the enemy ran about dazed and demented by the most awful upheaval in the history of warfare . . . I was struck dumb by what I was witnessing . . . Then I heard my section officer shouting, 'Fire, dammit, Fire!' . . . The bullets spurted out, and there I sat doing — quite mechanically — what I had been trained to do, traversing fire.

Euphemisms are everywhere. 'Heavy losses' mean dead friends. A dog-fight up above means pilots burning in their planes.

'We were outflanked.' 'I wrapped them in their blankets prior to removal.' The Northamptonshire Regiment 'resisted valiantly'. 'Our men held out until eight o'clock.' It was a 'heroic but helpless stand'. 'No Britisher can read without a pang of pity . . . how they held out against overwhelming odds. . . .'

And on and on. It all means death, with everything happening again and again, the advancing and retreating, their advancing and their retreating. Whether losses were massive, or light, exceptional or heavy, it was all so repetitive. A reader's mind is numbed, just as the soldiers' minds were numbed, day after day and week after week, as the remorselessness continued. 'C Company resisted valiantly until nearly all of them were casualties, and the survivors were surrounded and surrendered.' When would this bleeding war be over?

Passchendaele (or the Third Battle of Ypres) is the next major name, in terms of blood-letting and horror, after the Somme. It started on 31 July 1917 and ended that November, almost exactly a year since the Somme offensive had also ground to a halt. It was initiated because the French army was in increasing jeopardy, the Russian situation had become yet worse, and destruction of the Merchant Navy lifeline supplying Britain had become yet more traumatic. John Jellicoe, then Britain's First Sea Lord, was all for haste in conquering the Germans. Do not mention 1918 as a feasibility, he kept on saying, as there will be no 1918 on offer if the U-boats maintain their grip. For every four ships leaving Britain, only three returned. The Ypres salient, so much nearer the Channel than either the Somme or Loos, was particularly subject to water-logging if the weather grew severe, but the British had to chance their luck on that score. Delay until the spring, with the Americans then abundant, was impossible to contemplate.

Douglas Haig, still commander of the British armies, had reason for a certain optimism. The Somme's lessons had been learned. No more would the enemy's machine guns be permitted to cut swathes through British infantry quite so readily. Munitions and armaments were in good supply. The Royal Flying Corps was in better shape than ever, with its better aircraft no longer easy victims for German flyers. British artillery had developed its creeping barrage well; it now advanced skilfully as and when it should do so. Tanks were more plentiful, so too light machine guns, mortars, and grenades. Those mines at Messines had disrupted the German lines. Everything would be as fine as could be expected, provided the weather held — but it did not hold. The battle began on 31 July during the wettest summer ever known in that area. Autumn was no better. Men had difficulty even in reaching the front, let alone fighting an enemy. The wounded crawled into shell holes and, if unable to move, were then drowned when the water-level rose. Tanks became bogged, just as mules and men became embedded. It was not warfare, as generally understood. It was like nothing anyone had known. It was more mud than Armageddon. It was Passchendaele.

Duff Cooper wrote that soldiers in action normally expect progress by each evening, but those who fought in that desolation 'awoke at morning with no such hope'. The battle was 'similar to others, but longer than most, with conditions more unfavourable, the sufferings greater, and the results less demonstrable'. As for machine guns, they were 'not so overwhelmingly important, as at the Somme, despite the ground being speckled with German pill-boxes'. These concrete emplacements were an improvement on the old and relatively unprotected 'nests', and the British were rightly wary of them, treating them with caution — or grenades.

On the positive side, in Cooper's opinion, although the territorial objectives were not reached, the French army had been saved, Great Britain's tactical position had improved, the British coast had been protected, and the anti-submarine position had been bettered during the interim. Erich von Ludendorff, about to plan Germany's spring offensive of 1918, was more brutal in his assessment of that Third Battle of Ypres.

> It was no longer life at all. It was mere unspeakable suffering . . . Rifles and machine guns were jammed with mud . . . Despair was creeping into the rank and file.

Just as the Somme battle, adds Cooper, had broken the mainspring of the old German army, so did the autumn of 1917 undermine the resisting power of the German nation.

Both sides now possessed formidable numbers of machine guns. Both sides were skilled in the use of such weapons, whether they were of the lightweight kind or the heavier tripod variety. The machine gun had been incorporated into strategic thinking and had been generally adopted. Britain's Machine Gun Corps, despite its difficult birth, had grown in stature.

Machine guns had proved themselves yet more destructive of human life once they had been given opportunity. In that First World War, notably on the open land around the River Somme, they were given that opportunity as never before. They had killed and killed as they were meant to do. That was the purpose of this particular form of human inventiveness; there was no other. Its day had truly dawned.

# Chapter 15

# From Lewis
# to Browning

Samuel Colt, Richard Gatling, and Hiram Maxim, such a critical triumvirate in the business of rapid-firing weapons, were unequal in almost every other sphere. Colt, right from adolescence, pursued his revolving chambers obsessively. He became tremendously wealthy, and died young. Gatling, inventor and doctor, became forthright about revolving barrels, but less fixedly. He also became rich, although not overwhelmingly or flamboyantly, and died at eighty-five. As for Maxim, his gun was only one of his very many inventions, it gaining him a lot of money, much of which he lost on other ventures, and he died at seventy-six. The three men were all American-born, but their early years were spent entirely differently. They were each propelled by their personal dynamos, and not one was involved with the

428

military, save obliquely via the need to sell their wares.

Then along comes Isaac Lewis, quite distinct yet again from his three predecessors. He did not really have to struggle, as Colt had done so impecuniously, as Gatling had to do so lengthily, and as Maxim had to do most energetically against established rivals. Of course there were some initial difficulties, which all inventors have to face. Lewis was consistently 'slapped with rejections by ignorant hacks', but his progress in advancing his gun was relatively swift. He planned it in 1911, manufactured several examples in 1912, took these to Europe in 1913, started a major production line in 1914, welcomed the British adoption of his invention as standard light machine gun in 1915, and knew that 40,000 of his weapons were in service on many fronts by 1916. All gun men need a war to help them on their way, and Lewis's timing was fortuitous. He was also well acquainted with the military, having joined the U.S. Army aged twenty-two, and rising to colonel by his fifties. In 1913 he retired from this army life to pursue his growing business interests but sensibly retained and cultivated his military contacts.

Of all the machine guns produced for Britain's use during the First World War, the proportion of Lewis weapons altered from 3 per cent of the total in 1914 to 60 per cent in 1915, 65 per cent in 1916, 57 per cent in 1917, and 51 per cent in 1918. Throughout the conflict the average Lewis proportion of the machine gun total was 55 per cent. Contrarily the Vickers (formerly Maxim) guns, although providing 97 per cent of all rapid-firing weapons produced by the British in 1914, fell as a ratio to 32 per cent by 1918. The percentages varied as and when different tasks and tactics were developed and amended for the different guns. The more that Vickers weapons increased their range, the more they became a form of artillery. The more that infantry favoured the extremely lightweight Lewis weapons, the more they were welcomed in attack over the Vickers weapons, whose transport was always relatively cumbersome. Each Lewis gun weighed twenty-six pounds, as against much more than that for just the tripod of the Vickers weapon. By the war's ending, 133,104 Lewis weapons had been produced for British use, this huge figure affirming their very positive role. It has been estimated that between five and eight billion rounds were fired throughout the war solely by ground-based Lewis guns.

But the Germans had also decided they needed a light machine gun for their infantry as an alternative to the heavy, water-cooled, Maxim-type weapon. One example was the Parabellum, although the air force (and airships) had prior claim on it as on all lightweight products. There was also the Bergmann gun, which was ruggedly built, relatively cheap, and much admired by investigating ordnance men after the Armistice. In general, the Germans were quicker off the mark in desiring a lightweight machine gun, just as they had been quick to realise the merits of the heavier brand, notably in defence. Nevertheless, they admitted that the Lewis gun did sterling work on behalf of the Allies, and were keen to use the specimens they captured to bolster the 08/15s in their possession.

Isaac Newton Lewis, allegedly christened in honour of the British scientist, was born near New Salem, Pennsylvania, on 12 October 1858. This was three years before Colt's death and also three before Gatling started to think of a rapid-firing weapon. When aged twenty-one, Lewis was a teacher in Kansas, but wishing for a more active form of work. In the following year he was accepted (against strong competition) by the West Point Military Academy in New York state and graduated in 1884. Engineering and designing then became his dominant interest, with a range-finder being patented on his behalf four years later. He toured Europe at the start of the twentieth century, having been instructed to examine and assess all European ordnance. On his return, and after designing a much applauded harbour defence system for San Francisco, he unfortunately acquired enemies in Washington. The trouble seems to have occurred solely because he was not only successful but had also crossed swords with his superior officer. At all events, he was posted to distant and unrewarding locations. As other pioneering individuals have written following their similar experiences with officialdom, Lewis wondered: 'Why is it that some of the biggest men in military and government positions have the smallest minds?' Soon afterwards, following pressure from certain friendlier individuals with rather bigger minds, he was returned from the relative wilderness of his 'limbo posting' to the nation's capital.

Isaac Lewis's gun story truly starts with Samuel N. McClean, an inventive doctor of Cleveland, Ohio. He practised medicine for eleven years but then discovered that his creative work was more absorbing. Quite what a medical man was doing tinkering with machine guns can best be answered by remembering Dr Gatling. Many of McClean's words echo those of his therapeutic predecessor.

A machine gun is a noble thing as the mechanism which accomplishes the greatest amount of human destruction in the shortest possible time with the least difficulty . . . [It] may make war obsolete, for what rational man would throw his life away senselessly in front of one?

McClean's enthusiasm for nobility caused him to spend hundreds and thousands of investors' dollars on a nineteen-pound weapon. Additional investors managed to keep the business solvent during the first decade of the twentieth century, and everything changed when Lewis got to hear of it. McClean's commercial mismanagement forced him out of his own concern, and he went to work with General Motors. He therefore leaves the machine gun story, along with all his patents. These were taken over by the Automatic Arms Company, which was formed in 1910.

When Lewis joined this company's team, he started work to make McClean's good ideas more practical. In particular, he had to stop the gun from coming to a halt after firing only forty rounds. He worked hard, but the first official demonstration of his amended version was 'failure' and 'disaster'. These were the inventor's dismissive words before he hurried back to his drawing board. Only one month after that dismal showing, and as he wished for a more dramatic — and successful — exhibition, Lewis arranged for his latest weapon to be fired from an aircraft. This was not only prescient of him; it also achieved good publicity. Making a reliable gun from McClean's faulty efforts in so short a time was one astonishment. Putting it on board a flying machine was yet another.

On 7 June 1912, less than nine years after the Wrights' first brief flights at Kitty Hawk, an angled Lewis gun was fired from a Grahame-White two-seater biplane. This craft, together with its fixed armament, ascended from the Signal Corps Aviation School at College Park, Maryland (conveniently near to Washington). A cloth, six feet square, had been placed on the ground as an aiming point, and the aircraft was flown 250 feet above it. Lewis's gun had been bolted into position on the plane, and — astonishingly in those pioneering circumstances — several bullets found their mark, with one report even asserting five hits out of the forty-seven rounds fired. As there was no way for either the pilot or his gunner to see if success and accuracy had been achieved, with bullet impact on the ground or through the cloth quite invisible, the two men thought of firing at a nearby lake. They flew over it to get a better idea of their gun's behaviour, and were well pleased by their aiming capability, with splashes indicating where the bullets were arriving. (Coincidentally, this all occurred one week after Wilbur Wright, flight's crucial pioneer, had died from typhoid, aged only forty-five.)

An amateur cameraman was there at College Park to record the historic event, but he missed the actual flight. Instead he photographed the pilot and (another) gunner after the plane had landed, with newspapers then giving this picture and its story major coverage. Everyone who learned of it seemed delighted by the display, save for Washington's Board of Ordnance. Its director was patronising, stating that flying men should be allowed to have their fun, but junior army officers (such as that pilot) should never assist inventors to make money from their creations.

Lewis, still in the service, was stung, immediately replying that he would refuse any U.S. royalties arising from his weapon. Soon afterwards, perhaps encouraged to do so by that Ordnance affront, he considered the time had come for him to leave the army — which he did on 20 September 1913. It was also, in his opinion, time to sail for Europe, much as Colt, Gatling, and Maxim had done before him. Whereas Colt's first visit had been in 1849, Gatling's in 1867, and Maxim's in 1881 (before he had even made a gun), those three particular years had all been relatively peaceful. Europe in 1913 was wholly different, with the tinder-box just waiting for a spark. Indeed, an American-designed auto-loading pistol proved to be that detonator when a Serbian anarchist used one on 28 June 1914 to shoot dead the Hapsburg heir in Sarajevo. The war would begin five weeks later when Germany sent fifty-four divisions marching into Belgium.

Isaac Lewis took four guns with him as

he crossed the Atlantic nine months before that assassination, and his demonstrations with them worked well before eager audiences. A Belgian company at Liège soon offered to mass-produce his weapon, and Armes Automatiques Lewis was then created. Other offers for manufacture came from an English company and later, following these successes, from the Savage Arms Company of the United States. By early August 1914 Lewis was involved with half a dozen armament manufacturers, most notably the Birmingham Small Arms Company in England. Production then leapt ahead, with countries other than Britain excited by the new weapon. B.S.A. purchased more land to make room for another factory, and during March 1915 a hundred guns a week were being delivered. By the end of 1915, that number had risen to 300, and by March 1916 it was 500 per week. Isaac Lewis and his weapon were hardly making war obsolete, as McClean had hoped such lethal weapons would, because rational men were indeed flinging themselves at every kind of gun, and their lives were being thrown away in awesome numbers. Samuel McClean would not have understood, any more than the soldiers themselves understood, how such madness was occurring.

Lewis's income became immeasurably greater than his colonel's pay had been. However, he honoured his former pledge to Washington that he would make no money from his own government. He regularly forwarded cheques to the U.S. Treasury, as and when its armed services purchased his weaponry. His first big American contract was agreed in May 1917, only a month after President Wilson had signed the declaration of war, and .30-calibre Lewis's were then ordered in massive numbers from the Utica, N.Y., factory at $239.89 per gun. Interestingly, after the weapons had been assembled and tested, they were stripped down into their component parts for easier packing and transport. During reassembly in Europe no effort was made to use the same pieces from the original assembly for the same gun. Complete interchangeability of parts, desired from the eighteenth century onwards, admired as a possibility by Thomas Jefferson and so much advocated by ordnance men in the interim, had finally arrived.

McClean's original gun, as outlined in his patents, was heavy. It stood firmly upon a tripod, and was water-cooled. Isaac Lewis, as soon as he became involved, was determined on lightness, seeing no reason why automatic guns needed to be cumbersome. He favoured the notion of air cooling, thus getting rid of water's weight, and also welcomed a drum feed for the cartridges, as McClean had originally planned. Most significantly, he saw little reason for massive and concentrated firepower. The drum he designed contained forty-seven bullets, or six seconds' worth of firing. Such a lightweight weapon could be fired by a single individual — unlike Maxim's bulky arrangement, which needed a No.2 to organise the belted ammunition (and more companions to bring up the great quantities of cartridges being so speedily consumed). The lightness — twenty-six pounds and six ounces — of the Lewis meant that a single man could readily carry the gun. Its modest dimensions also made it relatively inconspicuous; the gun could serve in defence without being blatantly exposed.

The *Machine Gunners' Handbook*, essential reading for would-be gunners and their instructors, not only gives crucial information about the Lewis weapon, but also does so in a tone as revealing about the army's methods as about this aspect of its ordnance.

# LEWIS MACHINE GUN
## Method of imparting instruction.
### GENERAL DESCRIPTION

*Name.* — Lewis Machine Gun. .303.
Air-cooled and gas-operated.
*Weight.* — 25 lbs.
*The gun is worked by two forces:* —
1. The force of the explosion.
2. The return spring.

NOTE. — Do not talk too much about things that cannot be seen, wait for these until the gun is stripped.

*The Gun is divided into two portions:* —
1. The stationary portions.
2. The moving portions.

The *stationary* portions consist of: —
(a) The barrel group;
(b) The body group.

(a) The barrel group consists of: —

i. The *barrel.*
It is threaded at the front end to take the *barrel mouthpiece* which has a left-handed thread, to prevent it being detatched from the barrel during firing.

A *gas vent* is bored in it 4 inches from the muzzle, to allow the gas to pass into the gas chamber.

A square thread is cut at the rear end for attachment to the *body*.

A *stud* is placed in front of the square thread to . . .

And on and on for quite a few more pages, with the sergeant-instructor's clipped intonation when passing on the details still clearly audible.

The fact of air-cooling made the gun extremely suitable for use in aircraft. Two British fliers first test-fired a machine gun from a British aeroplane on 27 November 1913, some seventeen months after the similar American achievement. Once again officialdom was unimpressed, and those in charge made certain that the British planes crossing the Channel to go to war, as they did from 13 August 1914, were unarmed. Nine days afterwards a couple of British airmen, using their own initiative, ascended with a Lewis gun, fired at a German Albatross, achieved no visible hits and were rebuked on their return. Authority had decided that, as an aircraft's only purpose was reconnaissance, aerial combat would be a distraction from that important task. Therefore, with airborne machine guns strictly forbidden, certain pilots achieved unofficial firings with rifles, pistols and, on one occasion, a shotgun. No German aircraft were actually imperilled by such fusillades until 5 October 1914 when two French airmen in a Voisin 'pusher' achieved success. (Aircraft were either pulled by their propellers, the favoured system, or pushed by them, with the advantage of pushers being freedom for a machine gun at the front.) By this time German airmen were also armed, notably with a Mexican device known as a Mondragon. This was more of a self-loading rifle, and was soon supplanted by fully automatic weapons.

In 1914 the French did not consider airborne machine guns to be suitable for ground strafing, preferring the notion of flechettes. These six-inch steel darts could be dropped in bundles of 1,000 and, in theory, would then scatter to inflict great damage on massed infantry. If released from a height of 1,500 feet, it was believed they could go straight through a horse. Presumably a horse would merely stand there, not expecting aerial punishment, but the German military soon dispersed when seeing that steel arrows were about to come their way. This much-vaunted secret weapon (bringing back memories of the mitrailleuse) was soon replaced by machine guns when strafing was desired. In fact, this also was not often an agreeable option, with so many riflemen firing back, quite lethally, at the aircraft overhead.

For British aviators the airborne machine gun ruling vanished long before 1914 was over, with the lightweight air-cooled Lewis gun installed as the weapon of choice. Initially it could only be fired backwards, or down or up, because of the forward propeller, and the whole procedure of such combat was markedly haphazard. The first British aeroplane actually designed for aerial fighting was the Vickers FB5 Gun-Bus, the earliest of this type reaching France in February 1915. Blessed with a maximum speed of seventy miles an hour, this two-man pusher aircraft possessed a forward-firing machine gun operated by a gunner in an exposed compartment at the nose. Some French aircraft, from April 1915 onwards, could even fire forwards through the rotating propeller, but only because there were metallic deflector plates to prevent unwelcome damage to the spinning blades. These had been designed by Roland Garros (a famous French aviator who had set up an astonishing altitude record of 15,000 feet in 1912). He had learned that, at a normal rate of fire, only 2 per cent of bullets would need to be deflected — before they ricocheted harmlessly elsewhere. This system permitted him to be extremely successful in aerial combat. When ill fortune came his way, and he was shot down, the Germans were careful to examine his plane. Garros soon escaped, and fought again, but the Germans then considerably improved the crude Garros procedure for firing forwards.

Anthony H.G. Fokker was the man who took most note of the French deflector system, but disapprovingly. Instead he created a synchronised machine gun, cunningly designed to fire its bullets between the blades, and it was first developed for his Fokker monoplanes. Fokker, a Dutchman born in Java in 1890, was already designing aircraft and flying them when war broke out — and he was only twenty-four. The interrupter gear he devised for firing forward without damaging the propeller had originally been patented before the war by Franz Schneider, a Swiss engineer. As hardly anyone then thought of aircraft — as against airships — becoming fighting

444

machines, there was no interest in his idea. Fokker first offered his undoubtedly brilliant services to his own country, and then to France and Britain, but only Germany wished to employ him. Having done so, it was then sceptical about the Dutchman's interrupter ideas. After all, with propellers rotating at 1,200 times a minute, this meant that a six-inch space became available for bullets 2,400 times a minute. Oswald Boelke, on his way to becoming the first true fighter-pilot leader of the war, then courageously tried it out and was delighted that it worked. Afterwards Max Immelmann did so, again with great success, causing the General Staff to become hugely and suddenly enthusiastic. These two German pilots were both killed in 1916, but Fokker's innovative creation quickly led to the deaths of innumerable British fliers from August 1915 onwards. (The firing details about this system had actually been published in the April 1914 issue of *Scientific American*, but no one then had apparently noticed this article's significance.)

For some ten months after the Fokker monoplane's first success, in a period known as the Fokker Scourge, these forward-firing planes were outstandingly triumphant. The French attempted to rival the German capability by installing its Hotchkiss machine gunner in a false nose forward of the tractor (as against pusher) propeller of a Spad machine. A wire frame behind this gunner prevented him from leaning his head too far backwards into the whirring blades. Britain attempted to defy the Fokkers by introducing aircraft of similar ability, such as the DH2. This single-seater pusher fighter for the Royal Flying Corps was the first to be equally blessed as a forward firer, with its Lewis gun mounted forward of the pilot. The gun was not only slightly manoeuvrable, and firmly bolted to the plane, but it was also much more profitable for the pilot to aim himself, his aircraft, and his gun at an enemy aircraft than using a wide-ranging swivelling system.

By then this aerial Lewis machine gun possessed a drum containing ninety-six cartridges, as against the usual forty-seven-round drum for ground fighting. With weight always a problem for every form of aircraft, any lightening was appreciated. The stripped-down aerial Lewis, which no longer had a cooling jacket, only weighed seventeen and a half pounds, as against twenty-six pounds for the standard version. Each aircraft was equipped with ten or so spare ammunition drums, these adding a total of twenty-six pounds to the load, but of course this weight diminished as the bullets were consumed. Twin Lewis's were sometimes installed in parallel, but good fliers preferred a single weapon as this was easier to control and, of course, weighed half as much.

With aerial warfare growing ever more aggressive, and fighting on the ground showing no sign of lessening, the Lewis production line had to be extremely active. At Utica the American plant became yet more so after the United States had joined the conflict. By May 1918 this factory had delivered over 16,000 Lewis guns, with more than 10,000 of these specifically designed for aircraft use. In only six more months, leading up to the war's conclusion, that production figure had risen to 34,000. The infantry welcomed the weapon because it could be carried into action by one man, and could therefore be brought up promptly. Only a few seconds were necessary to change drums, and short bursts of firing were often all that were required. Just as magazines had extended a rifle's usefulness, by permitting a greater rate of firing, so did the Lewis gun go one step further. It was almost three times as heavy as a rifle but could fire its forty-seven bullets in the time a rifle needed to fire just one, the rifle's bolt having to be pulled back and then pushed forward to discharge each round. According to J. David Truby, in *The Lewis Gun*, Britain's General Staff concluded that the Lewis was the 'finest weapon for frontline trench strafing, both offensively and defensively'. Whether it was called a light machine gun or an automatic rifle — there was always dispute — this divergence of opinion emphasised its novel role. For soldiers, who cared little about nomenclature, it was a very handy device and good to employ.

When tanks were introduced, the Lewis gun often served as their secondary or even primary armament. There were three to five such weapons for every vehicle, these operating through ports at the front and on each side. This form of fire-power was taken to extremes with the later Mark V versions of Britain's new weapon. A dozen or so machine gunners were then employed. This may have worried the enemy, with so many bullets being launched their way, but such fire-power was not wildly welcomed, even by those within the tank. One veteran, according to

Truby, said the internal atmosphere soon contained '75 per cent exhaust fumes, 13 per cent cordite fumes, 10 per cent perspiration odour, and 2 per cent oxygen'.

This kind of adulteration occurred within three minutes of the attack and, by then, 'half the Lewis gunners were already returning their breakfasts'. If the tank took ten minutes to reach its objective, as was more than likely, 'not one member of the squad of gunners was [then] capable of lifting his weapon'. Apart from this undoubted defect, the Lewis guns protruding from each armoured machine tended to have their cooling jackets peppered with bullet holes before too long, and this damage rendered them useless. With the guns becoming impotent, the gunners insensible, and the tanks themselves often failing in their mobility, it becomes easier to understand why this wonder weapon did not achieve the immediate and longed-for victory which had been anticipated.

The third type of machine gun used in substantial numbers — 35,381 all told — by the British Army during the First World War was the Hotchkiss weapon. Its story is marginally more straightforward than those of the other two, and starts with a certain Baron Adolph von Odkolek, a captain in the Austrian army. Wishing to emulate Maxim's undoubted fame, and after circumventing all the Maxim patents, he too designed a rapid-firing weapon and sought to have it manufactured. At St Denis, France, Benjamin Berkeley Hotchkiss had set up business. He was yet another Colt-trained American who then chose to abandon the United States. Nineteen years later he died in 1885 aged fifty-nine, with his gun-making business then remaining as the Société Anonyme des Anciens Établissements, Hotchkiss et Cie. In France this organisation did well with a revolving-barrel machine gun, as well as a cannon shell, but the firm was struggling when the Austrian captain chose to visit it in 1893.

By then the company had appointed another American, Laurence V. Benét, as head designer. This man's father, prominent in developing cartridge cases, had risen to become the U.S. Army's Chief of Ordnance after the Civil War. Benét Senior then recommended that his son, Laurence, should try his luck in Europe. (There is a relentless pattern to the machine-gun story. Get born in America. Acquire that nation's enthusiasm and ability for invention. Start inventing. Create new designs. Realise that Europe holds more purchasing opportunity. And cross the Atlantic to take advantage of it.)

Having been a friend of Benjamin Hotchkiss many years earlier, the elder Benét suggested that his boy should join that man's French company, which by then had taken on board and promoted a young Frenchman named Henri Mercié. This apprentice had shown much skill and enterprise in looking after the company's power plant, a stationary ex-railway locomotive parked next to the factory. Neither the younger Benét nor Mercié was particularly excited by von Odkolek's weapon, but they realised it did possess a couple of merits covered by patents. These were then purchased outright, and the catalytic baron quickly disappears from the story, much as McClean would do. By 1895, after redesigning the Austrian captain's version, the Franco-American Hotchkiss team had created a simple (only thirty-eight parts), extremely lightweight (twenty pounds), gas-operated (as against recoil-operated) machine gun. In honour of their company's founder, they named this weapon the Hotchkiss. Confusingly, while this title was adopted by certain countries, such as Britain, others such as France and the

United States preferred to call it the Benét-Mercié (although those awkward accents tended to disappear in America). Whatever the name, the weapon was capable of slow automatic fire, up to 100 rounds per minute, or rapid fire of 500–600 rounds. Its cartridges were fed by metallic clips rather than canvas belts.

Laurence Benét was compelled to return home when the Spanish-American war broke out, and he was soon serving as ensign in the U.S. Navy. With that war's conclusion, and after his return to France, he learned that some of his company's Hotchkiss weapons had been sold to the French government. Its colonial department had expressed particular interest in the gun's air-cooled system because, when fighting in the hot and arid African territories, all water-cooled arrangements, as with the Maxim, were at a disadvantage. At more or less the same time, directly encouraged by the former naval ensign during his tour of duty, the United States was showing a modest interest in the weapon, and it initiated official trials at the start of the new century. Perhaps the Gatlings had helped to pave the way with their success in Cuba. Or perhaps the extreme lightness of the Benét, as against the far heavier and more cumbersome Gatling, had been more influential. As a third, and possibly greater incentive for adopting the Hotchkiss/Benét weapon, there was soon its triumphant use by the Japanese in their war against Russia, where the Hotchkiss had — in machine-gun terms — done very well indeed.

What did not go so well for the weapon was wholehearted American approval. (Once again the pattern prevails. Gatlings had been more speedily adopted in Europe, and Maxims were only half-heartedly welcomed in America.) The Benét-Mercié, as most U.S. documents now described the Hotchkiss weapon, was not officially adopted by Washington until 1909, but much wrangling then occurred over how it should be used. British disinterest in machine guns was distantly influential, and more so than German interest in rapid-firing weaponry — which, by then, was increasingly enthusiastic. The United States did possess over 200 Maxims but had not expressed much enthusiasm for them. Only in 1911 did the U.S. receive its first consignment of the Benét-Merciés but — once again — the guns did not meet with general approval. They failed to create as much fire-power as a group of riflemen equal in number to those who were necessary for working the gun.

Unfortunately, as Benét pointed out, the gunners had only very recently been introduced to the novel weapon. Therefore the comparison was hardly fair. It was also mounted on a bipod (good for lightness) rather than a tripod (better for stability). Therefore it did not shoot particularly accurately, even in the hands of experienced gunners. Captain Douglas MacArthur (to become renowned in World War Two and Korea) gathered thoughts about the gun from a general survey. These 'held a unanimity of opinion that in its present form the piece cannot be regarded as satisfactory'. The U.S. Congress also became involved, debating whether Britain's Vickers gun was not in fact to be preferred. For one reason or another, there was considerable delay. As David A. Armstrong put it in *Bullets and Bureaucrats*, this

> meant that in early 1917 the American army did not have a satisfactory machine gun in its inventory . . . During the last week of June 1917 the vanguard of the American Expeditionary Force landed in France . . . neither trained nor equipped for the fighting that had been going on in Europe for almost

three years . . . Illustrative of this condition were the machine-gun units, which were outfitted with the Benét-Mercié model 1909 gun, a weapon that had been officially recognised as unsatisfactory in 1913 and superseded by the Vickers gun in 1914.

Unable to get the Vickers guns it needed, the U.S. Army looked again at the Lewis gun, a weapon it had been offered in 1911 and had then rejected. It so happened that the U.S. was then also looking, rather more importantly, at a complete modernisation of the entire American military system. This, quite understandably, kept the General Staff fully occupied. As for machine guns, and their deployment and use, those decisions were compelled to wait until Americans were fighting in France and learning the hard way what was actually required. Just as the Japanese had discovered in 1904, and as the British had discovered rather less speedily after 1914, personal experience is always the best teacher. The Germans had learned by proxy, having earnestly studied events in Manchuria, and the Germans had a great machine-gun advantage when World War One began. They were only to lose the fight after their opponents had discovered such information for themselves.

The list of big names in the early history of the rapid-firing business is already lengthy — Samuel Colt, Elisha Root, Richard Gatling, William Gardner, Thorsten Nordenfelt, Hiram Maxim, Albert Vickers, Benjamin Hotchkiss, Isaac Lewis, Laurence Benét, Henri Mercié — but one more must now be added, a man often described as the very best gun-maker the world has ever seen.

John Moses Browning was born forty-one years after Colt, and thirty-seven after Gatling. He therefore arrived in a world more accustomed to personal weaponry. Indeed, his father was a professional Colt-trained gunsmith (yes, Colt again). Unlike the eastern gun-makers, he actually lived out west, where gunfire was such a familiar sound. Utah was very much frontier territory, with armament a crucial ingredient for individual defence, for hunting, for staying alive. People did need guns, and Browning senior was happy to supply them. The first repeating rifle was not only fashioned by him in his store, but then sold by him extensively. He had set up shop at 2461 Washington Avenue, Ogden, and he was prospering. Later he moved to a bigger establishment nearer the centre of town.

This inventive father was also a Mormon. He had travelled west with many others of his faith to escape persecution. The trek to Utah occurred after Joseph Smith, the Mormon founder, had been killed in jail by an assassin in 1847. The new Mormon leader of the day, Brigham Young, was then appointed governor of Utah territory. As for Browning, he soon put down roots not far to the north of the more famous Mormon settlement of Salt Lake City. Like others of his community, he practised polygamy, producing twelve children with his first wife, and then ten more with his next two wives. John Moses Browning, his famous son, was the first child of the second marriage.

J.M. Browning was therefore different from predecessor gun-makers, such as Colt and Gatling, having been born into the business. He received little formal schooling, but certainly learned about weapons, making his first rifle out of spare parts when ten years old. His upbringing occurred within a home whose frontage was part workshop and part sales department, and whose interior must have been more than occupied by all those siblings and their mothers. When he reached the age of twenty, J.M. Browning was shooting with a gun of his own construction which, according to his proud father, was the best that man had ever seen. The son's motto from an early age was 'Make it strong enough, then double it'. Having reached adulthood, he and four of his brothers, Matt, Ed, George, and Sam, set up business professionally. Life was hard, but their rifles were cheap (at $25 each) and very, very good.

Everything would change dramatically when T.G. Bennett, president of the Winchester Repeating Arms Company, encountered one of the Ogden weapons. He promptly travelled from New England across to Utah, quite an undertaking in the early 1880s, and not what presidents of large concerns often did, particularly without prior consultation. But he had seen the rifle, wished to meet its maker and wanted to involve him with the Winchester company. His arrival at the Ogden railroad station can perhaps best be described by reporting the various conversations which are supposed to have followed:

Bennett: Can you direct me to the
    Browning factory?
Attendant: There's no such thing here
    in Ogden.

Bennett: There has to be, and I've come 2,000 miles to find it.

Attendant: Perhaps you mean the store on Main Street?

Bennett (after arriving at the store): I'd like to talk with John Browning.

Man in store: That'll be my brother John; you'll find him upstairs.

Bennett (after going up, and then coming down): There's only one young man up there working at a lathe.

Man in store: Yup, that's him, that's my brother John.

The subsequent meeting transformed the Browning Brothers business, and certainly altered the finances of Bennett's company. For the sum of $8,000, Bennett bought the patents of the gun he had seen back home. The 'Winchester 1885' then became the most widely used single-shot gun of the era. As for John Browning, the massive injection of funds meant that, thenceforth, he could work full-time on gun design, and not have to worry about day-to-day business. The Winchester/Browning partnership would last for almost twenty years, most profitably for both sides. Bennett's impulsive train journey had paid off handsomely.

The Winchester factory at Hartford, Connecticut (yes, Hartford again) was busily churning out Win-Chest-Ers — as John Wayne drawled their name — during all that time. John Browning's brother Matthew, although interested in guns, was more of a marketing man, whereas John was more designer and creator. On their father's early death, these two then looked after the business, with 'J.M. Browning and Bro. Guns, Pistols, Amunition & Fishing Tackle', in large lettering above the front door.

The next rifle offered to Hartford became the 1886 Winchester. For its patent rights the Utah inventor was paid $50,000, causing him to exclaim that 'it was more money than there was in Ogden'. John Moses Browning had married in 1879 and would produce ten children (with a single wife). Thanks to Hartford, and with his finances in good order, he found the opportunity to take two years off from all gun activity. During that time he became a Mormon missionary, and toured the southern U.S. while promoting the Church of Latter-Day Saints. When that work was satisfactorily accomplished, he returned to gun-making and in 1892 he created the

1892 Winchester. This was much lighter than the weapon of 1886 and widely favoured by, among others, Robert Peary during his polar expeditions and Annie Oakley in her Wild West performances.

The Winchester Company continued to snap up the Browning designs, with ten more in the next two years. It often did so only to prevent any opposing company from getting hold of them. The weapons chosen by Bennett for mass production certainly did well, with the 1894 Winchester becoming the most popular lever-action gun of all time (more than five million of the model were made and sold). By 1900 Winchester had bought forty-four gun designs, but had only manufactured ten of them. Both Winchester and Browning were doing well out of the liaison, but the fact that Browning's guns were known as Winchesters may have irked. Anyhow, after wishing to become independent of Winchester, and having then failed to link up with Remingtons, another gun company, the man from Ogden, Utah — much to everyone's understandable surprise — chose to set up business with Fabrique Nationale, the Belgian armaments factory at Liège.

Not only did Browning promptly arrive

there, as one more U.S. gun man excited by Europe, but he swiftly revitalised this ailing company. For the next twenty years *'le maître'* (as they called him) would spend several months each year designing, creating, and manufacturing guns in Belgium. Overall he would register 128 patents and produce more than a hundred different weapons. Unlike Maxim and Gatling, who invented in other directions, but more like Colt, he was single-mindedly devoted to weaponry. His pistols became popular in Europe, and one of his creations had the dubious distinction of helping to precipitate World War One when Gavrilo Princip used a Browning automatic so lethally on 28 June 1914.

Browning's first gun designed for rapid fire was not such a revolutionary event in his life, as it was for Maxim and Gatling; it was merely one more kind of gun. Nevertheless it was distinct from his normal run of weaponry, and was allegedly inspired by reeds parting in front of a rifle's bullet when it hurtled past them. (Biographers have often made great play of John Browning's middle name being Moses, with that namesake of antiquity so linked to bulrushes.) At his workshop the machine gun's creator tested the reed observation in

1889 by placing a heavy square of iron in front of his gun's muzzle, with the bullet-sized hole in its centre directly aligned with the barrel. On firing the gun not only did the bullet hit that room's far wall, but so did the piece of iron. Plainly there was plenty of extra energy which could be used, and soon the world's first automatic *gas-operated* machine gun had been born. Initially, Browning kept the iron square at the muzzle, and attached it via a spring to the trigger beneath the bolt. Therefore every time a bullet was fired, the spring effectively pulled the trigger to fire another bullet, with all the work being done by the products of combustion. (Maxim's machine gun, activated by recoil and inspired by shoulder-bruising, was quite a different proposition.)

'The bullet nips smartly up the barrel hotly pursued by the expanding gases,' Browning gun instructors would proclaim, even in World War Two. They were right, of course, and the Browning weapon made use of some of that force to cause the recoil of the bolt. This novelty first saw service during the Mexican war of 1898, and was also reportedly 'useful' (as were Gatlings) during the Boxer Rebellion in China two years later.

When on 6 April 1917 the United States officially became a belligerent power on the Allied side in World War One, its relevant authorities belatedly asked inventors, such as John Browning, to submit ideas. At that time, due to years of indecision, the U.S. government only possessed a mixed — and very small — bag of ancient rapid-firing weapons. There were 670 Benét-Merciés, 282 Maxims (1904 model), and 158 Colts (model 1895). This was hardly an assembly with which to go to war. Lewis guns were already being manufactured in Europe and, from 1917 onwards, also in America, but estimates made in Washington at that anxious time suggested a requirement of 100,000 machine guns. U.S. industry eventually and magnificently set to work on mass production, notably on two of Browning's guns. These were made in considerable quantities, namely the .30 water-cooled machine gun and the .30 machine rifle (known as the B.A.R.). The first, with its heavy tripod, could be fired most easily from some fixed location, and the second could be carried by advancing infantry. As this lightweight automatic rifle could fire bursts of twenty rounds at a time, it was therefore extremely popular among regular infantry.

By June 1918 the Westinghouse production line, the most prolific of all those in the U.S. to be given an order, had manufactured 2,500 Brownings. By 1 August 1918 Westinghouse and Remingtons, another major producer, had created 10,000. By the time of the Armistice these two concerns had manufactured over 42,000. As for machine-gun production as a whole, the figure of 195,150 was given after the war's end, with 70,000 being delivered by June 1919. The figures are considerable, but production in such quantity only became a reality as that First World War was drawing to its close. Meanwhile, over in France, American troops were largely using British and French products. According to George M. Chinn, in his formidably impressive *The Machine Gun*, it was unfortunate that the 'clean lines and simplicity of construction of the Browning automatic machine guns . . . arrived too late to offer more than a token demonstration against an already defeated enemy'. The first use of these weapons in combat was by a small detachment of the 79th Division on 26 September 1918. General John Pershing, U.S. Commander-in-Chief, then reported enthusiastically about those Brownings.

During the five days my four guns were in action . . . they had very rough handling . . . placed in the mud . . . considerable grit, etc. got into the working parts of the guns . . . became rusty . . . [and] they fired perfectly . . . with only one stoppage.

John Browning, displaying an attitude not always found among weapon manufacturers during wartime, or in the wranglings which occur when peace arrives, suggested that the U.S. Government should set its own price for his contribution. He then received a flat fee of about one-tenth of the amount inventors would normally have been given for such work. (The U.S. government was therefore doing well out of both Lewis and Browning, getting very good deals from each of these undoubted patriots.) A letter of commendation from the Secretary of War referred to Browning's 'generous attitude': 'You have performed, as you must realize, a very distinct service to the country in these inventions . . .' He had indeed.

Other countries also wished to indulge themselves, however belatedly, in the inventions. Within Europe there was less interest in the heavy and water-cooled

Browning guns than in the lightweight versions. France's government asked for 15,000 of these even as the war was plainly about to end. General Pershing, although enthusiastic about John Browning's creations, thought a more powerful weapon should be created. This wish was immediately taken up by Colonel John H. Parker, head of the U.S. machine gun school at Gonducourt in France and the very same — then Lieutenant — Parker who had been so forthright with Gatling guns in Cuba two decades earlier. Word got back to Browning that a .50-calibre weapon should be constructed, and he immediately set to work.

One month before the war's end such a weapon was ready for testing. It did well, and the U.S. Chief of Ordnance recommended that the Winchester Repeating Arms Co. (still very much in business) should be given an order for 10,000 of these more powerful guns. This request was underscored by a recent realisation that the Germans, so consistently ahead in machine gun thinking, had created a yet more devastating gun. With 12.7-mm ammunition it could penetrate an inch of armour at 250 yards, and was therefore extremely useful against tanks. Browning's gun did not do so well, but it had been an astonishing achievement. The time from conception to delivery of his more powerful weapon had been only slightly more than a year. When asked how this had been achieved, Browning replied, 'One ounce of genius in a barrel of sweat (had) wrought the miracle.'

This extraordinary inventor fell ill on 26 November 1926. He was at Liège in Belgium supervising the manufacture of his guns, and he died later that same day at the age of seventy-one. The U.S. Secretary of War, promptly and officially, praised his great compatriot.

It is a fact to be recorded that no design of Mr. Browning's has ever proved a failure, nor has any model been discontinued . . . It is not thought that any other individual has contributed so much to the national security as Mr. Browning in the development of our machine guns and our automatic weapons to a state of military efficiency surpassing that of all nations.

During the summer of 1940, when the national security of Britain was again in deadly peril, its Hurricanes and Spitfires all had lethal weapons in their wings. Each aircraft carried eight Browning machine guns, these firing outside the propeller's arc at 1,200 rounds per minute. They proved to be triumphantly effective. Back in World War One, the .30-calibre Browning machine gun, specifically designed for aircraft use and designated the Model 1918, never actually experienced any fighting in the air. Not only was this weapon late in its arrival, but it possessed some weaknesses. The only machine gun used in aerial combat by the U.S. fliers was the modified Colt 95, then known as the Marlin (or Marlin Aircraft Machine Gun Model 1917–18) because it was manufactured by the Marlin-Rockwell Corporation.

But Germany had introduced a heavily armoured plane — an advance which was given prominence when Quentin Roosevelt, son of the rough-riding and presidential Theodore, attacked one of these aircraft from below. Bullets from his plane could be seen bouncing off the German armour whereas German bullets were soon the death of him. This weighty German protection meant that all rifle-calibre machine guns were henceforth less effective, making General Pershing's wish for a more powerful weapon yet more significant. Indeed, to leap ahead a little, the dominant aircraft gun used by the U.S. in World War Two was of .50 calibre. Contrarily, the eight Brownings in each Hurricane and Spitfire in 1940 were all of .303 calibre, and it is generally agreed that greater hitting power might have been of use.

By 1940, Maxim had been dead for twenty-four years, and Browning for fourteen. The famous airborne battle had been won by the few to whom so much was owed, but the creator of the world's first fully automatic gun and the inventor of a supreme successor were by no means irrelevant to that victory. Spitfires and Hurricanes were both excellent aircraft, but needed the Brownings in their wings. By then, it was a matter of course that rapid-firing guns would be involved, and that they would continue to serve as killing machines. They had done so in World War One, and certainly did so in its sequel. Indeed, although missiles were developed in World War Two, and then actively promoted when it ended, it is highly likely that airborne rapid-firing weapons will never go away.

# Chapter 16

# Civilian Death and Pips Squeaking

'War has been completely spoilt,' wrote Winston Churchill in 1930; 'It is all the fault of Democracy and Science.' This man, so adept at hitting nails on heads, was doing so once again. Science and technology were to blame for obliterating the pageantry and glory, and Democracy was at fault for removing everything else, the blind obedience, the unquestioning allegiance, the status of inequality. A fond hope that machine guns, by their ability to kill, might have had the power to banish warfare, once and for all, had disappeared for good. Instead the new weapons had merely transformed it, and stepped up the quantity of death. America's Civil War, whose arrival had first caused rapid firing to be vigorously proposed, had been a terrible slaughter but, sixty years later, World War One had shown what machine guns do once they had properly arrived. Churchill was quite right. Warfare had been spoilt absolutely.

The Great War, as all called it afterwards, initiated two other major ingredients which, thenceforth, would also never go away. The first of these was flight. It too had spoilt the former times, having transformed warfare in a manner unthinkable when Churchill had been charging with the 21st Lancers during the Battle of Omdurman. World War One had ended with Britain possessing 22,500 aircraft, making it the world's greatest air power. Britain had entered the conflict with about 180 machines, and Germany with 280. Almost all aviation thinking had then involved aerial reconnaissance which, as a practice, already had a lengthy history. The French had used balloons for this purpose in 1794, the Union Army had employed them in the U.S. Civil War, and the British had done likewise in South Africa when fighting against the Boers.

Aircraft could plainly perform the same task a great deal more effectively. The Wright brothers had taken to the air less than eleven years before the First World War began, but there had been extraordinarily swift advance — in speed and reliability — during that short time. The longest flight of those pioneering aviators at Kitty Hawk in 1903 had lasted for fifty-nine seconds, during which time their machine travelled over 852 feet (and at less than ten m.p.h. over the ground). Within five years, Wilbur Wright was achieving seventy-seven miles in two hours and twenty minutes (or thirty-three m.p.h.). Many other pioneers were also taking to the air in 1908, notably in Europe, and there was even the first fatality. Then, on 25 July 1909, Louis Blériot of France changed the world for ever by flying across the English Channel from Sangatte, near Calais, to land near Dover.

At that period in aviation's history there was considerable enthusiasm for the long-range capabilities of airships, these so much greater than those of aircraft. One year after Blériot's flight, which had ended in a gentle crash, the Germans had started a commercial airship service, named DELAG. This set out to carry passengers efficiently around Germany, and then did so. Meanwhile heavier-than-air machines, if this is a proper term for the delicate structures of wood, fabric, and even paper, were themselves advancing, but nothing like so efficiently and certainly not so safely. (DELAG never experienced a single injury during its four years of operations.) Charles Rolls, famous aeronaut of those days, made the first-ever non-stop double crossing of the English Channel in 1910, thus eclipsing Blériot, but he died shortly afterwards when his plane broke up in mid-air. The first all-metal aircraft flew in 1912, but a fatal accident then temporarily halted further testing with this type. A plane was flown under each of London's bridges across the Thames that same year, but was damaged on the return flight. One month later two members of the Royal Flying Corps were killed when they crashed near Salisbury, this accident occurring less than four months after the corps' formation. France, which possessed almost three times as many pilots as either Britain or Germany by 1912, even grounded Blériot monoplanes from further flying, as they had proved themselves too lethal, with alterations being officially demanded before they could fly again. In short, with mishaps and accidents seemingly in their nature, aircraft were experiencing a difficult and dangerous birth.

Airships were doing much better. W. Sefton Brancker, later to be Britain's Director of Civil Aviation — and later still to die in the crash of R101 — was one of many alarmed by the military threat posed by German airships. He visited that country in 1913, saw DELAG in service, and wondered what would happen should bombs ever take the place of passengers. He expressed no similar fears concerning aircraft. Long-distance and international flying plainly belonged to airships rather than the heavier-than-air devices, which often experienced difficulty even in leaving the ground and were adept in killing their occupants having done so.

The relevance of airships in a book about machine guns is that they diverted attention from the major issues of the Western Front. Hundreds of thousands of soldiers were being cut down by automatic fire, but a very few civilians were being killed by airship armament. Four East Anglians died from airship bombs on 19 January 1915, an event which terrified the nation, although 500 men were being killed *on average* every day in France. Even by the war's end, and after Gotha heavy bombers had been yet more punitive, only 1,500 British civilians had been killed from the air. The machine-gun toll had been one lesson from the war. For many people, such as civilians, the possibility of yet greater attack by future airborne forces was yet more disturbing.

To some extent H.G. Wells was to blame. In 1908 *The War in the Air* had been published. By then its author was extremely famous, having written *The Time Machine* in 1895, *The Invisible Man* in 1897, and *The War of the Worlds* one year later. In his terrifying account of aerial warfare the city of New York was virtually annihilated by a fleet of German airships.

[New York] was the first of the great cities of the Scientific Age to suffer by the enormous powers [of war from the air] . . . . As the airships sailed along they smashed up the city as a child will shatter its cities of brick and card. Below, they left ruins and blazing conflagrations and heaped and scattered dead; men, women, and children mixed together as though they had been no more than Moors, or Zulus, or Chinese. Lower New York was soon a furnace of crimson flames, from which there was no escape. Cars, railways, ferries, all had ceased, and never a light led the way of the distracted fugitives in that dusky confusion but the light of burning.

Only seven years after that book's publication airships were over London, and dropping bombs, but being shot down by aircraft rather more effectively than American aircraft had been able to damage some of Wells's marauders over Manhattan. Interestingly, Wells's defenders and attackers had all used machine guns against their enemy during his imagined war, the author having sensed their power. Whether it was airships or aircraft flying overhead, and dropping dreadful bombs, the fear was quickly installed that civilians were in terrible jeopardy. It was all very well for soldiers to die on some battlefield but much less well for ordinary people, living peacefully at home, to be subjected to sudden death. And air machines, of one sort or another, were becoming increasingly capable of delivering it.

Between 1909, which witnessed Blériot's crossing, and the outbreak of war in 1914, heavier-than-air flying had certainly advanced — there had been the first flight with two aboard, first airborne photography, first successful float-plane, first Channel crossing with passengers, and first take-off from a ship. Nevertheless the flying machines flown from Britain in August 1914 to serve with the British Expeditionary Force did not appear outstandingly brilliant as war machines. Certainly none was equipped with guns. That first assortment consisted of BE2s (speed seventy m.p.h., not very manoeuvrable, but more than 3,000 were to be produced), Blériots (which had killed five pilots before March 1912, and then two more even on their way to Dover), Farmans (the first of the bunch to see action), BE8s, and Avro 504s (one of which was shot down by ground fire only nine days later). The Royal Flying Corps had been officially initiated on 13 May 1912, and was therefore seeing active service within twenty-seven months of its formation.

Pre-war aviation progress had been swift, but the arrival of war hastened it tremendously. Britain first attacked Germany by air in October 1914. A four-engined bomber became operational in Russia in 1915. The Vickers Gun-Bus, with its forward-firing machine gun, reached France in February 1915, this being the first machine specifically designed for aerial combat. The Fokker Scourge of 1915–16 has already been mentioned, and it was only lessened when the DH2, the R.F.C.'s first single-seater fighter, entered service. Britain's Flying Corps continued to experience terrible losses, as during Bloody April of 1917 when over a third of the planes ready for action were lost in the month's first half. Machine guns did almost all the damage and on both sides these rapid-firing weapons were bonded with aircraft from the start of aerial warfare. The speeds involved, when aircraft met aircraft in the sky, demanded a rapid rate of fire if any effective damage was to be achieved.

Aviation's general willingness to accept and develop this new form of fighting stands in stark contrast to military reluctance concerning machine guns. Everything about flying was so new. There were no traditions to be upheld, no regimental customs. The initial assumption that aircraft were only good for observation was quickly amended, partly because their reconnaissance abilities were so speedily concluded when they could not defend themselves (as with kite balloons which, stationary and filled with hydrogen, were even more vulnerable to attack). All thinking about air warfare changed rapidly as the war progressed, and then continued to do so when the years of peace arrived. What on earth would happen in any future war?

In general, when that next war did arrive, civilian casualty figures were not quite so horrendous as had been feared, although far greater than during 1914–18. Britain lost 50,000 civilians in aerial attacks between 1939 and 1945, a thirty-five-fold increase over World War One, but it also lost (together with the Commonwealth) nine times as many individuals in the fighting. Germany suffered almost four million civilian deaths, mostly in air attacks from Britain, a number similar to those lost in its armed services. Russia's civilian dead totalled almost eight million, as against over twelve million for its military, but aerial bombardment was not the major factor for either quantity of death. Japan, the only nation to experience atomic bombs, suffered 350,000 civilian deaths in World War Two, as against 1.7 million for its military.

Never before had civilian casualties been so extreme, but the total damage from every kind of bombing was not so severe as had been feared. Almost all of Poland's 5.2 million civilian deaths, for example, were caused by means other than air attack. The war was the most lethal there had ever been — by far, but savagery on the ground was hugely more horrendous than death inflicted from the air. Machine guns, both in the air and on the ground, played a violent part in the ends of millions. The weapons were so widespread that death from a rapid-firing weapon had become conventional. Certainly no one has hazarded a guess as to the proportion of World War Two's total toll caused by automatic fire.

Similarly, no one can estimate the amount of mayhem caused to the environment, the homes obliterated, the ground polluted, the general destruction. Europe bore the brunt, with hardly a nation unscathed, but much of Asia also suffered horrendously. At least, during the First World War the damage was more confined. It was still possible to take a holiday in France, and not even hear the loathsomeness proceeding in the north. As for the front line with its trenches, that was a wasteland, with devastated towns, shattered trees, and death everywhere. 'When they make a wilderness they call it peace,' Tacitus had written 2,000 years earlier, but he never could have imagined the kind of shambles left behind in 1918 when the warring parties of industrialised nations decided to call it a day and go back home. There had never been a war like it in all the centuries of conflict between one community and another. It had been a true world war, with fifty-seven nations exchanging declarations of hostilities before, wearied from so much death, they chose to call a truce.

Britain's Duke of Wellington and France's Bonaparte would not have been totally at a loss during the U.S. Civil War. They might have been amazed at its wide-ranging scope, but the fighting was still mainly a matter of men shooting at each other with rifles while being assisted by artillery. Nor would the Boer War have been a complete astonishment to them. Firearms were then more accurate and more powerful, as was artillery, but troop deployment and the like would have been comprehensible to those two men who, eighty-five years earlier, had fought against each other. However, the stalemate of the trenches in World War One would have been quite bewildering, and the mental confusion induced in the old antagonists would then have been submerged completely by the three great alterations brought to prominence by that war — the machine gun, the aeroplane, and the tank. Six hundred rounds per minute from each gun, airborne activity in general, and an armour-plated gun platform moving stolidly across the ground were each distinct indicators that the old kind of war had been quite spoiled. The First World War was not only shocking in terms of numbers killed. It also shocked by introducing elements which would play their part, yet more aggressively, in every future war.

Machine guns, aircraft, and tanks, the three major novelties, were also accompanied by gas. First used by Germany on 22 April 1915, less than eight months after the war's beginning, it led to quantities of chlorine slowly drifting towards Allied trenches not far from Ypres. 'I saw an opaque green cloud, about 10 metres high,' wrote a witness afterwards, '[It was] thick near the ground, [and it] moved towards us, pushed by the wind. Almost immediately, we were suffocated . . .'

The German troops, equipped with rudimentary gas masks, then tore a four-mile gap in the Allied lines, but were halted by men behind the front not affected by the gas. According to Richard Holmes, in *The Western Front*, a German officer had prophesied that his country's use of this loathsome addition to war 'would earn Germany widespread criticism, but, having expressed their moral outrage, her enemies would follow suit'.

He was right. The British were appalled and outspoken concerning the 'Hun's' novel form of 'villainy', but promptly set up a gas contingent whose aim was to be equally foul to their German enemy. Britain used gas for the first time on 25 September 1915, with John French reporting that it was 'very successful', but mention gas attacks to the British, even now, and most of those asked will answer that they were exclusively perpetrated by the Germans.

Gas attacks in general, although damaging and often blinding, were unsuccessful in breaking the stalemate. They permitted advances, and small gains, but the intruders were then held up by troops uninfluenced by the gas. Its opaque green clouds were a fickle form of warfare, being diluted as they were dispersed, and most literally at the mercy of the winds. Both sides developed even more damaging gases, such as phosgene, which was eighteen times more powerful than chlorine. There was also mustard gas, an oily fluid which burned any skin with which it came into contact. There were even gas shells which released their poison upon detonation, and could therefore be lethal in their landing area.

The Allies had no defence whatsoever when the first gas clouds were wafted their way, but masks — primitive at first, and perhaps no more than a pad of wadding soaked in chemicals — were gradually improved. Soldiers without any form of protection against gas tended to die within 48 hours of an attack. About one million individuals (on both sides) were gassed during World War One, and 91,198 of them died. Many of those who survived were affected for the rest of their lives, with weakened lungs and often blindness reminding them of this terrible addition to warfare. All ground-based combatants in World War Two carried masks, and every British civilian was also issued with one (albeit an inferior version), but poison gas was never used during that later war, either militarily or against civilian populations.

There were some incidental, but certainly not irrelevant, consequences to the slaughter, a death toll brought about in large measure by the machine gun. The great sacrifice of lives caused anger to be directed almost wholly at Germany rather than at the national leaders for their conduct of the war, and the attrition it involved. During that war's fifty-two months almost 1,600 times as many British and

Commonwealth servicemen died as during the thirty-two inglorious months of the Boer War. Therefore Germany should be punished, its invasion of Belgium having initiated the fighting. Lloyd George, Britain's prime minister, wanted the 'German lemon to be squeezed until the pips squeak'. The French, who had lost proportionately even more men, were yet more demanding. It was this loss of life, so exacerbated by the machine gun, which boosted the demand for revenge. Germany must be made to pay.

When the Treaty of Versailles was reluctantly signed by the vanquished on 28 June 1919, the pips did indeed squeak. A first instalment of reparation would be 6,600 million pounds sterling, to be paid over the next forty-two years — and therefore up to 1963. Within the 200 pages and 75,000 words of the Treaty of Versailles, there was even a special ruling concerning machine guns, the cause of so much Allied death. The Germans were not permitted to create any 'sustained fire weapons'. (In the end they circumvented this particular stricture by developing air-cooled guns in Switzerland, each with changeable barrels, that then served as the MG34.)

It is easy to argue that the machine gun,

more than any other facet of the war, had created the lust for revenge at Versailles, it having been such a major cause of death. No one could forget those casualty lists, so lengthily inscribed in newspapers, and so awesome even for those whose loved ones were not among the names (a listing practice never carried out during World War Two).

Awareness at home of the casualty figures, and a desire for remembrance, were all too clear-cut in the post-war carvings upon memorials. No village or town within Britain was too poor, too small, or too uncaring (so it seems today) not to establish a reminder of its glorious dead, of those who had given their lives for others, and whose names would live for evermore. Of the 44,800 war memorials now existing within the United Kingdom 31,000 were erected after the First World War.

It was, of course, impossible for the survivors of the First World War not to know of the monstrous killing which had occurred, or of the machine guns which had been largely responsible. There were reminders at every turn. Schools listed those who had lain down their lives for their friends. The wounded were all too noticeable, being short of a limb, or two, or blind, or with a cruelly damaged face. Remembrance Day, with its two minutes of silence, was officially instituted, and it called a halt to the nation at the eleventh hour of the eleventh day of the eleventh month. Even trains would stop during the earlier years of that moment of quiet when memories were all too clear. There was such relief at the blood-letting having been concluded that questioning was minimal about its causes or the war's conduct as a whole. There could very well have been considerable enquiry. Why did so many have to die? Why were the enemy's machine guns given such dreadful opportunity?

The fact that the war of mechanical killing had so eclipsed every other form of war, with almost ten million perishing in total, suggested that any subsequent fight would be just as lethal, if not more so. Therefore appeasement was born. Everything should be done to prevent a repetition. One generation had been lost, and the next in line could not be allowed to follow suit. Tanks, aircraft, and tens of thousands of machine guns had demonstrated their lethal capabilities during that First World War. Worse still, they had been novel and largely undeveloped as machines of war, and would surely grow yet worse during the years ahead. Tanks would become faster, and better able to donate and withstand punishment. Aircraft would leap ahead, in speed, in armament, and in their ability to deliver death. As for machine guns, they would surely grow yet more competent. Perhaps every soldier would have one. If so, hundreds of rounds a minute, and therefore hundreds of possible deaths, would become a commonplace. Anything and everything should be done, by way of diplomacy and negotiation, of moderation and mitigation, to prevent a recurrence of the nightmare which had lasted for 1,568 days stretching from 1914 to 1918. Never, never again.

Rather than hold post-mortems about the war, and criticise the manner in which young lives had been expended, be joyful with the survivors, dance the Charleston, wear skimpy dresses, cut hair short, forget about the Kaiser, watch women vote, go to the pictures, worship Mary Pickford and Rudolph Valentino, relish jazz from Dixieland, know of flights to Paris every day, and above all — get on with life. The war was best forgotten.

Nevertheless the mood was different in the conquered and the conquering countries. Loss of life in each had been formidable, but only one side had arranged the peace. Within Germany there was fury at the Treaty of Versailles; the defeated nation could only watch while its economy collapsed. The great sacrifice on the Western Front had apparently been to no avail. Therefore listen to ranting from every political party, particularly the extremist groups. Blame civilians, such as Jews and capitalists, for allegedly stabbing the soldiers in the back. Oppose Bolshevism or favour it. Experience hunger. Plead poverty, justifiably, concerning the reparations demanded of Germany. Attempt to disobey the Versailles strictures. Keep weapons and the army as much as possible. The machine-gun war, as some were calling it, had never truly ended; it had merely entered a different phase.

The machine gun's day had certainly not receded. Tanks and aircraft all carried them, and would continue to do so. If there was to be a future war, there would be rapid-fire from every quarter. The machine gun would not have to be a stationary item, firing at those who advanced towards it. There would be large machine guns rattling out their bullets but, in general, the weapon would be much more mobile, carried in its lightweight versions by the infantry, and helping to ensure — both on the ground and from the air — a much more mobile war. Trenches had had their day. That stalemate would never be repeated. The First World War had been like none other, and any second global conflict would also be wholly different.

# Chapter 17

# Whatever Happens They Have Now All Got . . .

So what of Hartford, the place where so much of this rapid-fire story began? The factory did keep going after Sam Colt's death and was still functioning busily when his widow died at the start of the twentieth century. It continued to do so, making M16s at the very end, before all its armament production gradually ceased during the 1960s. No one then tore the old place down, a custom more widespread in the U.S. than, say, England. The city of Hartford, so aware of its historic past, could not do that, even if short of alternative ideas. It found the money, and the will, to restore the dome and prancing horse (which had always topped Colt's factory), and then ran out of steam. Sam's decision to return to his birthplace, to set up business by the Connecticut River, to purchase 250 acres, and successfully to initiate rapid fire, became a two-fold inspiration. Not only did he put Hartford on the map, making it the place to be for wholesale manufacturing, but he helped to introduce the notion of automatic weaponry.

Hartford's population today stands at 120,000, with the latest batch of new arrivals being Puerto Ricans. Many of these newcomers live in the dwellings, purportedly Germanic in their style, that were built when Sam Colt wanted his new workforce to feel at home as much as possible. Manufacturing in Hartford is still active, for example of helicopters, but the city's reputation as prime location for machine-made excellence has now been widely scattered around the United States.

Armsmear still exists — 'Drive by for a hint of what was once the Colts' domestic paradise,' states a local guidebook. The Church of the Good Shepherd, with its revolver motifs, is still resplendent, even if locked on most days. Richard Gatling's home, as already mentioned, is several apartments, and should be better known. He, above all, forged the link between a sound manufacturing base (Colt's) and rapid fire (the Gatling gun). As Hartford was once the wealthiest small city in the U.S., and the first to be fully lit by electricity, there are numerous legacies still standing of that golden age, such as fine buildings, a great railway station, the first ever city park to be conceived and paid for by its citizens, a supreme State Capitol (since 1972 a National Historic Landmark), the Ancient Burying Ground (one of the few sites surviving from the seventeenth century), and the ultra-Gothic cathedral built in 1828. There are also many derelict and unloved open spaces, either full or empty of parked cars. Two freeways are the greatest travesty. With a cavalier disregard for Hartford history, or indeed for anything save hastening vehicles from A to B, they have sliced through and over this venerable community.

Richard Jordan Gatling's inheritance in modern times is far less visible than Colt's. Parallels exist between their lives, but not many. Both men were profligate with cash, once some of it had come their way, and both continued to invent and improve while their lives were lasting. Gatling's millions were largely consumed by mistaken investments, many connected with the railway system. Only two of his creations ever brought major revenue his way, namely his gun and his wheat drill. Gatling's wish to invent a better gun was a steadfast compulsion, but less of a single fixation than with Colt. He also became interested in casting cannons, in gun boats, in flushing water closets, in the use of compressed air (for transferring energy), in cleaning systems, in cotton thinners, and in controlling horses without using hands. Along the way he also devised a brand new form of bicycle. With this machine not only did the rider's legs provide propulsion, as was customary, but the rider's arms did so as well. All steering was achieved by the rider swivelling his rump. The design was patented, as were all of Gatling's novelties, but — alas — not a single Gatling four-limb driven and buttock-governed bike was ever made.

Unlike Colt, Gatling enjoyed good health, and in February 1903 made an eight-mile journey by foot (to *Scientific American*'s offices in New York City) on the very day he died. His appearance for most of his life much resembled that of some genial family physician, but not one of his patented inventions related to medicine. After his death an obituary stated that, 'although best known as the inventor of a terrible death-dealing weapon, Dr Gatling was the gentlest and kindliest of men'. There had to be a better way, he thought, a less lethal way of fighting wars, and his solution was the Gatling gun. He earned some latter-day posterity when the U.S. Navy named a destroyer after him in 1943. His surname was also used, in abbreviated form, by Humphrey Bogart and his pals when busily snarling at each other while bringing their 'gats' to bear.

Eventually, and remarkably, some forty years after the inventor's death, his weapon made a come-back. The U.S. Army had officially retired the Gatling from its ordnance in 1911, having been slow to adopt it in the 1860s and then slow to abandon it half a century later. After World War Two, when aircraft were so very much faster than ever before, and were hurtling over their ground-based enemies so very fleetingly, it was suddenly realised that the multi-barrelled Gatling principle still had advantages. An aircraft flying at 500 miles an hour is covering the ground at 8.3 miles a minute, or 733 feet a second. Such speed gives little opportunity to fire at a target below. But however swift a machine gun may be, when using a single barrel, it is likely to be much speedier if several barrels can be brought into the equation. In 1945, with Gatling's idea officially resuscitated, an experimental firing rate of 5,800 rounds per minute was achieved and a few years later the even faster Vulcan gun was born. This weapon was then developed into the M61 20-mm. Its six barrels were able to launch a total of 7,200 rounds per minute, and this form of Vulcan was installed in the U.S. Air Force's F-104 and F-105 fighters and its B-52 and B-58 bombers. Not only would such a rate of fire be virtually impossible to achieve with a single barrel, but a single malfunctioning bullet in a solitary barrel would halt the entire mechanism. Not so with several barrels when the faulty one would simply be bypassed. As Paul Wahl and Don Toppel concluded, in their book on the Gatling gun:

> Thus, as the Vulcan Gun, the old Gatling has come full circle, after a century, from a mule-drawn carriage to a bulge on the hip of a supersonic jet fighter.

Hiram Stevens Maxim did not set up a manufacturing empire, as did Colt. He did not have his gun reinvigorated, as did Gatling. Indeed the best-known inheritance on his account lies with Belloc's awesome lines, 'Whatever happens we have got the Maxim gun, and they have not'. These were written in 1898, and it is not known whether Maxim grinned with pleasure at such fame or grimaced at their disarming implications. In fact, the next conflict, breaking out one year later in South Africa, was the first in which both antagonists possessed his weapon, although neither side found them much use in a landscape where the accurate and smoke-free magazine rifle was in its element.

Hiram Maxim's workshop at 57D Hatton Garden, to which royalty and others had paid such court, was demolished when Maxim vacated it for bigger premises in Kent. The current dwelling on that site, constructed in 1880, possesses one of London's blue plaques informing passers-by of the site's links with Maxim and automatic fire. As for Maxim's grave at West Norwood, lying within fifty yards of the cemetery's entrance, its wording gives no evidence whatsoever of the inventor's life, beyond his dates. It certainly says nothing about his role in sending others to their graves. There are three Maxim roads in London, with the diminutive one at Crayford undoubtedly named for him as he used a factory in that area. Otherwise the man has gone — save for his enduring legacy of automatic fire.

Even individuals with zero knowledge of such weaponry, or how rapid-firing guns altered the face of war so dreadfully, may well know of Colt, Gatling, and Maxim, even if uncertain of their actual nationalities or relevance to the machine gun's history. As Isaac Lewis said, after fame (and fortune) had come his way via his Lewis gun:

> One of man's immortal claims is the pride of his name. No one can take that away from my family or from my gun.

That particular inventor would assuredly have been pleased had he been able to know that his weapons also served widely in World War Two. Their distinctive rattle was also heard during the birth pangs of Israel, during the Nigerian Civil War of 1967–70, and in Vietnam. His gun therefore stayed in action for over sixty years, and the name of Lewis has resounded for all that time.

Other major names already mentioned in the machine-gun story — Benjamin Hotchkiss, Laurence Benét, Henri Mercié, John Browning, Albert Vickers, Thorsten Nordenfelt, William Gardner — did not occupy the pivotal positions of Colt, Gatling, and Maxim. A direct line did exist between 'le système Gribeauval' of the eighteenth century and the battlefields of the twentieth. The desire for uniformity of parts, initially seen as little more than an economy measure, worked its way through several decades and inventive individuals until it became an integral ingredient of killing machines. Having arrived, it has shown no intention of disappearing.

Machine guns have not made war obsolete, as some individuals had hoped rather too optimistically. Instead, both the guns and their manufacturers have proliferated, increasingly putting the less speedy single-shot or magazine-fed rifles in the shade. The machine gun is still ready to spew forth its brand of affliction; it has done so, generally, in the hands of servicemen, who have used it in wartime when murder becomes legitimate. One important exception to this rule, particularly in its early days, was well known to every cinema-goer in the 1930s. It was certainly well known to every hoodlum, hood, villain, gangster, or mere 'gen'leman' wishing to make a fast buck before the other guy got there faster. This was the Thompson sub-machine gun, or Tommy.

John Tagliaferro Thompson graduated

from West Point in 1882, and joined the Army's Ordnance Department eight years later. He retired from service life in 1914, wishing to perfect an automatic rifle, and then linked up with the Remington Arms Company. When America joined the First World War the inventive Thompson, by then a re-enlisted general, was in charge of the small arms supply for the U.S. expeditionary force. After the war he became the principal designer of a readily portable 'sub-machine gun' of .45 inch calibre and ten-pound weight, known as the M1921A. The Maxim, plus its variations, had done a considerable share of the killing in World War One, but it had become increasingly apparent that extremely lightweight machine guns would be useful in close-combat fighting. (Hence the 'sub' of this kind of weapon.)

Thompson's new gun was tested by the U.S. Army and Marine Corps, and *Scientific American* called it 'the most efficient man-killer of any firearm yet produced'. By then its creator had set up the Auto-Ordnance Corporation to market his weapon, and initially sold more of them to the law enforcement agencies, such as the police, than to the armed services or any other official operator. For these organisations, Thompson offered a bird-shot variety of bullet, which he claimed would damage but not kill. This humane aspiration did not excite the few buyers (in the biggest cities). They were more interested in killing the opposition than in wounding it.

At that time machine guns of all kinds could be sold legally to private citizens (even in Britain until 1920), and Thompson — still short of purchasers — chose to advertise his 'ideal weapon for protection'. Everyone in the protection business took note, such as those in the world of organised crime. Its leaders were making a bundle by recommending this form of care for its customers as a wise alternative to arson, to abduction of their families, or merely death. Thompson's publicity material stated that only 'responsible parties' could purchase his gun, but for lawless individuals gaining rich reward from the bootleg industry that was like requesting them to drive more slowly or shoot fewer rivals. Prohibition began on 16 January 1919 and on 25 September 1925 the new kind of gun first chattered its distinctive sound in civilian hands. Soon afterwards, impressed by the gun's desirable qualities, Al Capone purchased a few, and let the world know he had done so. Their most famous hour arrived on St Valentine's day 1929, when seven men were 'rubbed out', executed, and generally done to death by the Thompson gun. Roger Ford, in *The Grim Reaper*, tells a story of that shoot-out. Frank Gusenberg, one of the victims, had fourteen bullets in him when the police arrived. 'Who shot you, Frank?' asked a detective. 'Nobody shot me,' replied the dying Gusenberg, disdaining cooperation with the police even to the end. (No one was ever indicted for that crime.)

The West Point graduate and ex-Army general was disheartened by the renown his weapon was achieving, however much his sales were boosted by the underworld. Nevertheless Thompson continued working on his gun. His next creation, the M1928A1, was a better weapon, and did well in revolutionary Central America. Close-combat jungle fighting was not dissimilar to encounters in the back streets of Chicago, and the gun's growing reputation led to further sales. The Irish Republican Army was another purchaser, but modest armies and unlawful organisations formed a market too small for Thompson's commercial requirements. He struggled on valiantly, but at the end of the 1920s, with him no longer in control and his major financial backer abdicating, the Auto-Ordnance Corporation was sold.

Despite this setback, the gun itself did not die and neither did the corporation. They were both vigorously resuscitated by the arrival of World War Two and, in gun terms, became a huge success. Perhaps some of the military welcomed the weapon for its famed association with Cagney, Bogart, Raft and Co, as well as the real-life villains, like Ma Barker's family, Pretty Boy Floyd, Legs Diamond, Bonnie Parker and Clyde Barrow. John Thompson himself died aged eighty in 1940, without seeing his weapon's fulfilment in the service of the Allies fighting Germany.

By that time, with rearmament on almost every nation's agenda, with gun makers merrily borrowing or stealing everyone else's ideas, and with automatic weaponry more abundant and varied than ever before, the list of rapid-firing guns was formidable and numerous countries were involved in their manufacture. Machine-gun creation had certainly become commonplace since Hiram Maxim had introduced so many countries to the first fully automatic weapon they had ever seen. He had naturally stressed the unique characteristic of his merchandise, namely that it was automatic. He may indeed have called it an automatic gun, but machine gun became the name by which it was generally known. Before World War One, and certainly during it, everyone knew what was meant by a machine gun. Since then the full title has been gradually eroded, just as flying machines, steam locomotives, and horseless carriages have all acquired simpler descriptions. Rapid-firing weapons are now so commonplace, with keepers of the peace, breakers of the law, and the military in general, that 'machine' gun is a touch superfluous. They are just guns. As for all the progeny of this huge family, it would be easy to be drowned in its wealth of calibres, types, weights, rates of fire, and methods of operation, but a few of the offspring do stand out from the crowd, either for their fame, their novelty, or affection or dislike, with which they are remembered.

One such is the Sten. It was called cheap, and nasty, and a whole lot of other unflattering epithets — the Woolworth Special being one of them — but hundreds of thousands were to be made, derided, applauded, and used in every theatre of World War Two. Its most important characteristic was the price of manufacture, this being minimal — about £2. No wonder unkind adjectives came its way but, if the choice lay between no rapid-firing gun and one resembling pipework which plumbers would understand, there was no difficulty in assessing which option was preferable.

Thompson machine guns were available from the U.S., but at considerable expense, and so cheapness was the driving force when a team at the Royal Small Arms Factory, Enfield, set to work. They were not to care about precision engineering of all the parts, or about the weapon's appearance. Instead they were to design something simple, and easy to make, which would fire bullets with reasonable aplomb whenever the need arose. The 9-mm Sten first appeared in mid-1941, each costing about as much to make — when full-scale production was underway — as an agricultural labourer received for one week's work.

R.V. Shepherd and H.J. Turpin were its designers. Their surname initials, coupled with the first two letters of Enfield, gave the gun its name. Its greatest snag was the horizontally projecting thirty-two-round magazine, the object's lips being easily deformed. Also any dirt which entered the magazine tended to stay there. The gun could then jam, as it did most famously when Czech assassins aimed at Reinhard Heydrich, number two in the Gestapo, and had to use a hand-grenade instead. Conversely, it could often work in circumstances when more refined weaponry failed to operate owing, perhaps, to excessive cold. Throughout the war, various other marks of the Sten were created, and later models made the Mark 1 look positively resplendent. Firing the gun, for the uninitiated, caused the weapon to launch its final bullets more at the sky than at the ground. The Sten — by whatever name — could not have been so bad, with four million manufactured, with Germany copying it precisely (to become the MP3008) in the later stages of the war, and the weapon staying in service with the British Army until the 1960s.

One predecessor to the Sten was the Bren, a more conventional weapon and much respected. During the 1930s, although the Lewis gun was still in use, British officials looked around for a possible successor. Military attachés in other nations were asked to report on likely candidates. The Madsen was favoured; so too the Darne, the Vickers-Berthier (which had found favour with British troops in India), and the Browning automatic rifle, but opinions altered when the embassy in Prague sent back details and enthusiasm concerning the ZB26. Following much testing, this Czech weapon became the definite leader in the pack, provided a few alterations were introduced. These stipulated .303-calibre chambering — Britain's standard rifle size, plus a shortening of the barrel, and a modification of the stock, all of which meant a smoother action and a slightly increased rate of fire. It was then ready for introduction to the British Army, and was given the name of Bren. This stood for Brno — or Brunn in former times — where the gun originated, largely under the care of Vaclav Holek. It also stood for Enfield, where it would be made in England, despite that region's proximity to London and its vulnerability to air attack. (In fact, the establishment was largely unaffected.) The Bren saw service on both sides after the Germans had overrun Czechoslovakia, and had used the slightly different ZB30 as their Maschinengewehr 30. The Bren gun also did well in longevity, still serving the British Army in 1974.

Machine guns may be similar in their ability to despatch many rounds in a short time, but there is little similarity among the individuals who supplied the driving force behind them. Colt, Gatling, and Maxim were all quite distinct, and so too their successors, but then came the Russian Mikhail Kalashnikov, who was different yet again. Born in 1920, he was at a perfect age for call-up in World War Two. He had been a railway clerk, and soon became a tank commander, being commended for gallantry. He was badly wounded in 1941 and, after a lengthy spell in hospital, was invalided out of the service. He then started thinking about weapon design, and quickly produced two suggestions, neither of which was accepted. Nevertheless he persevered. In 1947 he designed an automatic rifle which was soon enthusiastically approved. After being accepted into the Soviet Army in 1953, it was given the name AK-47 (standing for Automatic Kalashnikov, with the inventor's sound proletarian origins entitling him to fame). It went on to become the most widespread, most sold, and most famous such weapon around the world. It served not only everywhere in the Soviet bloc, but also in China and other communist states. For freedom fighters and guerilla bands of all kinds, notably in Africa, it was the most desirable weapon, earning an extraordinary reputation — and almost becoming a synonym for machine gun.

Basically the AK-47's ingredients followed on from its inventor's decision to use a short (7.62mm) cartridge. The gun could therefore be smaller and more compact. There would be less recoil energy, and the reloading stroke (putting in another cartridge from the thirty-round magazine) would be abbreviated. A novel system for gas extraction from the barrel, plus a distinctive and quite different bolt action, are further distinguishing characteristics. Kalashnikov himself deplored his gun's considerable use by international terrorism, particularly as he was by then a deputy in the Supreme Soviet of the U.S.S.R.; but, like Thompson, he was to discover that there is not much a designer can do to prevent unwelcome sales.

Yet it is not necessary to be a gun designer to be unhappy about such subsequent events. There is, for example, the latter story of the Machine Gun Corps. The unit was born belatedly against opposition, and was then given additional cause for regret at its termination, an ending which underlined the former British attitude towards its style of war. When memorials were being erected up and down Britain, and were receiving their poppy wreaths every Remembrance Day, 'The Boy David' was created. This impressive sculpture would serve as a reminder of the 'suicide squad' whose casualties had been so intense. The larger-than-life-size sculpted youth (by Derwent Wood) was considered an appropriate subject, since the Judean king-to-be had so famously slaughtered ten thousand of the Philistines, most notably Goliath, whereas the jealous Saul had only managed thousands (I. Samuel xvii 7). Wood's statue was set up in 1925, and dedicated to the Machine Gun Corps, with two actual Vickers machine guns, each encased in bronze, forming part of the monument. The chosen site was by Grosvenor Place near London's Hyde Park Corner. Soon afterwards, the statue was dismantled as certain 'road improvements' were in force. (There was also talk that a nunnery, housed nearby, had objected to such blatant nakedness.)

Only in 1963, at the insistence of former machine-gun men, was the memorial resurrected and dedicated all over again. Its new location, within the central enclave of Hyde Park Corner, is considered favourable. That horribly apt quotation, vaunting

David's ten-fold superiority over Saul, is therefore still in place. The dismantling may have been quite justified for traffic reasons, but a certain suspicion has not been quite so easy either to remove or displace. The Machine Gun Corps itself was speedily disbanded after the First World War — and ceased to exist in 1922, the last unit of the corps being disbanded at the army camp of Shorncliffe on 15 July of that year. All of its records were stored there and, as it happened, they were totally destroyed by fire shortly afterwards. Shorncliffe, an ancient establishment lying within western Folkestone, lay close to fire-fighting services, and yet the conflagration was specific and complete. As one result of this destruction there could be no official history of the Machine Gun Corps, as all the requisite information had been incinerated. According to Dolf L. Goldsmith, in his comprehensive volume on the Vickers gun, there has been speculation about the fire, with some feeling that

> it was deliberately set on order of someone high in the Army hierarchy who considered that the Machine Gun Corps was not a 'proper regiment', and therefore a 'traitor' to the British Regi-

mental tradition, and as such, its records and deeds were not to be perpetuated . . . Two ex-M.G.C. officers who [had] announced themselves prepared to undertake this task were promptly posted to the Northwest Frontier and Burma respectively, where obviously no material support for such an enterprise was available.

The British Army had not liked the machine gun in the first place. The novel unit formed on the weapon's behalf was alien to the proper conduct of a war. If the speculation quoted by Goldsmith is valid, it is entirely in keeping with the original sentiment. Machine guns had had a controversial beginning. It was therefore apt and understandable that the Machine Gun Corps' abrupt conclusion should also be a matter of dissent. The passing of this misbegotten offspring was not mourned universally, save of course by those most involved, such as all the former members of the corps. They insisted that the memorial should be reinstated. And, four years after David's restoration, a new M.G. Corps banner was officially 'laid up for ever' in St Wulfram's Church, near Grantham in Lincolnshire, just down the road — as it were — from the training ground where so many of the corps' members first got to grips with the lethal weapon in their charge.

# Epilogue

The deadly effect of the devastating fire of machine guns was directly responsible for the trench warfare of 1915–18.

So wrote F.W.A. Hobart in the *Pictorial History of the Machine Gun*. Had there only been rifles, it might have been possible for either side to break through that stalemate. As it was, the machine guns could kill men with such impunity that they ruled the situation. Peter Chamberlain and Tony Gander, in their *Fact File* on the subject, wrote that

of all the hideous 'engines of war' produced in the twentieth century, none has exacted a more dreadful toll of human life than the machine gun . . . It reached the peak of its destructive powers during World War One, when the military and political course of the world for the next three decades was dictated by the dominance of the machine gun over the battlefield.

During the Second World War the weapon never regained the dominance it had held during the First. At once there is an apparent contradiction because rapid-firing weapons were far more commonplace during the later and yet more lethal conflict. They had come into their own formidably. Not every soldier possessed one, but every soldier expected to be assaulted by machine-gun fire in almost every fighting situation. Back in the trenches, a lone machine gun could hold up an attack, but it could not do so in the more open warfare which followed twenty-five years later. Strategy and tactics had been compelled to change. Men took cover, but mobility was all-important. In creating the Maginot Line, for example, the French had constructed the ultimate in defensive systems, but it proved to be quite useless when the Germans went round the back of it.

The existence of the machine gun, and the stalemate it induced, caused men to think in terms of the tank. The static situation also boosted interest in the aeroplane, so free in comparison, and so able to attack in quite a different manner. The machine gun also killed off the horse, no less effectively than it murdered men. And it severely fractured the old style of warfare, with romance, glory, and precious pageantry. Its influences went far beyond the ability to spew forth 600 rounds a minute.

The machine gun did reach the peak of its destructive powers during World War One, but it is hard to say what other peaks it has induced. It altered society, with the old subservience disintegrating or even vanishing. It certainly helped to spoil warfare, as Churchill had lamented. Yet when Hiram Maxim exulted in 'certain success ahead', after bullets had first leapt from his prototype, he could not possibly have known, or even suspected, what else lay ahead once his gun had truly come to pass.

The machine-gun story had its origins in 'le système Gribeauval' of the eighteenth century. It grew from strength to strength during the nineteenth century, and met its apotheosis in the utter misery of the twentieth, notably along the front line that sliced through Western Europe. No story ever truly ends, and the rapid-firing gun has still, assuredly, a terrible way to go.

'The good people of this wirld,' as Sam Colt phrased it so long ago, 'are very far from being satisfied with each other.'

They are indeed and now, unfortunately, have machine guns in their hands to help them express their discontent.

# Bibliography

*Airships in Peace and War* by R. P. Hearne (John Lane 1910)

*All Quiet on the Western Front* by Erich Maria Remarque (Putnam 1930)

*All Sir Garnet* by Joseph Lehmann (Cape 1964)

*Amazing Hiram Maxim, The* by Arthur Hawkey (Spellmount 2001)

*Army and Society, 1815–1914, The* by Edward Spears (Longman 1980)

*Blood Brothers: Hiram and Hudson Maxim* by Paul F. Mottelay (John Lane 1920)

*Boer War, The* by Thomas Pakenham (Weidenfeld and Nicolson 1979)

*Britain and Her Army, 1509–1970* by Corelli Barnett (Penguin 1970)

*Bullets and Bureaucrats; The Machine Gun and the U.S. Army* by David A. Armstrong (Greenwood Press 1992)

*Chronic Inventor, The; Life and Works of Hiram Maxim* by James E. Hamilton (J.E. Hamilton 1991)

*Collins Encyclopaedia of Military History* by R. and T. Dupuy (Harper & Row 1970)

*Colt; The Making of an American Legend* by William Hosley (University of Massachusetts Press 1996)

*Defence, A* by James Puckle (1718)

*Devil's Paintbrush, The* by Dolf L. Goldsmith (Collector Grade Publications 1993)

*Douglas Haig* by John Terraine (Hutchinson 1963)

*Dynamite Stories and Some Interesting Facts About Explosives* by Hiram Maxim (Stokes and Co. N.Y. 1916)

*Encyclopaedia of Firearms* by Ian V. Hogg (Quarto Publishing 1992)

*Fact File on Machine Guns* by Peter Chamberlain and Terry Gander (Macdonald and Jayne's 1974)

*Fire Power: British Army Weapons and the Theories of War* by Bidwell, S. and Graham, D. (Allen & Unwin 1982)

*First Day of the Somme, The* by Martin Middlebrook (Allen Lane 1971)

*First World War, The* by Martin Gilbert (Henry Holt & Co. 1994)

*Gallipoli* by John Masefield (Heinemann 1917)

*Gallipoli Diary* by Ian Hamilton (Edward Arnold 1930)

*Gatling, A Photographic Remembrance* by E. Frank Stephenson Jr. (Meherrin

River Press 1933)

*Gatling Gun, The* by Paul Wahl and Don Toppel (Arco Publishing Co. 1965)

*Gatling Gun and Flying Machine, The* by F. Roy Johnson and E. Frank Stephenson Jr. (Johnson Publishing Co. 1979)

*Gatlings at Santiago, The* by John H. Parker (Hudson Kimberly Publishing Co. 1898)

*Genius in the Family, A* by Hiram Percy Maxim (Michael Joseph 1936)

*Giant Airships, The* by Douglas Botting (Time-Life Books 1980)

*Goodbye to All That* by Robert Graves (Jonathan Cape 1929)

*Grand Old Lady of No Man's Land, The* by Dolf L. Goldsmith (Collector Grade Publications 1994)

*Great Contemporaries* by Winston Churchill (Thornton Butterworth 1937)

*Great War, The* by Jay Winter and Blaine Baggett (Penguin Studio 1996)

*Greenhill Military Small Arms Data Book, The* by Ian V. Hogg (Greenhill Books 1999)

*Grim Reaper, The* by Roger Ford (Sidgwick & Jackson 1996)

*Guilt at Versailles* by A. Lentin (Methuen 1985)

*Guinness Book of Air Facts and Feats, The*
(Guinness 1977)

*Haig* by Duff Cooper (Faber and Faber
1935)

*History and Memoir of the 33rd Battalion
Machine Gun Corps* by Sir Edward
Spiers (Waterlow Brothers 1919)

*History of the British Cavalry Vol. 3
1872–1898* (Secker and Warburg
1982)

*History of the First World War* by
B.H. Liddell Hart (Cassell 1970)

*History of Warfare, A* by Montgomery of
Alamein (Collins 1968)

*Imperial War Book of the Western Front,
The* (Sidgwick and Jackson 1993)

*Informal Record of 26 Machine Gun Training
Centre, An* ed. by S. R. Barney
(printed by W. H. Evans 1946)

*In Relief of Gordon* ed. by Adrian Preston
(Hutchinson 1967)

*Journey's End* by R. C. Sherriff and
V. Bartlett (Gollancz 1929)

*Kitchener* by John Pollack (Constable
1998)

*Kitchener's Army* by Peter Simkins
(Manchester University Press 1988)

*Lewis Gun, The* by J. David Truby
(Paladin Press, Colorado 1988)

*Life and Work of Sir Hiram Maxim, The* by

Paul F. Mottelay (John Lane 1920)

*Lore of Arms, The* by William Reid (Mitchell Beasley 1976)

*Machine Gun, The* by George M. Chinn (Bureau of Ordnance U.S. Navy 1951)

*Machine Gun, The* by Terry Gander (Patrick Stephens 1993)

*Machine Gunner, The* by Arthur Russell (Roundwood Press 1997)

*Machine Gunner 1914–18* by C. E. Crutchley (Bailey Brothers 1975)

*Machine Gunner's Handbook, The* by J. Bostok (W. H. Smith & Sons 1916)

*Machine Guns: Their History and Tactical Employment* by G. S. Hutchinson (Macmillan 1938)

*Machine Guns, A Pictorial, Tactical and Practical History* by Jim Thompson (Greenhill Books 1989)

*Machine Guns of World War One* by Robert Bruce (The Crowood Press 1997)

*My Life* by Hiram Maxim (Methuen 1915)

*My War Memories* by Erich Ludendorff (Hutchinson 1919)

*Pictorial History of the Machine Gun* by F.W.A. Hobart (Ian Allen 1971)

*Pollard's History of Firearms* ed. by Claude Blair (Country Life 1983)

*Price of Glory, The; Verdun 1916* by Alistair Horne (Penguin Books 1962)

*Private Papers of Douglas Haig* ed. by R. Blake (Eyre and Spottiswood 1952)

*Rapid Fire; The Development of Automatic Cannon, Machine Guns, and their Ammunition* by Anthony G. Williams (Airlife 2000)

*Realities of War* by Philip Gibbs (Heinemann 1920)

*Redcoat* by Richard Holmes (HarperCollins 2001)

*Revolt in Southern Rhodesia* by T. Tanger (Heinemann 1967)

*Rough Riders, The* by Theodore Roosevelt (Charles Scribner 1899)

*Russian Army and the Japanese War, The* by General Kuropatkin (John Murray 1909)

*Scramble for Africa, The* by Thomas Pakenham (Weidenfeld and Nicolson 1991)

*Shaka Zulu* by E.A. Ritter (Longmans Green 1955)

*Smoke and the Fire, The* by John Terraine (Sidgwick and Jackson 1981)

*Social History of the Machine Gun, The* by John Ellis (Pimlico 1993)

*Somme* by Lyn Macdonald (Michael Joseph 1983)

*Superiority of Fire* by C.H.B. Pridham
(Hutchinson 1945)

*Testament of Youth* by Vera Brittain
(Gollancz 1933)

*Travel in Space: A History of Aerial
Navigation* by E. Seton Valentine and
F. L. Tomlinson (Hurst & Blackett
1902)

*Trench Warfare* by Tony Ashworth (Pan
Books 2000)

*Vickers, A History* by J. D. Scott
(Weidenfeld and Nicolson 1963)

*Vickers Machine Gun, The* by Mike
Chappell (Wessex Military Publishing
1989)

*Victoria's Wars* by I.F.W. Beckett (Shire
Publications 1998)

*War Memoirs* by David Lloyd George
(Odhams Press 1938)

*Washing of the Spears, The* by Donald
Morris (Cape 1966)

*Western Front, The* by Richard Holmes
(B.B.C. Books 1999)

*When this Bloody War is Over: Soldiers'
Songs of the First World War* by Max
Arthur (Piatkus 2001)

*With a Machine Gun to Cambrai* by
George Coppard (Cassell 1980)

The employees of Thorndike Press hope you have enjoyed this Large Print book. All our Thorndike and Wheeler Large Print titles are designed for easy reading, and all our books are made to last. Other Thorndike Press Large Print books are available at your library, through selected bookstores, or directly from us.

For information about titles, please call:

(800) 223-1244

or visit our Web site at:

www.gale.com/thorndike
www.gale.com/wheeler

To share your comments, please write:

Publisher
Thorndike Press
295 Kennedy Memorial Drive
Waterville, ME   04901